BARCELONA ACCESS

Orientation

Dynamic, bold, seductive, and at times aloof, Barcelona is easy to get to know on the surface, but reveals its rich Mediterranean soul only to the savvy and persistent. You can take it at face value and simply delight in its considerable physical and cultural charms, or you can explore its 2000-year history, its avant-garde artistic currents, its trendiness, and its dedication to tradition to get a handle on just what makes this city tick. Either way, you'll be glad you came.

The city spreads across a plain bordered by the **Mediterranean**, the **Serra de Collserola**, and the **Llobregat** and **Besós** rivers. The old city, or **Ciutat Vella**, at the port end of town is a compact warren of narrow, old-world streets tailor-made for leisurely strolling. Above the **Plaça de Catalunya**, turn-of-the-20th-century Barcelona broadens into a facile grid of prosperous boulevards and chic shopping streets where the pace picks up considerably. Beyond that, the city has come to absorb former satellite villages like **Pedralbes** and **Gràcia** into the municipal fold.

Densely populated Barcelona tallies 1.7 million inhabitants within the city limits and some 3 million in the greater metropolitan area. Although the citizenry is rather reserved, they will assist you (language permitting) if asked, and then if they find you at all *simpático*, they'll probably launch into a lengthy tale or two about their fabulous city. For *barceloneses* deeply love their town and often have an intimate knowledge of it that spans its 2 millenia of existence.

One fundamental fact about Barcelona is that it is the capital of the autonomous region of Catalonia, which likes to set itself apart from the rest of Spain whenever and however possible. Likewise, Barcelona maintains a chronic rivalry with the national capital, Madrid. For although Barcelona is Spain's *second city* demographically, it has always considered itself Number One in industry, culture, commerce and the arts.

Emphatically proud of their city, the people of Barcelona like to throw global parties. In 1888 the city hosted the **Universal Exhibition** and in 1929 the **World's Fair**. Both were a fine excuse for urban development, as are now the upcoming **1992 Summer Olympic Games**. In preparing for them, Barcelona is reshaping itself daily. In fact, by the time you read this, Barcelona will have changed appreciably from what it was at this writing. Inevitably, then, you will find discrepancies between the information given here and the new reality you encounter. Please forgive them. Barcelona, ever known for its progressive vitality, is even more vital and volatile in the grip of pre-Olympic fever. Changes are occurring at lightning speed. All the more reason to keep going back.

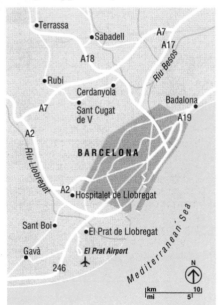

Since the beginning of this century Barcelona has been making a bid for the Olympic Games. In 1924 it lost to Paris, in 1936 to Berlin and in 1972 to Munich. Victory came on 17 October 1986 at 1:31PM, when the president of the International Olympic Committee, **Juan Antonio Samaranch**, pronounced the name of Barcelona as host city for the Games of the XXV Olympiad. Thousands of citizens flocked into the streets of the city to celebrate this honor and a gigantic municipal party ensued, which reached its climax at midnight with the return of the Barcelona delegation, led by **Mayor Pasqual Maragall**.

Airport

El Prat Airport

Barcelona's sole airport is currently undergoing a $150-million expansion to the design of **Peter Hodgkinson** of the **Taller Bofill**. El Prat is located 7.5 miles (12 kilometers) from the city and, depending on traffic, it can take 15-45 minutes to get into the center of town. When work is completed there will be 4 terminals—international, national, air-shuttle and a private air-taxi terminal—designed to accommodate 12 million passengers annually.

Major Airlines

Air France	KLM
Air India	Lufthansa
Alitalia	Pan Am
AUA	Sabena
Avianca	SAS
BEA	Swissair
BOAC	Tap Air Portugal
Finnair	TWA
Iberia	Varig
JAL	VIASA

Airport Information

Airport Information	379.24.54
	379.27.62
Flight Information	301.39.93
	370.10.11
Train to Estacío Central-Sants	322.41.42

Rental Cars

Atesa	302.28.32
Avis	379.40.26
Europcar	379.90.51
Hertz	370.57.72

To and From El Prat

Driving If you have a car, you can approach the city via the Castelldefels autoroute or the *Cinturó del*

Litoral (coastal expressway). Expect a 15-45 minute drive, depending on traffic.

Public Transportation The cheapest way to reach the city from El Prat is by train or bus. Trains travel from the airport to Estació Central Sants every half hour from 6AM to 11PM. The trip takes 15 minutes. Buses make the journey at night, as well as during the day starting at 7:15AM.

Taxicab The most convenient way to get into the city is by cab. A taxi from the airport to La Rambla costs about 1600 pesetas (about $17). See the Phonebook on page 6 for telephone numbers of major taxicab and limousine companies.

Trains If you come into Barcelona by train from Paris, Geneva or major Spanish cities, you will most likely arrive at the **Train Estació Barcelona Central-Sants**, which links up with the municipal metro system and is central enough to make taking a cab to your hotel a moderate expense.

Getting Around Town

Barcelona's municipal transport systems are easy to master. You can get around by metro, bus, funicular, cable car, taxi, train or on foot. Note that public transport fares are slightly higher on weekends and holidays. Given the city's frequent traffic congestion, the metro and walking are typically the quickest ways to get around. Walking is also the best way to get to know the city intimately. As soon as the city's ring roads are completed, getting around town will become a literal possibility. The mountain ring road will connect with the coastal ring road at a series of plazas and cloverleafs.

Public Transportation The **metro** is clean and safe and has stops within a few blocks of most major attractions. Consult the subway map on the inside back cover of this book. Service is efficient, comfortable and generally air-conditioned, and at several stations waiting passengers are treated to piped-in music. Use of the metro requires the purchase of a ticket or strip of tickets available at the ticket booths at most stations. If you're planning to ride often, purchase the more economical T-1 or T-2 strip of 10 tickets. The former entitles you to travel by bus, metro, *tramvía blau*, Montjuïc funicular and the FF.CC. de la Generalitat commuter train line within the city limits; the latter permits travel on all the same transport except the bus. Special 1-, 3- and 5-day passes (*abono temporales*) admit unlimited travel on the bus and metro networks. Metro hours are Monday through Thursday from 5AM-11PM; Friday, Saturday and holiday eves from 5AM-1AM;

weekday holidays from 6AM-11PM; and Sunday from 6AM-midnight.

Barcelona's color-coded **buses** are slower than the metro but more scenic. The areas they service are: red (center-city area); yellow (outer-city districts); green (city periphery); blue (night service in central areas). More than two numbers or letters indicate inter-city buses. Regular bus service is from 6:30AM-10PM; night service from 10PM-4AM.

The **Montjuïc funicular** runs between the Paral.lel metro stop (Line 3) and the amusement park at the top of Montjuïc on weekends throughout the year, daily in summer and during the Christmas holidays and Holy Week. The funicular and Montjuïc castle are linked by cable car weekends and holidays throughout the year and daily June to September and during the Christmas holidays.

The **Transbordador Aéreo del Puerto** or **Montjuïc Teleferic** links Barceloneta and Montjuïc, where it deposits you far from any museums, restaurants or sights, so consider this ride merely for its scenic value (it operates at an altitude of 1000 feet). It also has a terminus mid-way at the Moll de Barcelona in the vicinity of the Columbus monument.

The **tramvía blau** links the FF.CC. de la Generalitat at Avinguda Tibidabo with the **Tibidabo funicular** serving the amusement park at the top of Tibidabo Mountain (altitude 1600 feet or 500 meters).

Call 336.00.00 for general information on public transportation throughout Barcelona. Don't count on being helped in English on the first go-around, though.

Driving and Parking Given Barcelona's traffic congestion and the high cost of renting a car in Spain, we recommend taking the efficient public transportation or taxis within the city. If you want a car for excursions outside the city, try to book a fly/drive or other special package before you go. Parking garages are abundant and your best bet since parking space on the street is at a premium and the regulations border on the Byzantinely complex. For city traffic information call 421.33.33. For information on road condi-

Orientation

tions throughout Cataluña call 421.33.33 or 204.22.47. For information on road conditions throughout Spain call 91/441.72.22 (Madrid).

Taxicabs Most Barcelona taxis are black and yellow. A *Libre* sign and/or lit green roof light signals availability. Cabs may be hailed almost anywhere, but there are abundant taxi stands around town marked by prominent square *T* signs. Taxi drivers generally speak minimal English, so have your destination written down to ease your way. Also, many come from other parts of Spain and might not know every nook and cranny of the city. Taxi tariffs are usually posted inside the taxi, but even those fluent in Spanish will be hard pressed to decipher the nuances of the fare structure. Suffice it to say that there are zone rates. Additional charges apply when travelling to and from the airport or from a train station and for each sizeable bag. Surcharges apply at night, on weekends and on holidays.

FYI

Addresses Street names precede street numbers in Spain. The floor is indicated with a ^{0} sign. *Dcha.* means *right*, *izqda.*, *left*. *Planta baja* or just plain *baja* refers to the ground floor, which to Americans is the 1st floor. But in Barcelona, the 1st floor is not necessarily the American's 2nd floor. Older buildings have such floor designations as *pral* for *principal* and *entl.*^{0} for *entresuelo*. These are vestiges of yore when the former indicated the family's residential quarters and the latter the servant's quarters. As the terminology has not caught up with our less aristocratic times, finding the right floor is sometimes an adventure. Catalan street terminology also frequently differs from the Spanish. The following list should help you decipher maps and street signs. Because Barcelona street names can be rather lengthy, the abbreviations in parentheses have been used throughout the book.

Catalan	Spanish	English
avinguda (Av)	avenida	avenue
carrer (C)	calle	street
carretera (Ctra)	carretera	road, route, highway
cinturó	cinturón	ring road
passatge (Ptge)	pasaje	passage, alley
passeig (Pg)	paseo	boulevard, promenade
plaça (Pl)	plaza	plaza, square
ronda (Rda)	ronda	outer road, ring road
travessera (Trav)	travesía	short cross street
via	vía	road, route

Gran Via de les Corts Catalanes appears as Gran Via C.C.

Also, many street names contain prepositions and articles (e.g., *Passeig de Gràcia* and *Carrer de la Llacuna*), which, in the interest of terseness, will be omitted in the listings (e.g., *Pg Gràcia* and *C Llacuna*).

Typically, odd number addresses are on the west and north side of the streets, even numbers on the east and south, and numbers ascend from south to north and west to east. Also, natives tend to refer to the north side of the street as *el lado montaña* (the mountain side) and the south side as *el lado mar* (the sea side).

Climate Blessed with a mild microclimate, Barcelona averages temperatures of 50F (9C) in winter and 75F (23.5C) in summer. Annual rainfall is 23.6 inches, and annual sunshine totals about 2500 hours.

Eating Habits A typical Barcelona breakfast is coffee and a croissant. Between 10AM and 11AM most natives take a *bocadillo* (sandwich) break. Lunch and dinner are eaten later throughout Spain than in the US and the rest of Europe. Restaurants are usually open from 1-4PM for lunch and 8PM-midnight for dinner. At *cafeterias*, *mesones* and *tapas* (snacks or hors d'oeuvres) bars drinks and food are often slightly cheaper if consumed standing up at the bar rather than sitting at a table. This is not usually the case, however, at upscale restaurants that serve meals at the bar to lone diners or when the house is full. Some Barcelona restaurants have *communal* tables where unaccompanied patrons can opt to share a meal with other solo diners.

Electricity The norm is 220/230V, but you may find 110/120V lines in some hotels. To ensure that you're always properly shaved and/or coiffed, pack a converter or dual-voltage appliances and an adaptor plug for the 2-round-prong outlets found throughout Spain.

Holidays 1 Jan (New Year's Day); 6 Jan (Feast of the Three Kings); 1 May (Labor Day); 15 May (Pentecost); 24 June (Feast of St. John); 15 Aug (Assumption Day); 11 Sep (Cataluña Day); 12 Oct (Columbus Day); 1 Nov (All Souls' Day); 6 Dec (Constitution Day); 8 Dec (Feast of the Immaculate Conception); 25 Dec (Christmas); 26 Dec (Feast of St. Stephen).

Hours Banks vary their hours but are usually open Monday-Friday 8:30AM-2PM and Saturday 8:30AM-1PM (except in summer). Typical **office hours** are 9AM-1:30PM and 4-7PM, but in summer many switch to an 8AM-3PM schedule. Many shops still close at lunch, and store hours are individualistically diverse; *average* opening hours are 10AM-1:30PM and 5-8PM.

Markets Barcelona's temperate climate favors year-round open-air markets. Here are some of our favorites:

Books and Coins Market Sunday from 10AM-2PM at the Sant Antoni Market in Ronda de Sant Antoni.

Coins and Postage Stamps Market Sunday from 10AM-2PM in the Plaça Reial.

Els Encants (flea market) Monday, Wednesday, Friday and Saturday from 7AM to dusk at the Plaça de les Glòries Catalones.

Mercat Gòtic D'Antiguitats (antiques market) Thursday (non-holidays) from 9AM-8PM in the Gothic Quarter.

Mostra D'Art Art for sale every Saturday from 11AM-8PM and Sunday from 11AM-2:30PM in the Plaça de Sant Josep Oriol.

Money The Spanish deal in *pesetas*. Coins come in 1, 5, 10, 25, 50, 100, 200 and 500 denominations; bills in 500, 1000, 2000, 5000 and 10,000. Two convenient money exchange offices are located at the airport (daily 7AM-11PM) and at the Estació Barcelona Central-Sants (daily in winter 8AM-8PM and summer Monday-Saturday 8AM-10PM and Sunday 8AM-2PM, 4-10PM). Most banks will exchange money, but some charge a minimum fee (that can be as much as 500 *pesetas*) and a further commission on traveler's checks. There are also numerous *CHANGE* offices around town whose fees and commissions vary from those of the banks but whose services are offered during non-banking hours. Most hotels will also change your cash and traveler's checks, albeit at a lower rate than that offered at the bank but without bank fees.

Newspapers Barcelona's leading dailies are *La Vanguardia* and *El Periódico*. The national *El País*, Spain's leading daily, prints a Barcelona edition. *The Wall Street Journal, USA Today, The Times* (of London), the *Financial Times*, the *International Herald Tribune*, and other foreign-language newspapers are readily available along La Rambla and throughout the Eixample.

Pharmacies They are abundant and take turns providing round-the-clock service. When a pharmacy is closed, it is required to post the name and address of the nearest open one (known as the *farmacia de guardia*). A daily list of *farmacias de guardia* is found in *El País* and other local newspapers, or you can call 010 to find the nearest one.

Police The Municipal and Regional Police in Barcelona wear blue uniforms; the National Police wear brown. The police station at La Rambla, 43 (301.90.60) is open 24 hours, offers the services of interpreters, and will allow you to make any necessary collect calls. You will also find small, roving trailers around town marked *Oficina de Denuncias* where you can seek help or report a crime.

Politics Barcelona is the provincial capital of Barcelona province and the regional capital of **Catalunya** (*Cataluña* in Spanish, Catalonia in English). The regional government is oft referred to as *la Generalitat*.

Post Office The central post office is in **Plaça Antoni López** (318.38.31 or 302.75.63). Hours are M-F 9AM-10PM, Sa 9AM-2PM. Cards and letters to the US cost 75 *pesetas* (78 cents) and take a week or more to reach their destination.

Street Smarts Like most major cities, Barcelona has its share of street crime—mostly pickpocketing, purse-snatching and chain-snatching. To avoid being a victim, be aware at all times of who and what is around you and bear in mind the following common-sense suggestions:

Never lose sight of your luggage. Keep it all together and within reach.

Avoid handling large sums of money in public.

Don't leave personal documents or valuable items in a parked car.

Carry your purse, camera or video camera slung across your body or carry your purse with the clasp side against your body.

Don't carry your wallet in a back pants pocket or anywhere that it bulges temptingly.

Avoid people trying to sell you flowers or other articles. This is often a ploy paving the way for a pickpocket.

Carry just enough money for your daily expenses. Leave the rest in the hotel safe with other valuables.

If you are on a bus tour, make sure the driver is staying with the bus before you leave anything behind.

Tax IVA is the Spanish rendition of **VAT** (value-added tax). The 6 percent you pay in restaurants up to the 33 percent you pay on luxury items is mostly non-recoverable. Non-EC residents can, however, recover the IVA on single purchases costing over 54,300 *pesetas* (roughly $550). There are 2 possible procedures for doing so. If you are leaving from Barcelona's El Prat airport, you present the store's signed and stamped official bill, along with your passport and article(s) purchased, for endorsement at Spanish Customs *before* check in. The Customs official returns the duly signed blue copy of the bill to you for presentation at the Banco Exterior de España office inside the airport terminal where the tax is refunded to you in the currency of your choice. The other possibility is mailing the endorsed blue copy of the bill to the store, which will then send a refund check to your home.

Telephone The area code for Barcelona is 93 when calling from within Spain and 3 when calling from abroad. The Spanish equivalent of toll-free 800 numbers are toll-free 900 numbers.

For information regarding telephone numbers in Europe and the US or for placing operator-assisted calls from any phone other than a phone booth, dial 008 or 005, respectively. Dial 003 for local information, 009 for national information.

You can call internationally from a direct-dial phone or phone booth by dialing 07 and, after the tone, dialing the area code(s) and number. Because of the expense, however, calling direct from a phone booth entails arming yourself with an unwieldy quantity of coins.

Speaking of expense, most hotels commit highway robbery in placing surcharges of 25 percent or more on calls made from your room. At the public *locutorio* at Carrer Fontanella, 4, you can make international calls Monday-Saturday from 8:30AM-9PM. They accept credit-card payment and offer one Direct USA phone with an AT&T operator at the other end (of course, the line here is usually quite long).

Time Zone Barcelona is generally 6 hours ahead of Eastern time in the US, except in March and October,

Orientation

since Spain switches to and from daylight savings time several weeks before the US does. For much of March, then, there is a 7-hour difference and for much of October, a 5-hour difference.

Tipping No one in Spain feels obliged to tip, and no one expects to be tipped extravagantly. For taxi drivers, just round the fare up or add on 5-10 percent. Give porters 100-200 *pesetas* per bag. Almost all restaurants routinely tack on a service charge, so if you must leave something make it 5 percent—unless the service was truly outstanding. At bars and cafeterias tip 10-100 *pesetas*. As a general rule, the higher the bill, the lower the percentage you leave as a tip.

Touring Barcelona The following services will help you get the most out of your time in Barcelona:

Barcelona Guide Bureau Guides and interpreters available for customized city tours, specialized itineraries, and research and information services. Contact for information on full range of services. ♦ Fee. Via Laietana, 54, 6°5ª, 268.24.22

Barcelona Transports Turístics' Bus 100 This special tourist bus operates from the end of June to mid-September. Making 15 stops, it covers the city's most important sights on a 2-hour route. A half- or full-day ticket entitles you to unlimited travel on Bus 100 plus the *tramvia blau*, Tibidabo funicular, and Montjuïc funicular and cable car. It runs daily every half hour from 9AM-7:30PM. Tickets are available on the bus, at the ticket booths of major metro stops, and at the *Poble Espanyol's* information office.

Julià Tours Daily half-day and full-day city bus tours, plus nighttime flamenco and cabaret tours and seasonal bullfight outings depart from Ronda Universitat, 5. ♦ Fee. Ronda Universitat, 5, 317.64.54

Pullmantur Ditto. ♦ Fee. Gran Via de les Corts Catalanes, 635, 317.12.97

Tourist Information The following tourist offices offer basic maps and background materials and information on current exhibitions and cultural events:

Ajuntament de Barcelona M-F 9AM-8PM; Sa 8:30AM-2:30PM, 24 June-30 Sep. Pl. Sant Jaume. 302.42.00, ext 433

Centre de Informació M-Sa 9:30AM-9PM; Su 10AM-2PM, 24 June-30 Sep. Palau de la Virreina, La Rambla, 99. 301.77.75

Estació Barcelona Central-Sants Daily 8AM-8PM. Pl. Països Catalans, s/n. 490.91.71

Oficina de Informació Turística M-Sa 9:30AM-8PM; Su 9:30AM-3PM. El Prat Airport (International Arrival Hall) 325.58.29

Oficina de Informació Turística M-F 9AM-7PM; Sa 9AM-2PM. Gran Via C.C., 658. 301.74.43

During the summer, you will also find multilingual, uniformed *roving hosts* in the main squares and principal areas of tourism ready to assist you.

You can also dial 010, the 24-hour information hotline, to find out what's happening in the city.

Phonebook

Emergencies

Ambulance	300.20.00
Dentist (emergency)	302.66.82
Doctor (emergency)	212.85.85
Municipal Police	092
National Police	091
Pharmacy (24 hr)	010
Police (regional)	300.22.96

Visitor's Information

Hotline	010
Tourist Office	301.74.43

Consulates

Canadian Consulate	209.06.34
UK Consulate	322.21.51
US Consulate	319.95.50

Credit Cards

American Express	217.00.70
Diners Club	302.14.28
Visa, MasterCard and Access	315.25.12

Lost and Found

City Hall	301.39.23
Public Transport	318.52.93

Transportation

Airport	379.24.54
	379.27.62
Airport Information	370.10.11
	301.39.93
City Traffic Information	421.33.33
Road Conditions/Cataluña	421.33.33
	204.22.47
Road Conditions/Spain	91/441.72.22

Car Rental

Avis

(airport)	379.40.26
(in town)	900/13.57.90

Europcar

(airport)	379.90.51
(in town)	410.93.12
	439.83.00

Hertz

(airport)	370.57.72
(in town)	237.37.37

Atesa

(airport)	302.28.32
(in town)	237.81.40

Car Services/Limousines

Carey	429.13.88
Contreras	423.85.48
Ferré	352.17.03
Public Transportation	336.00.00
RENFE (Spanish Railways)	322.41.42
FF.CC. de la Generalitat (commuter railway)	205.15.15

Taxis

	330.08.04
	300.11.11
	212.22.22
	387.10.00
	322.11.12
	357.77.55

Local Lingos

Sometimes even Spaniards are at a loss for words in Barcelona, the capital of Cataluñya, where Catalan, the region's native language (prohibited during the Franco years) is not only now an officially sanctioned second language but the language of patriotic choice among city dwellers. While some characterize it as a mere hybrid of Spanish and French, don't ever let a local hear you say this. It is, in fact, a separate branch of the Romance language group and bears a strong resemblance to Provençal. In varying dialects it is spoken throughout the Balearic Islands (Majorca, Ibiza and Menorca), and down into Valencia. To give you some idea of how strongly Catalans feel about their language, some local Olympic officials were considering substituting it for Spanish during the Olympic Games. Everyone in Barcelona does speak Spanish, however, so if you have mastered that tongue you'll have no problem talking your way around town.

Since all streets, squares, parks and promenades will eventually bear their proper Catalan names, addresses throughout this guide will be in Catalan except in those increasingly rare instances when a sight, street or locale is still most commonly known by its Spanish name. In all cases, prevailing usage will dictate which language is used in this guide. If it is advisable to give both the Catalan and Spanish renditions, the Spanish will appear in parentheses.

Below is a brief glossary of common words and expressions in Spanish and Catalan that might come in handy.

Basic Grub

English	Spanish	Catalan
breakfast	desayuno	esmorzar, or desdejuni
lunch	comida, or almuerzo	dinar
dinner	cena	sopar
bread	pan	pa
butter	mantequilla	mantega
cheese	queso	formatge
salt	sal	sal
pepper	pimienta	pevre
sugar	azúcar	sucre
salad	ensalada	amanida
fruit	fruta	fruita
vegetables	verdura	verdura
garlic	ajo	all

Orientation

English	Spanish	Catalan
rice	arroz	arròs
beef	carne de vaca	carn de bou
lamb (roast)	cordero (asado)	xai (rostit)
pork	cerdo	porc
rabbit	conejo	conill
veal	ternera	vedella
shellfish	marisco	marisc
fish	pescado	peix
dessert	postre	postres
ice cream	helado	gelat
beer	cerveza	cervesa
water	agua	aigua
wine	vino	vi
menu*	carta	carta

(*menu in Spanish and Catalan refers to a set 3-course meal at a discount price)

Timewise

English	Spanish	Catalan
morning	mañana	matí
midday/noon	mediodía	migdia
evening	tarde	tarda
night	noche	nit
yesterday	ayer	ahir
today	hoy	avui
tomorrow	mañana	demà
day	día	dia
week	semana	setmana
early	temprano	aviat
late	tarde	tard

Spacewise

English	Spanish	Catalan
near	cerca	prop
far	lejos	lluny
large	grande	gran
small	pequeño	petit
downstairs	abajo	a baix, or sota
upstairs	arriba	a dalt, or dalt

Room rap

English	Spanish	Catalan
room	habitación	habitació
bathroom	baño	bany
bed	cama	llit
hot water	agua caliente	aigua calenta
sink	lavabo	lavabo

Orientation

By the Numbers

English	Spanish	Catalan
one	uno	u, or un
two	dos	dos, or dues
three	tres	tres
four	cuatro	quatre
five	cinco	cinc
six	seis	sis
seven	siete	set
eight	ocho	vuit
nine	nueve	nou
ten	diez	deu
twenty	veinte	vint
thirty	treinta	trenta
forty	cuarenta	quaranta
fifty	cincuenta	cinquanta
sixty	sesenta	seixanta
seventy	setenta	setanta
eighty	ochenta	vuitanta
ninety	noventa	noranta
one hundred	cien/ciento	cent
one thousand	mil	mil

By the Week

English	Spanish	Catalan
week	semana	setmana
Monday	lunes	dilluns
Tuesday	martes	dimarts
Wednesday	miércoles	dimecres
Thursday	jueves	dijous
Friday	viernes	divendres
Saturday	sábado	dissabte
Sunday	domingo	diumenge

Travelspeak

English	Spanish	Catalan
I don't understand	No entiendo	No ho entenc
Do you speak English?	¿Habla inglés?	Parla inglés?
Do you have...	¿Tiene algo...	En té de...

English	Spanish	Catalan
a cheaper one?	más barato?	més bon preu?
a larger one?	más grande?	més gran?
a smaller one	más pequeño?	més petit?
another color?	de otro color?	un altre color?
a little	un poco	una mica
a lot	mucho	força
too much/too many	demasiado	massa
How much?	¿Cuánto?	Quant?
What time...?	¿A qué hora...	A quina? hora...?
Where is...?	¿Dónde está...?	On és...?
How do I get to...?	¿Para ir a...?	Per anar a...?
on the left	a la izquierda	a l'esquerra
on the right	a la derecha	a la dreta
open	abierto	obert
closed	cerrado	tancat
exchange (money)	cambio	canvi
bank	banco	banc
pharmacy	farmacia	farmàcia
bad	mal	malament
expensive	caro	car
more	más	més
to pay	pagar	pagar
to eat	comer	menjar
to drink	beber	beure
to order	pedir	demanar
bill/check	cuenta	compte
price	precio	preu
money	dinero	diners
traveler's check	cheque de viaje	xec de viatje
guidebook	guía	guia
newspaper	periódico	periòdic, or diari
magazine	revista	reviste
map	mapa	mapa
post office	correos	correus
postcard	tarjeta postal	targeta postal
stamp	sello	segell
driver's license	carnet de conducir	carnet de conducir
customs	aduana	duana
passport	pasaporte	passaport

In 1714 Barcelona's population was 30,000. At the beginning of the 10th century, it was 600,000. Now it's almost 2 million in the municipality proper and almost 4 million in the greater metropolitan area. Surprisingly its population density is almost as high as that of Bombay.

Barcelona in 1 to 7 Days

Stroll along **La Rambla**, taking in the **Columbus Monument, Museu Marítim, Palau Güell, La Boquería Market** and **Gran Teatre del Liceu.**

Take a round-trip ride in the **Transbordador Aéreo del Puerto** for the view.

Lunch at Casa Leopoldo

Coffee at **Cafè de L'Opera.**

Museu Picasso.

Cathedral or **Sagrada Familia.**

Dinner at **Restaurant 7 Portes.**

If there's an event of some kind at the **Palau de la Música Catalana,** go.

Have a *cava* nightcap at **La Cava del Palau.**

Sagrada Familia or **Cathedral** (whichever you didn't do on DAY 1).

Stroll along **Passeig de Gràcia,** taking in the **Mançana de la Discòrdia** and Gaudí's **Casa Milà.**

Browse in **Vinçon** and **Bulevard Rosa.**

Lunch at **El Gran Colmado.**

Museu d'Art de Catalunya.

Fundació Miró.

Olympic Ring.

Poble Espanyol (consider having dinner here and a drink in **Las Torres de Avila**).

Museu-Monestir de Pedralbes.

Museu Palau Reial de Pedralbes.

Lunch at **Restaurante Reno** (pricey) or **Tramonti 1980** (moderate).

Stroll around the **Barri Gòtic,** taking in the **Saló del Tinell, Capilla de Santa Agueda, Museu Frederic Marès, Museu de l'Historia de la Ciutat, Palau de la Generalitat** and **Casa de la Ciutat.**

Go antiquing along **Carrer de la Palla.**

Dinner at **Botafumeiro** (pricey) or **La Dentelliére** (moderate).

Go dancing at **La Paloma** or take in a show at **El Molino.**

Stroll around **La Ribera,** taking in the **Iglesia de Santa María del Mar,** the **Museu Textil i d'Indumentària,** and the **Parc de la Ciutadella.**

Lunch at **Reial Club Marítim de Barcelona** (stunning view), or one of the restaurants in **Barceloneta.**

Stroll along the **Moll de la Fusta** and take a trip to the breakwater and back in a *golondrina.*

Dinner at **Passadis del Pep** (pricey, make reservations well in advance).

After-dinner drinks at **Velvet.**

Stroll the streets of the **Eixample** and revel in the Modernist spectacle.

Fundació Antoni Tàpies.

Browse in **b.d. Ediciones de Diseño.**

Lunch at **La Masia** atop **Tibidabo Mountain** (great views).

Parc Güell (more good views).

Casa Vicens.

Dinner at **El Dorado Petit.**

A day trip to **Montserrat Monastery.**

Hear the boys' choir daily 1PM.

Take the funicular to the top of **Sant Jeróni.**

Cocktails at **Boadas.**

Dinner at **Azulete.**

A day trip to **Sitges.**

Dinner at **Neichel.**

Drinks at **Nick Havanna.**

P.S. If you're in town on a Thursday, Saturday or Sunday, don't miss seeing the **Cathedral** illuminated at night and the illuminated **Fuentes de Montjuïc** (illuminated on Thursday, June to September only).

La Rambla/ El Raval/ Barrio Chino

Like the roots of a resilient, flourishing oak, the streets of Barcelona's oldest disricts are haphazard and gnarled. Like a taproot, **La Rambla** runs down the center from the **Plaça de Catalunya** to the sea. A broad boulevard graced with a tree-lined central promenade, this is Barcelona's most compelling urban feature. Not because it is beautiful, ancient or even particularly historic, but because it is undeniably theatrical. Buskers, businesspeople, streetwalkers, tourists, transvestites, drug dealers, gypsies, newsstands, flower stalls, cafes, the opera house, porno palaces, the down-and-out and the upwardly mobile comprise a veritable open-air museum of mankind and its constructs. Locals deny they ever come here (absolutely untrue) and visitors can't seem to keep away from the singular blend of class and crass.

Formerly (and still variously) known as *Las Ramblas* and *Les Rambles*, the linguistic powers that be seem to have settled on the name *La Rambla* for the time being, despite the fact that it is actually comprised of 5 contiguous *Ramblas*— **La Rambla de Canaletes, La Rambla dels Estudis, La Rambla de Sant Josep, La Rambla dels Caputxins** and **La Rambla de Santa Mònica.** Some say that in its natural state La Rambla was a some-time stream for run-off after heavy rains; others say it never carried a drop of water to the sea. But no one would disagree that for some time now it has been Barcelona's most charismatic street.

In the 13th century, it marked the western limits of Barcelona just beyond the Roman city walls. In 1553, the first of a string of convents and monasteries was built along its western side. In the surrounding streets, as one would expect of a port city, were numerous houses of ill repute. Thus, early on La Rambla exhibited a complex, even contradictory, personality. And so the saga continues.

By the mid-19th century, only bits and pieces of La Rambla's convent past remained. It had now become a most prized and prestigious address, the social hub of a city whose cultural and economic sophistication gave rise to the elegant and ambitious **Gran Teatre del Liceu** (the municipal opera house) and the famed **Cafè de L'Òpera** across the way where intellectuals sipped coffee and debated politics.

Well rid of its restrictive city walls by 1860, Barcelona expanded beyond its gnarled core, and the prestige moved out to the broad, new boulevards of the Eixample. La Rambla's cachet steadily eroded, finally bottoming out in the last few decades when its lower reaches, always studded with bars and brothels, branched out into the world of drugs.

Through all its ups and downs, La Rambla has remained prime tourist turf. Now indications are that its stock is on the rise again. Among the dozen hotels along La Rambla, a number are survivors of the street's changing fortunes, but 2 newcomers—the deluxe **Ramada Renaissance** and the chichi **Rivoli Rambla**— point the way to a gentrified future. The Japanese too, are in on the act with the construction of a luxury *smart* building midway between the **Plaça de Catalunya** and the **Columbus Monument**. The Teatre del Liceu is planning an expansion, shops are putting on more upscale faces, and the city plans to broaden La Rambla's lateral and central sidewalks.

Meanwhile, such entrenched fixtures as the **Hotel Oriente** and the tarnished Cafè de L'Opera will likely hang on for awhile to keep the mix interesting. While an ambitious campaign to eliminate the street's seedier elements has met with some success, the contrasts that have made La Rambla a legend seem destined to endure at least through the '90s.

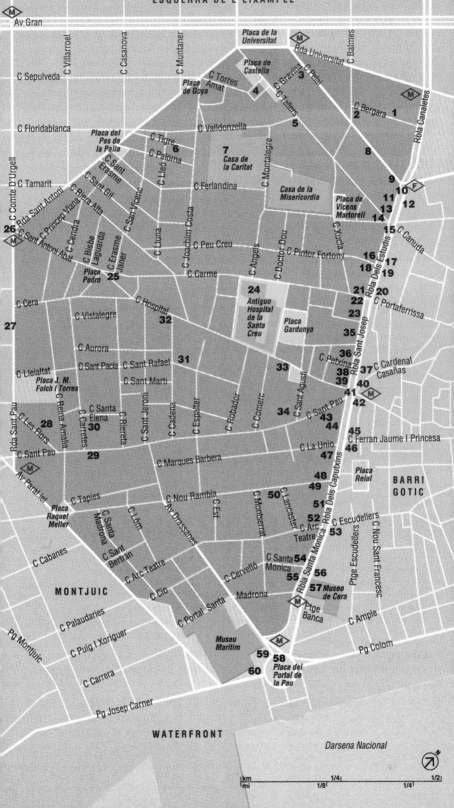

That area west of La Rambla bordered by **Avinguda del Paral.lel, Ronda de Sant Pau** and **Ronda de Sant Antoni** is commonly known as **El Raval** (from the Spanish *arrabal*, meaning outskirts or suburbs). Though its narrow streets suggest a medieval birth, this working-class barrio dates largely from the mid-19th century. The southern half between **Carrer de Hospital** and Avinguda del Paral.lel has been dubbed the **Barrio Chino** even though there's nothing the least bit Chinese, or even Oriental, about it. Clearly it once put someone in mind of the poverty, cramped quarters and dirty dealings of a downtrodden Chinatown somewhere in the world. Nobel-prize-winning author **Camilo José Cela** once characterized the Barrio Chino as an area of *cheap love and cognac on tap*. Bars do abound, prostitutes are clearly on the prowl, and drug deals do regularly go down, but the barrio's reputation is far worse than its bite and should not deter exploration, except at night.

Once denoted by such well-earned barrio nicknames as El Raval, Barrio Chino and Barri Gòtic, the *root systems* of Barcelona extending from the old port to the Plaça de Catalunya and from the Ronda de Sant Pau to the Parc de la Ciutadella have recently been lumped together under the new, homogenized designation of **Ciutat Vella** (Old City) that rides roughshod over the colorfully distinct personalities of these different neighborhoods. Fortunately habits die hard, especially linguistic ones, and the old monikers tenaciously linger on the lips of a municipal citizenry that can't quite get used to calling a spade a garden tool.

1 Hotel Ducs de Bergara $$$ (1898, **Emili Sala i Cortés**; renovation of facade 1988, **Román Arañó**) A real charmer outfitted with exquisite taste, this hotel occupies the Modernist **Casa Emília Carles vda. de Tolrà** noted for its ample use of decorative wrought iron. Combining furnishings of the last century with the sophisticated amenities of this one, the hotel's 58 rooms offer satellite color TV, air conditioning, direct-dial phones and minibars. The hotel's central stairway is simply splendid, and the public areas are oases of gracious comfort. ♦ C Bergara, 11 (Pl Catalunya-C Balmes) 301.51.51; fax 317.34.42

2 Hotel Residencia Regina $$ The 102 spacious, air-conditioned, rejuvenated rooms at this member of the Best Western reservations system have phones, TVs, minibars and vest-pocket baths. Also offers the full complement of room service, bar, snack bar and restaurant. ♦ C Bergara, 4 (C Balmes) 301.32.32; fax 318.23.26 (reservations can also be made through Marketing Ahead, 433 5th Ave, New York NY 10016; 212/686.9213; fax 212/686.0271)

3 Hotel Gravina $$ Sixty small rooms with glitzy baths. The public areas, abundantly dressed in marble, are rendered in a contemporary interpretation of Art Deco. Externally the building exhibits a pastiche of stylistic currents. TV, air conditioning, minibar, telephone and parking offered. ♦ C Gravina, 12 (C Pelai) 301.68.68; fax 317.28.38

4 Antigua Iglesia del Convent dels Paüls (1716; restored 1949) All that remains of a former convent complex, this church features a single nave flanked by lateral chapels, an upper gallery, an apse chamfered where it meets the nave, and a crowning cupola externally adorned with yellow and green glass tiles. Over a century of internal modifications have resulted in a mixture of Baroque and Neoclassical motifs. Its current external aspect is the result of a restoration that included the completion of one of the towers, the addition of the arched entranceway and recovering the facades. ♦ Pl Castella (C Tallers-C Torres i Amat)

5 Hotel Mesón Castilla $ A commendable place to stay for those on a budget. Air conditioning was added during the recent renovation of its 60 budget rooms with bath and phone. Parking facilities and an ample breakfast buffet are added incentives. ♦ C Valldonzella, 5 (C Tallers-C Montalegre) 318.21.82

6 La Paloma A lively holdover from the days when dancing was a chic form of socializing. Remember the waltz, samba, fox trot? You can dance them all at this Belle Epoque hall that still conserves the wonderfully effusive stage dressing of **Salvador Alarma**. Tradition and sentiment bring the *barcelonses* here for all manner of family celebrations and social functions. The music is live and the industrial-sized dance floor is typically packed buttock to buttock. ♦ Cover. C Tigre, 27 (C Lleó-C Joaquín Costa) 301.68.97

Restaurants/Nightlife: Red **Hotels:** Blue
Shops/Parks: Green **Sights/Culture:** Black

7 Casa de la Caritat (House of Charity)

(1700s; rehabilitation of the Pati Manning 1988, **Andreu Bosch, Josep María Botey** and **Lluís Cuspinera**; rehabilitation of l'Edifici Pati de les Dones, **Piñón i Viaplana**; Museu d'Art Contemporanea 1992, **Richard Meier & Partners**) No original elements remain of the 14th-century Carthusian convent that occupied this site. In the 18th century the bulk of the current facade, the **Chapel of Sto. Tómas**, and the cloisters known as **Pati Manning** (1743) were built. Notable are the cloisters' ceramic decoration and distinctive, bi-level construction with 2 upper-level arches corresponding to each lower one—a Barcelona structural tradition also found in the **Casa de Convalencia** and the **Convento de la Mercèd**. For a while during the 18th century the **Seminario Tridentino** was installed here. Then in 1769 a poorhouse moved in. Subsequently the premises were expanded to their current dimensions—an entire city block. In the late 18th century its occupants were mostly young women who learned domestic chores and religion in preparation for marriage. The House of Charity, as such, was founded in 1802 by Royal Order to continue the work of sheltering beggars and providing them with occupational training. Toward the end of the 19th century it housed increasing numbers of children—orphans or paupers—and functioned in part as a reformatory. Ultimately abandoned in 1956 when its services moved to the outskirts of the city, it is today being reborn to embrace 3 entities—the **Centre d'Estudis i Recursos Culturals de la Diputació de Barcelona**, the **Centre de Cultural Contemporània de Barcelona**, and the future **Museo d'Art Contemporanea**. The first, occupying the Pati Manning, offers a library, training programs, and myriad cultural activities aimed at stimulating local and regional culture and at improving the services offered by the Department of Culture. The second, in **l'Edifici Pati de les Dones**, is dedicated to studying the dynamics of urban life. The museum, designed by Richard Meier & Partners, will be a showcase for contemporary art and additionally offer educational services, a children's studio, a library, a book shop and a cafe. The structure's projected vertical gallery parallel to the main facade will filter and diffuse natural light over the various exhibition areas. ♦ C Montalegre, 5-9 (C Valldonzella-C Ferlandina) 301.01.74 (Centre d'Estudis); 412.07.81 (Centre de Cultural Contemporània de Barcelona)

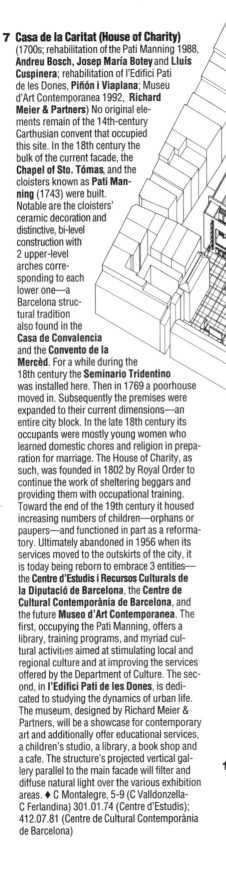

Museo d'Art Contemporanea

RICHARD MEIER & PARTNERS

8 C&A

(1915, **Lluís Homs, Eduard Ferrés** and **Ignasi Mas**; renovation 1987) After a fire destroyed the El Siglo department store in La Rambla on Christmas Day in 1932, it moved here for half a century. Now the C&A department store has taken over this principally Modernist building (one of Barcelona's first reinforced concrete buildings) known as **Can Damians** (for its first commercial occupants), a highly original structure difficult to pigeonhole stylistically. Some see a Secessionist (a Germanic version of Modernism) influence and foreshadowings of Art Deco. Some don't. Perhaps it might best be deemed a structure on the transitional cusp. In any case, its crowning ball and monumental caryatids (male and female) exude a lot of charisma. Though of comparatively little interest these days, the building won the Town Hall prize for the best commercial building of 1915. ♦ C Pelai, 54 (C Jovellanos-La Rambla) 317.99.39

9 Zara

The latest fashion concepts for men, women and children at unfashionably reasonable prices. This Spanish chain has now gone worldwide. ♦ C Pelai (La Rambla) 301.09.78. Also at: Rambla Catalunya at C Aragó

10 La Rambla de Canaletes

Natives refer to this portion of La Rambla stretching from the Plaça de Catalunya to Carrer Bonsuccés as *dels ocells* (of the birds) because of the numerous stands selling animals and, in particular, birds. It is also home to a legendary fountain of the same name.

10 Font de Canaletes This diminutive, 19th-century iron fountain gave its name to the upper reaches of La Rambla and is a landmark among those who know the city well. A plaque recalls the legend: whoever drinks from the fountain will always return to Barcelona. Since pollution struck its waters, however, the legend has dried up. Still, the fountain remains a favorite rendezvous spot among locals and a prime venue for rehashing the triumphs and blunders of the most recent soccer match.
♦ Pl Catalunya-C Tallers

11 Burger King $ If fast-food chains are a sign of progress, Barcelona has indeed arrived.

La Rambla/El Raval/Barrio Chino

Pizza Hut, McDonald's, Kentucky Fried Chicken...they're all here in multiples. On this particular site in 1916 **Esteve Sala** founded the bar **Canaletes**. The current interior decor retains much of the distinctive character of the former bar, but the exterior metallic adornments that once distinguished the facade were lost in the transition. ♦ La Rambla, 135 (Pl Catalunya) 302.54.29. Also at: Pg Gràcia, 4. 317.18.57

cortefiel

12 Cortefiel One of Spain's most widespread chain of clothiers for men and women offering fashions that in quality and flair range from average to a cut above. ♦ La Rambla, 138 (Pl Catalunya-C Santa Anna) 317.47.12

12 Hotel Continental $$ Among Barcelona's budget hotels, the 32 rooms here offer such charms as old fashioned high beds (some of them brass) and furniture that looks like it's been in the family for generations. The floral wallpaper and florid carpets often clash, but somehow that only makes it more endearing. All rooms have baths, phone and TV. A cosmetic renovation is planned in preparation for the Olympics. ♦ La Rambla, 138 (Pl Catalunya-C Santa Anna) 301.25.70; fax 302.73.60

12 Banca Jover Serving Spain's banking needs since 1737. ♦ La Rambla, 134 (Pl Catalunya-C Santa Anna) 318.22.66

13 I. Llobet Y Cia., S.C. Musical Emporium (1911) Worn, red-leather tomes filled with musical scores line the walls of this tiny shop, one of 2 music stores in La Rambla. It also sells musical instruments and accessories. The bevelled door is adorned with a muse of a certain Modernist air. ♦ La Rambla, 129 (Pl Catalunya-C Tallers) 317.63.38

13 Hotel Lloret $ A cozy, low-cost outpost where each of the 52 rooms has its own personality but some have limited plumbing (sinks only). The management is friendly and the rooms are spotless. The building dates from the mid-19th century. ♦ La Rambla, 125 (C Tallers) 317.33.6

14 Boadas Established by **Miguel Boadas**, a native of Havana, in 1933, this classic cocktail bar dressed in wood and brass exudes a Roaring '20s vitality and is popular with people of all ages, professions and political persuasions. Here they still shake, mix and stir cocktails with old-fashioned aplomb, and a board announces the cocktail of the day. Among the house specials are the *mohito* (served just as it is in Havana's own Floridita and Bodeguita de en Medio) and the Alexander. Then there are such house inventions as the *Tele/exprés* and *Joan Miró*. Portraits and caricatures share wall space with framed words of praise from **Joan Miró** and other prominent passing presences. The drawing behind the bar is by **Ricard Opisso**. ♦ C Tallers, 1 (La Rambla) 318.95.92

14 Hotel Royal $$$ Businesslike in demeanor, the 108 rooms in this 8-story, modern structure offer air conditioning, minibars, televisions and telephones. Lone travelers who like to take baths take note—a number of singles lack tubs. Parking on premises. ♦ La Rambla, 117-119 (C Bonsuccés) 318.73.29; fax 317.31.79

Within the Hotel Royal:

El Recó de la Poma ★$$ Known simply to locals as *la poma* (the apple), this 2-tiered restaurant offers an upscale version of fast-food fare. Those in a hurry should stay downstairs where the menu offers salads, pizza, pasta and a smattering of Catalan specialties. Upstairs the menu expands to include more Catalan and Spanish offerings, a number of them prepared before your eyes on the open grill.
♦ Pizzeria/Grill ♦ 301.94.00

At last count there were 18 kiosks selling flowers, 10 selling birds and 14 selling newspapers and magazines in La Rambla.

15 La Rambla dels Estudis This section of La Rambla running from Carrer Bonsuccés to Carrer del Carme got its name from **l'Estudi General,** the university, built here in the middle of the 16th century by the architect **Barsa**. In 1536, **Emperor Charles V** laid its first stone; in 1843, it was finally torn down. Of the vast number of convents and churches that survived in this part of La Rambla into the 18th century, only the **Iglesia de Betlem** remains.

16 Edifici de la Reial Academia de Ciències i Arts de Barcelona (1883, **Josep Domènech i Estapà**) Don't miss the noteworthy coffered ceilings inside this early Modernist structure. In addition to the **Royal Academy of Sciences and the Arts**, it now houses **Viena** (★$), whose winsome old-world facade and sprightly interior decor lure passersby into a world of tasty, Germanic-influenced fast food, and where some evenings the harried after-work crowd is serenaded by the baby grand piano in the upper gallery. This 19th-century building also houses the **Teatre Català de la Comèdia**; the **Teatre Poliorama**, dating from the early 1900s and remodeled in 1985 by the architects **Bohigas, Martorell** and **Mackay**; and an official retailer of **Majorica Pearls**. ◆ La Rambla, 115 (C Bonsuccés-C Pintor Fortuny)

16 Ramada Renaissance $$$$ (1957; remodelled 1988) For comfort, convenience and central location, this 5-star hotel simply can't be beat. The hotel of choice for such diverse shining lights as **Michael Jackson, Phil Collins, Julio Iglesias,** the **Rolling Stones, Tina Turner, Prince, Madonna, David Bowie, Pavarotti, Plácido Domingo, Bruce Springsteen** and **Peter O'Toole,** it lacks no imaginable service or amenity—including reserving for its guests a block of tickets to performances at the nearby **Liceu**. All 203 rooms (some non-smoking) have a writing desk and, upon request, can be outfitted with a personal computer, printer, fax, telephone with private number, and a Minitel PC. A separate reception desk, bar and restaurant serve the **Renaissance Club** executive rooms offering additional luxury amenities. Generous terraces are standard on the 6th floor. No. 918 is the sweetest suite. In addition to being the *home of the stars* in Barcelona, the Ramada is the home of the **Harvard Alumnae Association**, half of whose Spanish members reside in Barcelona. The Ramada's **El Patio** (★★$$) restaurant offers an international menu with Spanish accents and musical accompaniment at dinner. Long ago **El Siglo**, then the Bloomingdale's of Barcelona, stood on this site. It burned down Christmas Day 1932. Later, the **Carrer del Pintor Fortuny** was constructed and subsequently the 5-star **Hotel Manila**, which in its day also catered to the stars who came to perform at the Liceu and **Palau de la Música**. Having deteriorated along with La Rambla, the Manila was completely remodelled within by Ramada in 1987. Its Neoclassical facade was, however, meticulously retained by municipal decree. ◆ Deluxe ◆ La Rambla, 111 (C Pintor Fortuny) 318.62.00, reservations 318.44.32, toll-free 900/318.318 (Spain), 800/228.2828 (US); fax 301.77.76

La Rambla/El Raval/Barrio Chino

17 Hotel Rivoli Rambla $$$ (1920s; renovation 1989, **Alberto Esquerdo**) Built to house the **German Consulate**, this Art Deco building was acquired by the **Banco Popular Español** after the Spanish Civil War and later converted into the **Hotel Príncipe**. After its recent renovation and conversion into the 87-room, 4-star Rivoli Rambla, it was endowed with some furnishings, textiles and sculptures recalling the building's Roaring '20s birth. The rooms are elegant in a Minimalist way, and the public areas striking in their mix of marble and vivid colors. The 6th- and 7th-floor rooms are a cut above. The Suite Opera, the Rivoli's ultimate indulgence, is especially appealing to those who like bathrooms with a lot of character. Minitel PCs are standard in all suites. Among its more sybaritic amenities are a whirlpool, sauna and tanning table. The only drawbacks here are inconsistent service and poor sound insulation between rooms. ◆ La Rambla dels Estudis, 128 (C Canuda-C Portaferrissa) 302.66.43; fax 317.50.53

Within the Hotel Rivoli Rambla:

Le Brut ★★$$$$ Great care is taken with the food at this restaurant on the mezzanine level. Guests enjoy an ample buffet breakfast tailored to an array of international breakfast customs. ◆ Spanish/Catalan

Blue Moon Bar The multilingual cocktail conversation at this lobby-level piano bar attests to Barcelona's cosmopolitan cachet.

The Catalan **Narcís Monturiol** invented the submarine in 1858 and then associated himself with **Josep Missé** and **Josep Oliu** to bring about its construction in a Barcelona shipyard. Its inaugural immersion took place on 23 July 1859 in the port of Barcelona, when these 3 men became the first humans to descend in a submarine, named the *Ictíneo*, and make an underwater journey lasting nearly half an hour. On 29 September 1859, the official demonstration for the local authorities and the public proved the submarine's capacity to descend to nearly 66 feet and travel at a speed of 3 knots. Why the Spanish government failed to pursue this maritime breakthrough is unclear, but some maintain that certain government officials were bribed by England, then ruler of the waves, to suppress the development of such a formidable seafaring weapon.

18 Edificio de Tabacos de Filipinas (1880, **Josep Oriol Mestres**; facade, **Josep Maria Sagnier**) Built by the same architect that gave us the **Gran Teatre del Liceu**, this monument to the flourishing 19th-century tobacco trade now houses a monument to the flourishing 20th-century banking trade, the **Banco de Santander**. The corner statue of the painter **Fortuny** was done in 1942 by the sculptors **Miquel** and **Llucià Oslé**. ◆ La Rambla (C Pintor Fortuny)

19 Moka Restaurant Cafeteria ★$$ Spain's version of the standard American diner, this is an ultra-famous Barcelona pit stop. The house

specialty is *paella valenciana*. ◆ Diner ◆ La Rambla, 126 (C Canuda-C Portaferrissa) 302.68.86

Hotel
MONTECARLO

20 Hotel Montecarlo $$ A solid choice for middle-of-the-road comfort and cost, the 77 well-scrubbed rooms here come with baths and are being spruced up for the Games to further offer air conditioning, TV and telephone. Until the second half of the 1960s, the daily newspaper *El Correo Catalán* occupied one floor of the hotel. ◆ La Rambla dels Estudis, 124 (C Canuda-C Portaferrissa) 317.58.00; fax 317.57.50

20 Palau Moja (1790, **Josep Mas i Dordal** and **Pau Mas i Dordal**) Construction began in 1774, but the front and rear facades respectively facing La Rambla and the garden were not completed until 1790. The severely Neoclassical facades were once decorated with colorful murals. The garden facade was decorated in the 18th century by **F. Pla** *El Vigatà* the same man who adorned the ceilings of the **Ateneu**; the Rambla facade was decorated by **Josep Flaugier** at the beginning of the 19th century. In 1790 El Vigatà also decorated the interior walls with historical scenes and adorned the ceilings with allegorical depictions. During Barcelona's brief domination by the French (1808-13), **Chebrun**, the prefect of Barcelona, resided here. Successively, the building has been adapted to modern exigencies. In 1934 the garden was sacrificed to the downscale **Sepu** department store and the murals by Flaugier on the Rambla facade were destroyed; the only things conserved were the loggia built by **Antoní Rovira i Trías** in 1856 and the murals of El Vigatà dating from 1785. His decorative mural within has also been preserved. Recently the victim of several suspicious fires, the building has been restored to house outposts of the **Cultural Department of the Generalitat**. One of these is a bookstore offering official publications; another, a data bank of cultural information. ◆ La Rambla, 118 (C Portaferrisa)

21 Iglesia de Betlem (1732, **Josep Juli**) One of the rare reminders of the days when La Rambla was a network of convents and monasteries, this church is an example of traditional Catalan Gothic architecture—its semicircular apse and central nave are flanked by side chapels. The structure supersedes a 16th-century Jesuit church that burned down in 1671. The exterior, whose lower half is adorned with raised, diamond-shaped stones, and the main portal retain their original aspects, albeit sullied with the soot of centuries. Though sizeable, the church inside is rather plain by Spanish standards. Much of the interior was lost to a fire in 1936, but it was reconstructed in the original form. During the Christmas season there is always a display of crèches here. ◆ C Carme, 2 (La Rambla)

22 Restaurant Quo Vadis ★★★$$$ At this Barcelona fixture dating from the mid-60s, the solicitous waiters seem more like valets or butlers. In season, succulent mushroom melanges and hearty game dishes headline the menu, which all year round places savory emphasis on grilled and roasted meats.
◆ Catalan ◆ C Carme, 7 (La Rambla-C Cabres) Reservations recommended. 302.40.72

23 La Rambla de Sant Josep (aka La Rambla de les Flors) Since Corpus Christi day in 1853, 18 flower stalls have earned this part of La Rambla from Carrer del Carme to Pla de la Boquería its colloquial epithet, *La Rambla of the Flowers*. In the 19th century this was the only place in Barcelona where you could buy flowers, and each stand had its loyal clientele. From among its florists the legendary Modernist painter **Ramon Casas** plucked the woman who would be not only his best model but also his wife. Today's flower stalls mingle with large kiosks selling newspapers and books.

24 Antiguo Hospital de la Santa Creu (15th-16th c) This complex of buildings occupying a full square block is vintage medieval Barcelona and an oasis of quiet in the bustling cityscape. Its late 10th-century origins make it one of the oldest hospital sites in the world. In 1024 an already existing refuge became a shelter and hospital for pilgrims. At the beginning of the 15th century, the **Consell de Cent**, Barcelona's governing body, decided to streamline the city's hospital care and administration by fusing the most important municipal hospitals into a single entity on this site. In the process, part of the existing **Hospital d'En Colom** was tranformed into a church whose current vaulting was an 18th-century addition and whose Gothic cloister, the work of **Guillem Abiell**, was never completely closed off as planned, making further expansion of the premises possible. By the beginning of the 20th century, however, all expansion possibilities had been exhausted, and the **Hospital Sta. Creu i Sant Pau** built by **Domènech i Montaner** in the Eixample, took over the functions of this one. The beautiful Gothic hospital itself functioned as such until 1926 (on 7 June of that year, shortly before it ceased its ministrations, famed architect **Antoni Gaudí** died here) and now houses the **Biblioteca de Catalunya**, the **Institut d'Estudis Catalans**, the **Escola Massany** of the arts and the **Escola Universitaria de Biblioteconomia i Documentació**. Beautiful 17th-century polychrome tiles depicting scenes from the life of **Sant Pau**, founder of the institution, grace the Biblioteca's vestibule. In the patio beyond the vestible stands a 17th-century statue of Sant Pau by **Lluís Bonifàs**. A beautiful Baroque cross graces the complex's gardens. ◆ Bounded by C Hospital, C Carme, C Floristes Rambla and C Egipcíaques

On the Antiguo Hospital de la Santa Creu grounds:

Casa de Convalescéncia (1680) The 2nd story of the central cloister was built in 1674 by **Josep Juli** and **Andreu Bosch**. The patio, chapel, entranceway and other areas are decorated with tiles by famous ceramic masters of the period, and most of the sculptural work is by **Lluís Bonifàs**. All was restored before installing the **Institut d'Estudis Catalans**.

Antiguo Col.legi de Cirugia (1764, **Ventura Rodríguez** and **Pere Virgili**; restored 1929) This former school of surgery fronted by a Neoclassical facade now houses the **Real Acadèmia de Medicina y Cirugia** where you can still find the circular classroom with the marble table where dissections were once demonstrated. One of the building's lateral walls contains a 1955 bust of **Sir Alexander Fleming**, discoverer of penicillin, by **Josep M. Benedito**.

P.S. Two sheds on the old hospital grounds still house, as in days of yore, amanuenses that assist people in writing letters or filling out income tax declaration forms.

25 **Obelisco de Santa Eulàlia** (1685, **C. Tremulles** and **Lluís Bonifàs**; reconstructed 1952, **Frederic Marès**) Situated in the Plaça del Pedró near where the martyr **Santa Eulàlia**, one of the city's 2 patron saints, was crucified and where, according to legend, a timely snowfall piously covered her nude body. The original 17th-century statue of the saint was destroyed in the turmoil of the Civil War in 1936. Using the salvaged head as a reference, **Frederic Marès** rebuilt it. The fountain at her feet, dating from 1826, was the first to supply water to the barrio. ◆ Pl Pedró

25 **Bodega Pedró** An ample selection of all types of wines and heady libations—bottled or from the barrel. ◆ Pl Pedró, 6. 329.60.54

26 **Mercat de Sant Antoni** (1882, **Antoní Rovira i Trías** and **Josep M. Cornet i Mas**) A masterpiece of Barcelona's brand of ironwork architecture, this market is technically situated at the edge of the Eixample but fits more logically into this itinerary. Occupying a full city block, it is the only market constructed according to the original guidelines laid down by the **Plan Cerdà** (see Eixample chapter).

Laid out in the form of a Greek cross diagonal to the surrounding streets, it fulfills the geometric ideals of the Cerdà layout in creating a central area that has the same form as an Eixample intersection, thus suggesting a structural analogy between public building and the municipality it serves. This, coupled with the market's ornamental appeal without and pleasing graduation of ceiling heights within, makes it a work of singular architectural interest. On Sunday mornings it is of singular interest to collectors of second-hand books, coins and antique comics. ◆ C Comte d'Urgell (C Tamarit-C Comte Borrell-C Manso)

27 **Olympic Projects Exhibit** An out-of-the-way and rather dry display of models of the numerous municipal projects spurred by the Olympic Games—including the airport, roadways and Olympic facilities—along with audiovisual presentations on same in various languages. ◆ Free. M-F 9AM-8PM; closed holidays. Rda Sant Pau, 43-45 (C Marqués Campo Sagrado-C Parlament) 329.00.66

28 **Can Isidre (Casa Isidro)** ★★★$$$$ One of Barcelona's most prestigious restaurants, offering a surprisingly large selection of Catalan dishes in a small, bistro-like setting. The food is simple and abundant and meals traditionally start off with a series of *tapas*, including strips of pork loin cured like ham or fried whitebait. The rare Catalan sea creature *espardenyes* is offered here, and you shouldn't miss the monkfish (*rape*) teamed with a romesco sauce of hazelnuts, almonds, dried sweet peppers and tomatoes or the fresh salmon with Bordeaux wine. Photos of regular patrons—among them the King and Queen of Spain—adorn the walls. ◆ C Les Flors, 12 (Rda Sant Pau-C Sant Pau) Reservations essential. 241.11.39

29 **Monasterio de Sant Pau del Camp** (12th-13th c) Legend has it that **Sant Paulí** himself founded a religious community on these premises in the 5th century. Recorded history mentions something as far back as the 10th century. In any event, the marble capitals of the main door are Visigothic. True to the Catalan Gothic architectural tradition of the 13th and 14th centuries, the western facade of the church forms an angle with the abbatial dwelling. The main facade exhibits many Romanesque elements and terminates in fortress-like fashion. The prominent features of the facade are the Visigothic capitals and the hand of God in the center dating from a time when the use of human images was religiously frowned upon. The overall construction is in the form of a cross, with 3 apses and an octagonal tower crowned in the 18th century with a bell gable. Inside the church are a beautiful mosaic floor and cavernous altar, but most attractive is its small 13th-century cloister (impressively restored) with triple arches and a central fountain and garden. In fact, this

---

Restaurants/Nightlife: Red   Hotels: Blue
Shops/Parks: Green   **Sights/Culture:** Black

diminutive cloister is one of Barcelona's choicest treasures—an urban oasis offering the countryside peace of a thousand years ago in the midst of a populous barrio. Since the days of the Napoleonic invasions, this church has served as a hospital and barracks. Not until 1908 did it again function as a church. Damage done by some fires was repaired at the turn of the century, and in 1930 all buildings annexed to the church were torn down in accordance with the remodelling plans of architect **Josep Goday**, who is responsible for what little you see today. ♦ C Sant Pau, 101 (C Abat Safont-C Hort Sant Pau)

La Rambla/El Raval/Barrio Chino

29 Grupo Escolar *Collasso i Gil* (1932, **Josep Goday i Casais**) An unappealing, Scandinavian starkness characterizes this school designed at a time when the spartan virtues of Nordic design were cropping up in the work of certain Barcelona architects. ♦ C Sant Pau, 101 (C Abat Safont-C Hort Sant Pau)

30 Bar Restaurante *Mesón David* $ Well suited to a quick lunch in rustic surroundings. Specialties include octopus, *cocido gallego* (Galician stew) and roast lamb. ♦ Catalan/Spanish ♦ C Carretes, 63 (C Santa Elena) 241.59.34

31 Casa Leopoldo ★★★$$$ Don't let the downscale demeanor fool you. Founded to feed visitors to the 1929 World's Fair, this is one of Barcelona's most touted (and rightly so) spots for seafood. Beautiful tilework helps transform the mundane space into a rather pleasant eatery where the focus is definitely on fine food rather than decorative frills. The traditional house specialties are *parrillada de mariscos* and *parrillada de pescados*, platters of assorted shellfish and fish, respectively, typically followed by a single fish dish as a main course. ♦ Catalan/Seafood ♦ C San Rafael, 24 (C Cadena) 241.30.14

32 Farmacia del Dr. Sastre Marqués (remodelled 1905, **Puig i Cadafalch**) In 1973 a last-ditch effort saved this building from being demolished and replaced by an apartment building. The pharmacy dates from 1855, and its facades still conserve, albeit in a deteriorated state, Puig i Cadafalch's turn-of-the-century *sgraffito* designs of flowers and garlands. ♦ C Hospital, 109 (C Cadena)

33 Hotel San Agustín $ A strong contender for best of breed within the budget category. Ceiling beams and air conditioning (a rare find among downscale digs) speak for the blend of charm and comfort to be found in its 71 newly renovated rooms equipped with phones and baths. The front desk staff is extremely friendly and the food in the restaurant is every bit as good as it is economical. ♦ Pl Sant Agustí, 3 (C Hospital) 318.17.08; fax 217.29.28

34 Iglesia de Sant Agustí Nou (1752, **Alexandre de Rez, Pere Bertran** and **Pere Costa**) Construction of this church, formerly part of a convent complex, began in 1728 but proceeded at a snail's pace with less ambitious plans kicking in 20 years later, hence its perennially unfinished appearance. In fact, the lower reaches of the facade were completed just several years ago. Within are 3 naves and notable paintings by **Claudi Lorenzale**. On 7 November 1971 this church entered the annals of recent history by hosting the first planning session of **l'Assemblea de Catalunya** dedicated to creating a common platform against the Franco dictatorship based on liberty, amnesty and autonomy. Several participants were later arrested. ♦ Pl Sant Agustí, 2 (C Sant Agustí-C Floristes)

35 Palau de la Virreina (1778, **Josep Ausich**; sculptor, **Carles Grau**) In 1771, **Manuel Amat i Junyent**, viceroy of Peru, sent plans from Lima for a house to be built in La Rambla. Josep Ausich adapted those plans to the realities of the real estate and charged the sculptor Carles Grau with the task of adorning the facade, the double interior staircase whose unusual arches sport hanging capitals (typical of Barcelona), and the ornamental motifs of the central patio. The interior towers, visible from the street, are characteristic of the uppercrust Barcelona residences of the period. The reason the palace is today known as *Virreina* rather than *Virrey* is that the poor viceroy died days before moving in. His wife (whom the gallant viceroy married when his nephew left the family-chosen bride standing at the altar) enjoyed it long enough to bestow her title upon it, however. City Hall bought it in 1944. Between 1983 and 1987 it was modernized by councilwoman **Maria Aurèlia Capmany** to serve as headquarters of the **Town Hall Department of Culture**. It frequently stages important art exhibitions and contains a bookstore specializing in the arts. Where now you find **Casa Beethoven**, the information office, and the bookstore selling municipal publications, amanuenses once redacted letters for the illiterate. ♦ M-Sa 10AM-2PM, 4:30-9PM; Su 9:30AM-2PM. La Rambla, 99 (C Carme-C Petxina)

Within the Palau de la Virreina:

Casa Beethoven This small music shop is always packed with music aficionados in search of all manner of sheet music. A bulletin board brimming with music-related offers and solicitations attests to its status as a kind of clearing house for Barcelona's music enthusiasts. ♦ La Rambla, 97 (C Carme-C Petxina) 301.48.26

Some say La Rambla was once a torrent whose Latin name was *arenno*, which under later Moorish rule became *ramla* and eventually *La Rambla*.

36 Plaça de Sant Josep (1840, **Josep Mas i Vila**; metallic roof ca 1870) An architecturally harmonious group of houses were once in the forefront of this plaza dating from the Romantic era. Later, their uniform facades equipped with lovely terraces perched atop unfluted Ionic columns were hidden by the ironwork of the current covered market building. After a fire in 1835 destroyed the 16th-century **Convento de las Carmelitas Descalzas de San José**, this property reverted to the city, which erected a large porticoed plaza to accommodate the numerous street vendors impeding then, as now, the flow of traffic along La Rambla. Although typically attributed to **F. Daniel Molina i Casamajó**, stylistically and chronologically this plaza is more likely the work of Josep Mas i Vila, then a municipal architect. Inaugurated on the Feast Day of San José in 1840, it failed to serve its projected purpose because the vendors themselves objected; they wanted a covered space in which to pursue their activities. Thirty years later their wishes were granted. The **Mercat de Sant Josep**, the market popularly known as *La Boquería*, is a must on any Barcelona itinerary. If it's fresh, canned, or in any way edible, you'll find it here beyond the 1914 gateway. To watch the patrons size up the wares is to know that they are eminently demanding. ♦ La Rambla, 85-89 (C Carme-C Petxina)

Within the Mercat de Sant Josep:

Bar Pinocho ★$ A diminutive Barcelona landmark where the morning finds market vendors and their customers crowding each other for coffee and a bite of breakfast. At lunch the gregarious owner **Juanito** helps you select your meal directly from what his wife's got cooking on the stove. ♦ Catalan ♦ 317.17.31

Restaurante Garduña ★$$ At the opposite end of the market from Pinocho, this restaurant offers an ample selection of wines and a market-fresh menu highlighting grilled seafood. All is served up with a wonderfully cozy, country-quaint decor. ♦ Seafood ♦ C Morera, 17-19. 302.43.23

37 Paraguas For over 100 years a purveyor of umbrellas hand-crafted on the premises. Custom orders welcome. A great place to buy some souvenir Spanish fans as well. ♦ La Rambla, 104 (C Portaferrissa-C Boquería) 301.33.26

38 Escribà Behind the eye-catching Art Nouveau (i.e., Modernist) exterior lurk some tempting confections. In 1820 a pasta factory was founded here. In 1902 the premises were remodelled by **Antoni Ros Güell** in a quintessentially Modernist vein to accommodate the grocery store **Antigua Casa Figueras**. Note the enamelled mosaics, the wrought iron, the leaded stained-glass windows, and the plinth festooned with stone. Several years ago the groceries made way for Escribà's delicate pastries and fine chocolates, but the Modernist facade with its mosaic lettering lingers on by law. The original Patisseria Escribà located at Gran Via C.C. (546.254.75.35) has been in business since 1906. ♦ La Rambla, 83 (C Petxina) 301.60.27

La Rambla/El Raval/Barrio Chino

38 El Turia $ A popular lunch spot for actors, artists and other barrio regulars who appreciate its home-style, home-priced cooking. Some dishes are delicious—e.g., the *conejo al escabeche* (rabbit marinated in vinegar and spices)—others so-so. Avoid the *paella*; try the flan. Beyond that, it's mostly grilled meats and dishes dressed with tomato sauce. The ambience is amiable both upstairs and down. ♦ Spanish ♦ C Petxina, 7 (C Cabres-La Rambla) 317.95.09

39 Restaurant Egipte $$ The most sophisticated of 3 restaurants by the same name in the same vicinity, this one sports a few kitschy decorative flourishes, including a ceiling adorned with a painted sky and garlands of painted flowers. The service is friendly, the ambience pleasant, but the food is spotty. Avoid the rabbit. ♦ Spanish/Catalan ♦ La Rambla, 79 (C Petxina-C Hospital) 317.95.45. Also at: Jerusalem, 3 and 12. 317.74.80 and 301.62.08

39 La Casa Genové (1911, **Enric Sagnier Villavecchia**) One of a handful of Modernist buildings in La Rambla, this former pharmacy of Dr. Genové ceased ministering to the sick in 1974 and was subsequently and fittingly resuscitated to house the offices of **Promoció de Ciutat Vella, S.A**, a municipal organization fostering the promotion and promotion of the *Old City* as a new concept. ♦ La Rambla, 77 (C Petxina-C Hospital)

Restaurants/Nightlife: Red   Hotels: Blue
Shops/Parks: Green   Sights/Culture: Black

19

40 Casa Bruno Quadros (1885, **Josep Vilaseca**; modification and restoration 1980; restoration of facade 1988) In 1883 Josep Vilaseca i Casanovas supervised the alteration of a building dating from the beginning of the 19th century. Most probably the modification was due to the renovation of a store called **Botiga Bruno Cuadros** that occupied a large part of the structure. The alteration affected the facade decoration, the interior configuration, and included the construction of an additional floor. Representative of the architect's eclectic bent, the whimsical facade contains Egyptian references, especially in its balconies and the

La Rambla/El Raval/Barrio Chino

columned gallery of the upper floor, which also echoes the Catalan Gothic and Baroque traditions. All this together with abundant Oriental motifs that reach their most prominent expression in the former store's commercial emblem—a Chinese dragon protruding from the corner above an inclined umbrella and a cast-iron lamp—makes it an intriguing exercise in eclecticism. Now home to the **Caixa de Sabadell**, a bank, this building's recent restoration has considerably toned up this stretch of La Rambla. ♦ La Rambla (Pl Boquería)

41 Rambla dels Caputxins In terms of urban construction and development, this portion of La Rambla stretching from Pla de la Boquería to Plaça del Teatre is the oldest. Until late in the 18th century it was dominated by convents and religious schools. It started taking on its current contours in the first half of the 19th century when, in 1824, **Carrer de Ferran** was opened and soon became Barcelona's hub of luxury. Here you'll find the **Gran Teatre del Liceu** and its predecessor, the **Teatre Principal**, Barcelona's first theater.

42 Pla de la Boquería (aka Pla de l'Os) The mid-point of La Rambla, this plaza, at its center, is distinguished by a circular **Joan Miró** mosaic dating from 1976. The plaza got its name from the tables (*taules de bocateria*) where, as early as 1217, meat was sold. In the 14th century the plaza was paved with stone. At one point it was a prime spot for public hangings. In 1704 the first houses along La Rambla were built in this vicinity. By 1781 there were street lamps here and chairs to rent for brief respites (a custom still common along La Rambla). Now a much-travelled pedestrian crossroad, this plaza is at its most animated when there is a performance at the neighboring **Gran Teatre del Liceu**.

42 Hotel Residencia Internacional $$ What this place lacks in charm it makes up for in location and price. Travelers on a budget love it here and greatly appreciate the laundry service and singular breakfast view of La Rambla. Among the 60 newly renovated, ever-clean rooms with phones (some with shower only, no tub) are a goodly number of triples and quads. ♦ La Rambla, 78-80 (Pl Boquería) 302.25.66; fax 317.61.90

43 Hotel España $ (1900, **Lluís Domènech i Montaner**) Truly captivating here are the restaurant decor and the cafeteria's 4-meter-high chimney by the sculptor **Eusebio Arnau**. Elsewhere, neglect has tarnished many of the Modernist decorative embellishments imparted by such masters as **Ramon Casas** and **Pau Gargallo**. Walk in the hotel and have a look around. Check out the mosaic patterns on the stair landings. But don't even think about staying in its down-in-the-mouth rooms. ♦ C San Pau, 9 and 11 (Les Penedides) 318.17.58

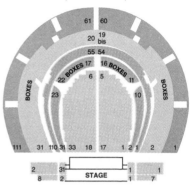

44 Gran Teatre del Liceu (1847, **Miquel Garriga i Roca**; reconstruction 1862, **Josep Oriol Mestres i Esplugas**) A rather unprepossessing facade masks the Victorian exuberance within. Barcelona's famed opera house came into being thanks to a group known as the **Liceo Filarmónico Dramático Barcelonés de S.M. la Reina Doña Isabel II**, which, in 1844, was ceded this ground for its headquarters. Shares in the project were purchased by individuals who then became part owners of the theater and were thus entitled to a permanent seat for all productions—a privilege that was handed down through the generations. Some *barceloneses* still hold these shares, which today simply entitle them to purchase tickets in advance of public sale. With an auditorium just slightly larger than that of Milan's Scala (and still among the largest in Europe), the lavish theater made its debut on 4 April 1847 with an audience of 4000. At the time Barcelona's population was only 250,000, so the theater was quite large for the city of its day and, as such, a telling barometer of Barcelona's cultural and economic status. Constructed without a single column, the auditorium was then an architectural innovation. To prove to a doubting public that all would not collapse when the house was full, sacks of stones were put in all the seats for several weeks during 1845. On 17 April 1847 **Donizetti**'s *Ana Bolena* was the first opera performed here. On 9 April 1861 the theater was totally destroyed by fire, but it opened a little less than a year later after rapid reconstruction under the guidance of Josep Oriol Mestres. In 1874 he remodelled the Rambla facade, and in 1898 **Salvador Viñals** superimposed upon it his iron-and-glass marquee. The current aspect of the auditorium and stage are the result of a significant renovation undertaken in 1883 by **Pere Falqués**, who imparted a Baroque demeanor to the loges, which all have anterooms of differing, highly individualized decor. Overall, the style of the theater is eclectic. Neoclassical columns and stairs adorn the vestibule; Rococo lamps light up the **Hall of Mirrors** where people congregate during intermissions. The lamps in the auditorium (which now often resounds with the native talents of **Montserrat Caballé** and **José Carreras**) are the original gas lamps turned upside down. The central chandelier, removed during the Civil War, was not replaced so no patron's view would be obstructed. In fact, management is so cognizant of disgruntled patrons that only 2600 tickets of a possible 2700 are sold. Plans to expand the theater are in the air, but neighboring merchants and residents who stand to lose stores and homes are trying to stop it. Guided half-hour tours are offered Monday to Friday at 11:30AM and 12:15PM. Opera season runs from November to March; ballet season is in the spring, with a new mini-season running from the first week of September to the last week of October. ♦ Seats 2600. Admission. La Rambla, 61-65 (C Sant Pau-C La Unió) 318.92.77

Within the Gran Teatre del Liceu:

Cercle del Liceu You can only get in here accompanied by a member, so try your darndest to meet one! The Cercle del Liceu is a very exclusive club in the English style comprised of some 1200 male-only members. Created to foster friendship and conversation lasting beyond that of the theater's boxes and Hall of Mirrors, the club was established in 1847 and its facilities inaugurated on 17 February 1848. Apart from a passion for music, gambling was once an integral part of the Cercle's daily life. The series of rooms it occupies within the opera house are an enclave of luxurious Modernist splendor. Outstanding among their many treasures are the impressively carved and couched elevator manufactured by the Cardellach Company and the rotunda containing a group of 12 oil paintings by **Ramon Casas** depicting different musical genres and, true to Modernist principles, using women as the main protagonists (a touch of irony in this staunchly masculine preserve).

Gran Teatre del Liceu

45 Cafè de L'Òpera When La Rambla was riding high, this was *the* posh place for coffee and conversation. Now, with over 100 years under its belt, it is decidedly less polished and posh, but no less popular. ♦ La Rambla, 74 (C Boquería-C Ferran) 317.75.85

La Rambla/El Raval/Barrio Chino

45 McDonald's $ Occupying part of the old Beristain armory, this is one half of a major-league, fast-food double-header. ♦ La Rambla, 62 (C Ferran)

46 Kentucky Fried Chicken $ (1914, **Puig i Cadafalch**) This is the other half, installed in a virtually unknown building (**El Miele**) by this well-known architect. ♦ La Rambla, 60 (C Ferran)

47 Hotel Oriente $$ (1670, **Pere Serra i Bosch**; 1882, **Juli Marial**) About a century and a half ago this hotel inserted itself into the basic structures of the **Colegio de San Buenaventura**, founded by the Franciscans in 1652. Today's banquet hall was yesterday's cloister; surrounding it are the old monastic galleries. Poor lighting is the main drawback to the 142 otherwise adequate rooms with baths of recent vintage and telephones. To get an inkling of the hotel's former cachet, take a peak at the restaurant and downstairs sitting room. ♦ La Rambla, 45-47 (C Unió-C Nou Rambla) 302.25.58; fax 412.38.19

47 Guardia Urbana (18th c, **Narcís Serra**) In May 1989 the local cops installed their HQ in the former **Convent of Santo Angel**, whose 18th-century cloister was preserved. ♦ La Rambla, 43 (C Unió-C Nou Rambla)

Some renowned Catalan opera singers of the past are **Maria Barrientos, Conxita Supervia** and **Francesc Viñas**. Today's world-class opera stars include **Montserrat Caballé, Victoria de los Angeles** and **José Carreras**.

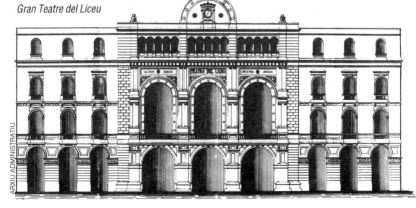

ARXIU ADMINISTRATIU

48 Hotel Gaudí $$ Matter-of-fact, air-conditioned accommodations made pleasant by a light and breezy decor. The 71 rooms have baths and telephones. ♦ C Nou Rambla, 12 (La Rambla-C Lancaster) 317.90.32

Palau Güell

CAIXA DE PENSIONS FOUNDATION

49 Palau Güell (1890, **Antoni Gaudí i Cornet**) Though no longer home to the **Museu de les Arts de l'Espectacle**, the name still sticks and this former mansion continues to stage sporadic exhibitions related to the theater and to house a theater arts library and archives. Its greater interest, however, lies in its Gaudí pedigree. Built for **Eusebi Güell Bacigalupi**, Gaudí's patron, it represents the beginning of Gaudí's full-blown creativity (he was 34 at the time), and combines Gothic elements with some Arabic flourishes. Linked by a passageway to the house of Eusebi's father, it was designed as an extension of the family residence to accommodate social gatherings, private concerts and house guests. It was Gaudí's great debut work for Güell and was built from stone from the owner's own Garraf quarries. Spatially interesting, its play of the horizontal and vertical creates a fluid interior distinguished by a marble staircase leading to a central, first-floor (our 2nd) salon that extends up to the perforated cupola. All in all, it would have made a great setting for episodes of *Dark Shadows*. The white-stone exterior suggests a fortress-castle. The cylindrical grill of the facade carries the Catalonian coat of arms topped by an eagle. The curious tombstones on the ground floor date from 1634 and were extracted from the **Capella dels Comediants** (now gone) within the nearby church of **Santa Mònica**. Don't miss the ceramic and stone mosaic decoration of the terrace's 19 chimneys—a Gaudí trademark.

In 1984 the Palau Güell was designated a World Heritage structure by UNESCO. ♦ Admission. Daily 11AM-2PM, 5-8PM; closed holidays. C Nou Rambla, 3-5 (La Rambla-C Lancaster) 317.39.74

50 Bodega Bohemia Since 1893 the Bohemia has been famed for giving performers past their prime a tiny stage to cling to. A tenacious feature in the Barcelona night, this vestigial cabaret bar sometimes finds bold patrons showcasing their singing talents as well. ♦ No cover. C Lancaster, 2 (C Nou Rambla) 302.50.61

51 Tablao Flamenco Cordobés Like bullfighting, flamenco is not indigenous to this part of Spain. Still, tourists demand it and owner **Luis Amade**, a native of Andalucia, flamenco's home, is happy to oblige with a reasonable approximation of the real thing. ♦ La Rambla, 35 (C Nou Rambla-C Arc Teatre) 317.66.53

52 Teatre Principal (1778, **Francisco Cabrer**; facade 1866, **Francesc Daniel Molina i Casamajó**) Site of Barcelona's first theater, created in 1603 to help raise money for the **Hospital de la Santa Creu**. For many years Barcelona's only theater, it was first known as the **Teatro de la Santa Cruz** because of its charitable beginnings. In 1815 it began offering regular opera performances. Until the appearance of the **Gran Teatre del Liceu** in 1847, it had a monopoly on all city productions. In 1802 it was enlarged and in 1847 substantially reformed to accommodate an audience of 2000. Eventually, however, newer, more luxurious theaters proved insurmountable competition and the theater declined to its present deplorable state. A series of fires, mutilations and vulgar decorations across the centuries further contributed to creating the eyesore we see today sadly adorned with 4 decaying busts of actors and actresses dating from 1933. Though it looks utterly abandoned, it houses a pool and snooker hall and a dance school under the auspices of the Teatre del Liceu. ♦ La Rambla, 27-29 (C Arc Teatre)

53 La Rambla de Santa Mònica Stretching from Plaça del Teatre to Plaça Portal de la Pau, this is Barcelona's version of New York's pre-gentrified 42nd Street, the place where the Barrio Chino's undesirable elements spill on to La Rambla. Unsavory by day and largely unsafe by night, it is an area of sleazy sex shops and shows. On holidays and weekends, however, a high-quality craft market takes over its lower reaches.

53 Monumento a Frederic Soler (1900, **Falqués**; sculpture 1906, **Agustí Querol**) Honors **Serafí Pitarra** (or simply Pitarra), pseudonym for **Frederic Soler** (1839-95), the father of modern Catalan theater. Fashioned of large blocks of stone and marble, it is a hybrid of the Baroque and Modernist traditions. ♦ Pl Teatre

Restaurants/Nightlife: Red   **Hotels:** Blue
Shops/Parks: Green   **Sights/Culture:** Black

54 Pastís After **Quime Ballester** and **Carme Pericás** returned from a visit to Marseilles, they opened this bar in May 1947. Ever since, it has been a shrine to their memories of France, a place where **Edith Piaf** lives on in recorded song and dusty art, and the namesake liqueur can be found in a few equally dusty bottles. The dark, drunken paintings are by the late Quime. The dingy, dark walls are by neglect. Still, the Pastís is a Barcelona landmark all the more beloved for its grunginess. Pastís patrons cover a broad spectrum of humanity, and the puritan of sensibility should be aware that transvestite prostitutes are part of the parade regularly passing by its windows. ♦ C Santa Mónica, 4 (Ptge Lluîs Cutchet-La Rambla) 318.79.80

55 Centre D'Art Santa Mònica (17th c; recent adaptation, **Helio Piñón** and **Albert Viaplana**) Within this ugly concrete shell resides the remnants of the 17th-century cloister of the **Convento de Santa Mònica**, now covered and most attractively incorporated into the downstairs exhibition space. The lofty artistic purposes of this public gallery contrast sharply with the baser instincts catered to by the surrounding streetwalkers and sex shops. ♦ Free. M-Sa 11AM-2PM, 4-8PM; Su, holidays 11AM-3PM. La Rambla, 7 (C Santa Mònica-C Portal Santa Madrona) 412.12.72

56 Casa March de Reus (1780, **Joan Soler i Faneca**) Like the Centre d'Art Santa Mònica across the way, this is the property of the **Catalonian Department of Culture**. One of the first structures built after the last bit of wall that reached to the Drassanes was torn down in 1775, it features a central patio and rear garden. The Neoclassical facade dating from the 18th century is very simple. Built for the businessperson March de Reus, it passed through many hands before being taken over by the **Conselleria de Cultura de la Generalitat**. During the Napoleonic occupation of Barcelona, **General Duhesme** installed himself here. In the 19th and early 20th century the **Banco de España** did likewise. ♦ La Rambla, 8 (Pl Teatre-Ptge Banca)

56 Hostal Marítima $ A favored, no-frills refuge for young people run by **Vittorio Rosellini**, an exuberant Italian who takes meticulous care with cleanliness and the clientele he accepts. The 16 high-ceilinged rooms have the bare minimum of functional furnishings, but the friendliness and comraderie fostered by Rosellini himself helps mitigate the meager amenities. They will do your laundry here, but you'll have to journey to the reception area for a bath. If you're traveling with friends, there are a number of triple and quad rooms available. ♦ La Rambla, 4 (Ptge Banca-C Escudellers) 302.31.52

Famed Catalan cellist **Pau Casals** founded the Casals Orchestra and the Worker's Concert Association in Barcelona. Casals refused to return to Catalunya during the period of the Franco dictatorship, and proclaimed throughout the world his unwavering Catalan *nationality*.

57 Museu de Cera Over 300 figures populate this wax museum and the neighboring **Expomuseu** devoted exclusively to figures from the worlds of witchcraft and the occult. ♦ Admission; children under 11 discount. M-F 10AM-1:30PM, 4-7:30PM, Sa-Su, holidays 10AM-8PM, winter; daily 10AM-8PM, summer. Ptge Banca, 7 (Pl Teatre-Pl Portal Pau) 317.26.49

La Rambla/El Raval/Barrio Chino

58 Plaça del Portal de la Pau At No. 5 the archives of the **Gobierno Militar** (Military Government) and the **Farmacia Militar** occupy the former **Banco de Barcelona** building whose passing presence (1844-1931) lingers in a lintel carrying sculptures by **Venanci Vallmitjana**. At No. 2 the **Sector Naval de Catalunya** and **Comandancia Militar de Marina** occupy a building dating from the 1950s.

59 Drassanes Reials (14th-17th c) The most complete surviving example of a medieval shipyard known today. Although constructed in multiple phases over a protracted period of time (7 bays date from the 14th century and 3 from the 17th century), there was a surprising consistency in the construction methods and structural forms used. Built by **King Pere el Gran** for the construction and repair of ships, the structure passed into the hands of the military in 1663 and adaptations were made to convert it into barracks and an arsenal. The outer wall dates from 1681. Nearby stands the 1971 sculpture by **Ros Sabaté** of a sailing ship that commemorates the Battle of Lepanto. ♦ Pl Portal Pau, 1

Within the Drassanes Reials:

Museu Marítim An original **Amerigo Vespucci** map, a replica of **Don Juan** of Austria's *La Galera Real*, a model of the world's first submarine invented by **Narcís Monturiol**, and a collection of antique figureheads are the starring attractions at this museum inaugurated in 1941. ♦ Admission. Tu-Sa 9:30AM-1PM, 4-7PM; Su, holidays 10AM-2PM. 301.18.71

60 Monumento a la Batalla de Lepanto (1971, **Ros Sabaté**) Few people know that alongside the **Drassanes Reials** stands this attractive sculpture of a sailing ship commemorating the decisive Battle of Lepanto, a 1571 naval clash between forces of the Ottoman Empire and various Christian powers in which **Miguel de Cervantes**, author of the legendary *Don Quixote de la Mancha*, was wounded. During this battle the combined forces of Greece, Austria, Spain and Venice stopped the Ottoman Turks from snatching Cyprus from Venice. The Turkish navy lay in the Gulf of Patras off the coast of Lepanto, Greece. Two hundred ships under the leadership of **Don Juan** of Austria attacked them and thus helped to turn the tide in favor of the allied Christians, who eventually defeated the Muslim Turks. ♦ Drassanes Reials

Barri Gòtic

The **Barri Gòtic** (Gothic Quarter), known long ago as the **Cathedral Quarter**, is a misnomer of sorts, a touristically convenient designation imposed on a by no means wholly Gothic part of **La Ciutat Vella**. In fact, in the 1920s, so the anecdote goes, a visitor asked a shopkeeper in Barcelona's Eixample where the Barri Gòtic was and the man replied, *Well, sir, it's the one they are building around the Cathedral.* There is much truth in the rejoinder. For example, the facade of the **Cathedral** itself, the barrio's architectural and spiritual omphalos, dates from the 20th century. Beyond that there are few truly Gothic buildings in the quarter and several that have actually been *imported* from other areas of the city and rebuilt here stone by stone to enhance the neighborhood's *Gothic* cachet. Most deserving of the *Gothic* moniker are the **El Call** and **Sant Just** sections of the quarter.

Though architecturally unsound, the term Gothic Quarter does suit these streets in spirit. This, after all, is where it was at during the 13th and 14th centuries when Barcelona was a major player in the Iberian and Mediterranean worlds, and the patina of past prominence still clings to many of its structures. For 5 centuries this was also the seat of power for the Catalan Monarchs, and it is today the headquarters of both the municipal and regional governments.

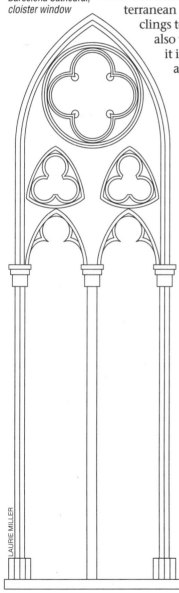

Barcelona Cathedral, cloister window

Well beneath the bustle of these contemporary bureaucracies reside the ancient remains of the Roman city of Barcino and its Visigothic successor, some of which can be seen in situ in the basement of the **Museu d'Historia de la Ciutat**. In fact, the Barri Gòtic is studded with numerous remains of the ancient fortifications and palaces built by the Romans on what they called *Mons Taber*.

Around the Cathedral and throughout the barrio's most delectable squares, buskers frequently gather to scatter their musical fairy dust through the surrounding alleyways. Their presence is especially magical at dusk when people bustling in and out of the shops on their way home from work are frozen, spellbound, in their tracks by the compelling strains of Strauss, Mozart, Albéñiz or an Andean band.

Culturally speaking, the Barri Gòtic is home to the **Ateneu Barcelonés**, the famous turn-of-the-century cafe-cum-culture club **Els Quatre Gats**, and **Sala Parés**, Spain's oldest art gallery. **Joan Miró** was born in this barrio; **Pitarra**, the father of the Catalan theater, lived and worked here; and for years **Picasso** drew inspiration from its richly textured streets.

Wall-to-wall cobblestones, gurgling fountains, vintage stores of yore, growing ranks of chic shops—it all adds up to our favorite area of Barcelona for aimless wandering. No matter how many times we meander through these streets in the company of our medieval reveries, it will simply never be enough.

LAURIE MILLER

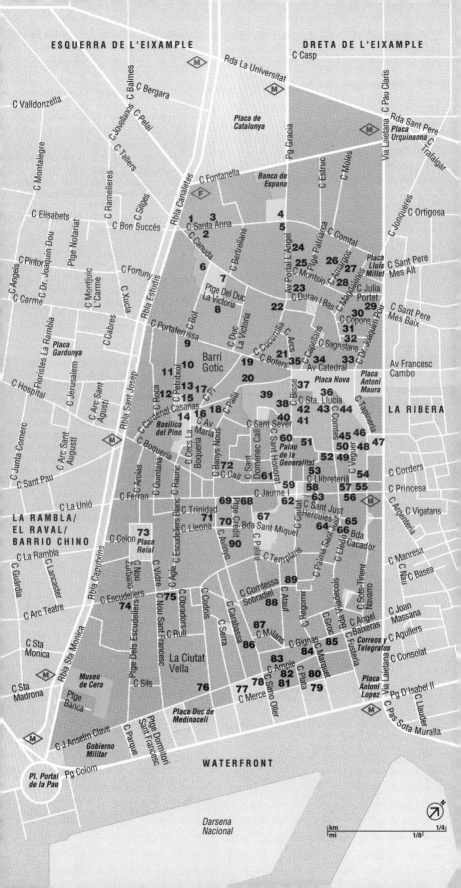

1 Self Naturista ★$ As the name suggests, you serve yourself at this cafeteria where the hearty, wholesome, healthy and, yes, *good* vegetarian choices appeal to the health-conscious and residual hippies of our day. Don't miss the fresh fruit juices. ♦ Vegetarian ♦ C Santa Anna, 11-15 (La Rambla-Av Portal L'Angel) 318.23.88

2 Amadeu Vidal Quite literally for the birds. Besides the standard inventory of dogs, cats, tropical fish and the various paraphernalia they require, this pet shop specializes in rare

Barri Gòtic

species of birds, many of whom sing. ♦ C Santa Anna, 14 (La Rambla-Av Portal L'Angel) 302.52.93

3 Casa Elena Castellano (1907, **Jaume Torres Grau**) Most notable in this building housing a hotel and apartments is the floral ornamentation that is so genuinely Modernist. You can visit the richly decorated vestibule with its white-tile wainscoting, *sgraffito*-covered walls, sculptured and painted ceiling, wrought-iron bannisters, and etched-glass doors. A fine example of the high-quality craftsmanship of the period's artisans. ♦ C Santa Anna, 21 (La Rambla-Av Portal L'Angel)

3 Pedro Alonso Purveyor of gloves, fans, costume jewelry and motorcycle apparel. Go figure. ♦ C Santa Anna, 27 (La Rambla-Av Portal L'Angel) 317.60.85

4 Iglesia de Santa Anna (12th-15th c) Tucked away in the **Placeta de Ramón Amadeu** between the entrance to a candy store and a photo shop, this church stands ringed by trees at a quiet, contemplative remove from the bustle of old-world Barcelona. A flower stand just inside the portal adds a further grace note of serenity to the scene. With the construction of this church in the middle of the 12th century, the complex of structures spawned by the **Santo Sepulcro de Santa Anna** convent, built in 1141, was completed. Built in the form of a Greek cross with a quadrangular apse, the church's most striking features are the 3-bell tower and the carved door of the main entrance dating from 1300. In 1420, this complex officially became the **Santa Anna Monastery**, which commissioned further construction lasting until the end of the 15th century. The cloister and **Sala Capitular** (the chapter house that is now the baptismal chapel) date from this period. By 1872 time and neglect had destroyed the convent that originally gave rise to the church. ♦ C Santa Anna, 27-29 (La Rambla-Av Portal L'Angel)

5 Galerías Preciados (1926, **Arnau Calvet**) Throughout Spain this department store plays Gimbels to El Corte Ingles' Macy's. Here it is housed in a building that won Calvet the municipal prize for the best piece of architecture of 1926. The building first housed the department store **Jorba**, which in 1964 was bought by the Preciados chain. ♦ Av Portal L'Angel, 19-21 (C Santa Anna). 317.00.00. Also at: Av Diagonal, 471-473. 322.30.11

6 Ateneu Barcelonés (1796, **Josep Francesc Ferrer de Llupià**, **Barón de Sabassona**; renovation to install the Ateneu 1906, **Josep Font i Gumà** and **Josep Mª. Jujol i Gibert**) Conceived and built by the Baron himself as the **Palacio Sabassona**, its original medieval style with Classical overtones has been modified so many times that little remains of its original personality except for the interior staircase opening onto the patio, the romantic rear garden, and the pictorial ceiling ornamentation of the 2nd-floor library, which is the work of **F. Pla** *El Vigatà*, who also worked on the **Palau Moja** in La Rambla. The most significant transformations occurred in 1906, when the palacio was adapted to the needs of the Ateneu, and in 1968, when it was enlarged and modernized. The Ateneu, founded in 1860, is essentially a private library/social club. Its 300,000-volume library is the third most important in the city. Technically, non-members are prohibited from entering its chummy domain, but a polite request is usually greeted with gracious permission to have a look around. Adjoining the rear garden is a salon where chess is played and serious thoughts are coined amidst swirling smoke. A foot-worn marble staircase leads to the dark-wood world of serious study in the upper library. Note the wooden elevator with bevelled glass windows. ♦ C Canuda, 6 (Pl Vila Madrid) 318.86.34

7 Plaça Vila de Madrid (1958) The Carmelite convent that once stood on this site was torn down by the city's Republican government in the early 20th century. When development work was undertaken in 1957, it struck upon a Roman necropolis below. The **Fuente de la Maja** in the plaza's upper level is by sculptor **Lluís Montané Mollfulleda**, whose subject pays homage to the Spanish capital, Madrid, famed for its *majas* (elegant young ladies). At the bottom of the steps leading to the lower level you'll find some Roman tombs.

8 Govinda ★★$$ Enchiladas and pizzas mingle with Govinda's mostly Indian, strictly vegetarian menu. The various *thalis* (trays laden with a variety of Indian dishes) are the house specialty. Try the fresh fruit and vegetable juices and drink to your health. ♦ Indian/Vegetarian ♦ Pl Vila Madrid 4-5 (C D'En Bot-C Duc Victoria) 318.77.29

On Christmas Eve, 1213 **St. Francis of Assisi** created Christianity's first manger scene in Barcelona. Since then crèches have been an important part of the city's Christmas festivities.

9 Carrer Portaferrissa In recent years this straight, narrow street has become a boutique-lined shopping artery with vast indoor malls branching off either side. **Galerias Malda** extends from just beyond C Petritxol all the way through to the Pl del Pi and **Gralla Hall** extends in and up in the vicinity of Pl de la Cucurulla.

10 Beardsley A browser's wonderland, this shop's eclectic inventory includes woolens, leather goods, flasks, glassware, stationery, quality gift items, occasional furniture and assorted antiques. Take special note of the stainless-steel tins for storing and pouring olive oil and the modern coffee pots by Barcelona's famous architect-designer **Ricardo Bofill**. ◆ C Petritxol, 12 (C Portaferrissa-Pl Pi) 301.05.76

SALA $\mathbf{P}$ ARÉS

11 Sala Parés Spain's oldest art gallery, this is sacred ground for any connoisseur of the art of our century. It was here that **Ramon Casas** and **Santiago Rusiñol** spearheaded the revival of Catalan painting. Together with sculptor **Clarasó**, they exhibited a sizeable collection of their Parisian creations—notably influenced by the French Impressionists—which served to light the artistic fuse of the Catalan Modernist movement. **Joan Parés**, an interior decorator, established **Casa Parés** on this spot in 1840 to sell painting materials. As an added come-on he also displayed paintings and drawings. When the house at No. 3 next door was built, it was agreed by all that its patio could be used for exhibitions. Joan's son **Joan Babtista** inaugurated it as an exhibition gallery in 1877. Thus was Sala Parés born. After the original house at No. 5 was demolished, the new building erected here in 1884 included a back patio for exhibitions, which has been incorporated into the present gallery. In those days exhibitions always opened on Sunday, and it became a tradition after attending mass and before plunging into a *patisseria* to drop by here for a look at the state of the arts. In 1869 an exhibition of posters by foreign artists was held; it included such heavy-hitters as **Cheret, Léfèvre, Grosset, Toulouse-Lautrec, Hiland Ellis, Price** and **Hardy**. In 1897 the gallery held its first musical performance featuring **Pau Casals** and **Carles Vidiella**. A 1901 exhibition of drawings in charcoal, pencil and pastel featured some illustrations by **Picasso**. Indeed, Sala Parés had the honor of being the first gallery to publicly exhibit Picasso in Barcelona. Early in the 20th century the gallery fell into decline and in 1925 it was taken over by **Joan Antoni Maragall**. Improvements were made without altering the architecture, and the first exhibition under the new management included works by **Salvador Dalí** and **Pau Gargallo**. At the end of the 1930s, the gallery entered into a relationship with Christie's. In

1966 it gobbled up the house at No. 8. ◆ M-Sa 10AM-1:30PM, 4-8PM; Su 11AM-1:30PM. C Petritxol, 5 and 8 (C Portaferrissa-Pl Pi) 318.70.20; fax 317.30.10

12 Juan Soler Founded in 1898, this is the only shop specializing in passementerie left in the city. Here you'll find every kind of feather, frill and froufrou imaginable, from industrial-strength brocades to bolt after bolt of sexy, sequin-studded cloth. If you're handy with needle and thread, come and let your imagination run wild. ◆ Pl Pi, 2 (C Petritxol) 318.64.93

13 Ganiveteria Roca, S.A. Although this shop dates from 1911, it remains on the cutting edge of scissor, knife and shaving accessory technology. Behind its beautiful *sgraffito*-graced facade awaits a battalion of Swiss army

knives, menacing daggers, and an ample selection of camping and hunting knives—not to mention the biggest butcher knives we've ever seen. ◆ Pl Pi, 3 (C Petritxol) 302.12.41

14 Iglesia de Santa Maria del Pi (14th-15th c) Work on the current church began around 1322, and the nave was completed in the second half of the 14th century. The finishing touches were added in the 15th century under the guiding artistic vision of **Guillem Abiell** and **Francesc Basset**. The **Sala Capitular** (now the **Capella del Santíssim Sacrament**), completed in 1486, was the work of **Bartomeu Mas**, who very likely also finished off the massive bell tower. The church's single nave culminates in a 7-sided apse and is flanked by lateral chapels. The stone wall of the 14th-century facade is perforated only by the main door and a large rose window (some say the largest in the world). The impressive 15th-century bell tower, 177 feet high, is now partly obscured by structures of more recent vintage. Like the **Iglesia Santa Maria del Mar** and the **Monasterio de Pedralbes**, this is a representative example of the Catalan Gothic vernacular applied to religious architecture, which is characterized by a unitary interior space and a compact, largely horizontal exterior whose solid facades contain few airy respites and are largely devoid of ornamentation. During Spain's period of Muslim rule, this was the only Barcelona church open to Christian worship. ◆ Pl Pi (Pl Sant Josep Oriol)

15 Plaça del Pi A lone pine marks the plaza to which it gave its name. Along with the adjoining Plaça Sant Josep Oriol, it became a city square in the early 19th century when parochial cemeteries within the city walls were abolished for reasons of hygiene. The statue of **Angel Giumerà** by **Josep Cardona** was installed in 1983. Occasionally you'll find here a flock of stands offering an array of fancy and home-grown foodstuffs. At other times it's a popular spot for buskers. Interesting among the surrounding buildings are the **Casa de la**

Congregació de la Puríssima Sang at No. 1, which dates from 1342 and was rehabilitated in the 18th century; the **Gremi de Revenedors** at No. 3, whose *sgraffito* designs have been restored; and the **Palacio Maldà Castellvell** at No. 4, which dates from the 17th century and houses the **Maldà** mall. At the end of the 19th century it was the headquarters of the **Fomento del Trabajo Nacional**, and one of its meetings was the occasion of the first terrorist bombing in Barcelona. During the Civil War (1936-39), it was the only place to attend Mass in the city.

16 Plaça Sant Josep Oriol Adjoining the Plaça del Pi at its southeast corner, this square is frequently brimming with artists showcasing their creations. Of interest among its sur-

Barri Gòtic

rounding buildings is the **Palacio Fiveller** at No. 4, which dates from 1571 and is now the headquarters of the **Institut Agrícola Català de Sant Isidre**.

17 Bar del Pi A classic, old-world bar that in fine weather, and when the Plaça Sant Josep Oriol is devoid of art for sale, sets up outdoor tables in the square. ♦ Pl Sant Josep Oriol, 1 (Pl Pi) 302.21.23

17 Molsa One of the city's better craft shops, Molsa offers an assortment of new and antique pottery, beautiful linens, and other appealing odds and ends. ♦ Pl Sant Josep Oriol, 1 (Pl Pi) 302.31.03

17 La Xicra A funky place to indulge in a hot chocolate or coffee and a pastry. But by far its finest feature is the old-world cafe aura that sustains conversations for hour upon hour. As in those days of yore, you can pick up the day's paper, conveniently mounted on a wooden stick, and just kick back. If you don't read Spanish, bring your own reading material. Typically, the atmosphere is agreeably capped off with classical music. ♦ Pl Sant Josep Oriol, 2 (C Pi) 318.07.86

18 Makoki Collectors of comics take note. Most of the vintage publications are in Spanish, however. ♦ Pl Sant Josep Oriol, 4 (C Palla-C Av María) 301.79.37

Restaurants/Nightlife: Red   **Hotels:** Blue
Shops/Parks: Green   **Sights/Culture:** Black

19 Charcutería *La Pineda* The aged atmosphere of this vintage *deli* is every bit as savory as the sausages, cheeses, cold cuts and pâtés. A smattering of chairs and tables accommodates customers who want to grab a quick bite. ♦ C Pi, 16 (Pl Sant Josep Oriol-C Portaferrissa) 302.43.93

20 Carrer de la Palla A sedate, curving street that skirts the ancient Roman walls and is lined with antique shops, art galleries and vanguard bookstores. Check out the antiquary **Artur Ramon**—he often hosts unusual exhibitions. At the Plaça Nova end of the street you'll clearly see a stretch of the old Roman walls.

21 Real Círculo Artístico/Institut Barcelonés de Arte A group of local artists maintain studios here and hold exhibitions. The restaurant within is open to the public. ♦ C Arcs, 5 (Pl Nova-Av Portal L'Angel) 318.78.66

22 La Hormiga de Oro, S.A. Offers all manner of enlightening books on Barcelona in diverse languages. Also a polyglot assortment of newspapers. ♦ Av Portal L'Angel, 5 (C Arcs-C Canuda) 302.39.42

23 Pensión Arosa $ Staying in this 7-room pension is a little like bedding down with family or friends that have a spare room. The extent of the bathroom facilities accompanying each room varies, but there is one double with a complete bath. The front rooms have balconies. Some rooms can accommodate up to 4. The entrance is several elevator-less flights up. All is clean, comfortable and quiet. ♦ Av Portal L'Angel, 14, 1º (C Duran i Bas-C Montsió) No credit cards. 317.36.87

24 Catalana de Gas i Electricitat (1895, **Josep Domènech Estapà**) Monumental and eclectic, this office building, like others by the same architect (i.e., the **Edifici de la Reial Academia de Ciències i Arts de Barcelona** in La Rambla) reflects his very personal style at the edge of Modernism. Its ornamental exuberance is of Classical inspiration. ♦ Av Portal L'Angel, 20-22 (C Comtal-C Montsió)

25 Casa Martí *Els Quatre Gats* (1896, **Josep Puig i Cadafalch**) One of this well-known Modernist architect's first important structures (and his first in Barcelona), this 4-story brick building vaguely echoes the Catalan Gothic style mingled with decorative elements drawn from a broader European Gothic genre. The pedestal at the corner bears the date *1896* along with an image of Sant Jordi and the dragon, an emblem that appears, almost in the manner of an architectural signature, in almost all of Puig's works. But Casa Martí's architectural significance is somewhat overshadowed by the fleeting but vibrant fame of the hybrid cafe-concert and *cervecería* Els Quatre Gats installed in the ground floor from 1897 to 1903. This was *the* meeting place of its day for the Modernist masters from all walks of artistic life, the tavern of choice for the group known as *Els Quatre Gats* (the 4 cats) founded by **Ramon Casas, Santiago Rusiñol**

and **Miquel Utrillo** and administered by **Pere Romeu**. Eventually **Picasso, Nonell, Carlos Vazquez, Anglada Camarasa** and many more joined this cultural circle. In fact, on 1 February 1900 Picasso presented here his first individual exhibition comprised of 24 portraits of Els Quatre Gats regulars. But even the eponymous magazine spawned by this dynamic group of artists could not prevent the financial demise of the cafe nor the spiritual demise of the group. From 1903 until the Civil War, the **Cercle Artístic de Sant Lluc** occupied the premises, which now, after many years of abandonment, once again house an appealing cafe-restaurant. The decorative mementos of its Modernist vitality have either disappeared or been installed in the **Museu D'Art Modern**, however. ◆ C Montsio, 3 bis (Ptge Patriarca)

Within Casa Martí:

Els 4 Gats ★$$$ A charming cafe-restaurant where one can have aperitifs and tapas as a prelude to romantic dining underscored by live piano music. In such a pretty and cultured setting, even if the food were somewhat lacking (which it's not, and you can't go wrong with the fish), the ambience would completely overrule any dissatisfaction. Even the bathroom decor in colorful ceramics is delightful. ◆ Catalan ◆ 302.41.40

26 El Pati $$ The variety of reasonably priced dishes here makes it popular with neighborhood workers of all professions. Pizza and pasta are the headliners, but at midday there is a daily 3-course lunch of assorted Spanish specialties. The main drawback is the high-decibel noise level. ◆ Italian/Spanish ◆ C Amargós, 13 (C Comtal-C Montsió) 302.00.36

27 Incas An inviting shop devoted to the arts and crafts of Ecuador, Bolivia and Peru. ◆ C Amargós, 16 (C Comtal-C Montsió) 412.26.86. Also at: Boquería, 21. 301.97.34

28 Restaurant Can Pescallunes ★★$$ The Catalan cuisine here borrows a bit from the French, and the mix is most satisfying. The châteaubriand and sole are solid choices, as are the dessert crepes. ◆ Catalan/French ◆ C Magdalenes, 23 (C Tomás Mieres) 318.54.83

29 Formatgeria Cannes ★$ A small eatery where dining is based on an assortment of over 30 Spanish cheeses and 20 national and

regional sausages and cold cuts that can be washed down with some of Valladolid's finest wines. ◆ C Doctor Joaquin Pou, 4 (C Copons-Vía Laietana) 302.50.71

30 La Odisea ★★★$$$$ Strange to think that some of Catalunya's most notorious communists helped found this enclave of luxurious, gourmet dining. Poet-chef **Antonio Ferre Taratiel** claims a loyal following of artistic patrons that avidly discuss the state of their arts over his fine *crema de cangrejos* or duck liver. ◆ Mediterranean ◆ C Copons, 7 (C Ripoll-C Doctor Joaquin Pou) Reservations essential. 302.36.92

31 Bar Restaurant Llivia ★$ Although brief, the menu here is market-fresh. Don't miss the *anchoas* (anchovies) or *navajas a la plancha* (razor clams). ◆ Catalan ◆ C Copons, 2 (C Ripoll) 318.10.78

32 Nostromo $$$ A nautical theme prevails at this combination restaurant-cafe-bookstore. The bar is in the form of a boat, and most of the magazines and books for sale and/or perusal deal with maritime topics. The downstairs dining area occupies old wine cellars restored in very good taste. Most charming among them is the circular one. Unfortunately, the cuisine does not attain the same enchanting level as the ambience. It redeems itself somewhat in the dessert department with its cakes and *creme catalana*. ◆ Catalan ◆ C Ripoll, 16 (C Misser Ferrer) 412.24.55

32 Hotel R. Regencia Colón $$ Tour groups and individual travelers looking for comfort in a central location at a comfortable price love the 50 newly renovated rooms here offering air conditioning, phones, music, TVs and minibars. Lone travelers should note that single rooms come with just a shower and W.C. ♦ C Sagristans, 13-17 (C Ripoll-C Doctor Joaquin Pou) 318.98.58; fax 317.28.22 (reservations can be made through Marketing Ahead, 433 5th Ave, New York NY 10016; 212/686.9213; fax 212/686.0271)

33 Hotel Colón $$$ One of our favorites because it overlooks the Cathedral, has a homey feel to it, and has a cozy bar that is really more like a living room. Converted from a private mansion into a hotel in 1951 (retaining the stones

Barri Gòtic

of the original facade), it has recently been completely renovated and redecorated in floral prints and breezy pastels. Its 200 rooms vary in size and decor, and those in the know opt for one on the 4th or 5th floor (exterior rooms on the 5th floor have pleasant, ample terraces). Room 406 has a particularly splendid balcony view of the Cathedral that has been enjoyed by such illustrious guests as **Tennesee Williams** and **Joan Miró**. All rooms are air conditioned and have direct-dial phones, music, TV and minibar. ♦ Av Catedral, 7 (C Doctor Joaquin Pou) 301.14.04; fax 317.29.15 (reservations can be made through Marketing Ahead, 433 5th Ave, New York NY 10016; 212/686.9213; fax 212/686.0271)

34 Gotic Ceramics have always been a leading Spanish craft, and this shop brings together creations from across the land, including those of the famed house of Lladró. ♦ Av Catedral, 3 (C Capellans-C Doctor Joaquin Pou) 318.06.27

35 Muralla Romana (Roman Walls) (3rd-4th c) Fragments of the old Roman city walls, which to a great extent have been reconstructed, frame the medieval heart of Barcelona. The lower portions of the current walls, comprised of large stone blocks, were erected between AD 270 and 310 and topped in the 12th century with a more refined construction of small stones. In their entirety, the walls had a rectangular configuration with chamferred corners, a citadel facing the sea, and a perimeter of 4166 feet. A series of towers topped the wall. The location of the gates and recent archaeological findings point to an ancient urban organization along the lines of the Roman *castrum*: the longest road (**Decumanus Maximus**) ran from the current Plaça Nova to the gate located in today's Plaça del Regomir; the second major road (**Cardo Maximus**) ran from the Plaça de l'Angel to the city gate located between the current streets Call and Ferran. ♦ Pl Nova (Av Catedral-C Tapinería-C Sotstinent Navarro-Pl Traginers)

35 Col.legi D'Arquitectes De Catalunya I Demarcació de Barcelona (1962, **Xavier Busquets i Sindreu**) Headquarters of the association of professional architects of Catalunya, this eyesore of a building, distinguished by a weather-beaten **Picasso** mural in concrete, symbolizes everything the professionals working within should be striving against. One of the city's first *skyscrapers*, its boxy, unadorned modernity is a blatant affront to the medieval beauty it borders. Allegedly conceived as an expression of Barcelona's modern spirit at a time when the municipal architecture seemed unable to lift itself from the doldrums of mediocrity it had fallen into after the Civil War, Busquets' design, which beat out several others, inflicted upon the city a version of the day's prevailing International style with no regard for integrating the building with its surroundings. Nevertheless, it serves its functional purposes and stages enlightening exhibitions. The facade murals designed by Picasso were sandblasted into existence by the Norwegian **Carl Nesjar**. Inside, the small bookstore on the downstairs cafeteria-bar offers a choice selection of publications in various languages, mostly about architecture and the arts. ♦ Pl Nova, 5 (C Capellans-C Arcs) 301.50.00

36 Casas de L'Ardiaca y Del Degà (remodeling of l'Ardiaca Despià 1510; remodeling of Casa del Degà 1559) In the early 15th century **Archdeacon Lluís Desplà** had these 2 edifices combined in a single structure patterned after the *palacios* of the day. In the last century both buildings underwent frequent changes until 1870, when they were acquired by **Jorge Altimira** at public auction. Under the technical tutelage of **Josep Garriga**, their remodeling and further fusion resulted in a splendidly eccentric structure. Most propitious among the many alterations this entailed was the conversion of the patio into cloisters. After the building became the seat of the **Sede del Colegio de Abogados** (headquarters of the law school) in 1895, **Domènech i Montaner** was charged with its decoration in 1902. The most playful of his adornments is the Modernist mailbox featuring a sculptured swallow and turtle, the former symbolizing the desire that the mail move swiftly, the latter acknowledging the reality that it ain't always so. Every Corpus Christi celebration includes the spectacle of an egg dancing on the waters of the courtyard's curious mushroom fountain. Today the **Institut Municipal d'Historia** and its library occupy the premises. ♦ C Santa Llúcia, 1 (Pl Seu)

For more than 500 years **Mons Taber** (now more or less the **Barri Gòtic**) was the seat of the Catalan monarchy. The **Cathedral** and the **Palau Reial** are the 2 surviving architectural pillars of this period.

37 Portal del Bisbe Leading off the Plaça Nova, this main entrance to a bygone Barcelona, flanked by 2 round towers of the ancient Roman wall, is the city's oldest gate. ♦ Pl Nova (C Irurita)

38 Palau Episcopal (13th c, Romanesque gallery; expansion and facade facing Pl Nova 1784, **Josep Mas i Dordal** and **Pau Mas i Dordal**) Work began on the Bishop's palace in the late 12th century. Remaining of that original construction are the patio and the Romanesque gallery of the northwestern wing, which has undergone considerable reconstruction and whose coffered ceiling and 13th-century mural are well worth viewing. In 1784, the patio was completed along with the Neoclassical facade facing the Plaça Nova and the facade facing C Bisbe with its *sgraffito* decoration. The facade facing the Pl Garriga i Bachs was not completed until 1928. ♦ C Bisbe, 5 (Pl Nova, 1)

39 Casas Gremiales dels Sabaters i Calderers (16th c) In the Plaça de Sant Felip Neri stand 2 adjacent houses that were moved here and restored several years ago. The Casa dels Calderers adjoining the church was a private residence adapted as a guild headquarters in the 16th century, occasioning the addition of some dignified Renaissance ornamentation. Originally built in the C de la Bòria, this house was actually relocated twice. This appears to be its final resting place. The Casa dels Sabaters, built in 1565, is also a Renaissance work that moved here from the C de la Corribia in 1943. ♦ Pl Sant Felip Neri

39 Iglesia de Sant Felip Neri (1752) An example of Counter Reformation Baroque church architecture, this church with a central nave and lateral chapels has much the feel of a fortress about it. Still visible on its facade are the scars of Civil War machine-gun fire. Few know that 20 children died here in January 1938 during Fascist bombing. It's worth a look inside to see the Baroque altar by **Ignasi Vergara**. The highly simplistic facade of the convent next door, which surrounds a 2-story patio, was largely rebuilt during the second half of the 18th century. ♦ Pl Sant Felip Neri

40 Museu del Calçat Antic (Museum of Antique Shoes) Here you'll find a brief précis of the history of footwear from the sandal of a Roman slave to the glitzy pumps in which some celebrities pranced their way to stardom. ♦ Admission. Tu-Sa 11:30AM-2PM; Su, holidays 10AM-2PM. Pl Sant Felip Neri. 302.26.80

40 Iglesia de San Sever (1705, **Jaume Arnaudies** and **Joan Fiter**) Externally very similar to the Iglesia de Sant Felip Neri, this church is noted for its well-preserved Baroque interior, one of the few remaining in the city. The carved wood and polychromatic work within are characteristic of a southern Baroque style that emerged with the Counter Reformation and are the work of sculptor **Escarabatxeres**, who also adorned the door and facade. ♦ C Sant Sever, 9 (Pl D'A. Garriga i Bachs)

41 Plaça D'A. Garriga i Bachs The figures along the wall are **Josep Llimona**'s monument to the **Mártires de la Independencia**, the heroes who opposed the Napoleonic occupation of Barcelona. The curious angelic grace note is the work of **Vicenç Navarro**.

42 Capilla de Santa Llúcia (1268) Its construction commissioned by **Bishop Arnau de Gurb**, this chapel quite possibly formed part of the **Palau Episcopal** before being incorporated as a Cathedral entrance leading to the cloisters. This adaptation likely resulted in the loss of the semicircular apse characteristic of the Romanesque chapels of the period which, like this one, comprise a single nave covered with slightly pointed vaulting. For those who are interested, Santa Llúcia is the patron saint

of seamstresses and, not surprisingly, those who suffer from problems of sight. ♦ C Santa Llúcia, 2 (C Bisbe)

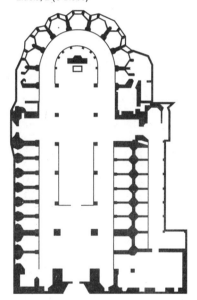

43 Catedral de Barcelona (14th-15th c; main facade and dome 1913, **Josep Oriol Mestres i Esplugas** and **August Font i Carreras**) The first religious structure on this site was a basilica with 3 naves destroyed in the Moor's attack led by Al-Mansur in 925; its remains are now on display in the **Museu d'Història de la Ciutat**. Around 1046 a new cathedral, of which some Romanesque elements remain, was built. Work on the current basilica, which was 6 centuries in the making, began in 1298, with the bulk of the work completed between 1365 and 1388 under the direction of **Bernat Roca**, who also started work on the cloisters. The final structure contains 3 cruciform aisles and 29 lateral chapels. Of special note are: the main altar dating from the 14th century; the medieval and Renaissance flourishes of the choir, completed in 1459; the crypt of **Santa Eulàlia**, one of the 2 municipal patron saints, with its white alabaster sepulchre by **Jaume Fabre**; and the **Sala Capitular**, the Cathedral's most notably Gothic feature, designed by **Arnau Bargués** in 1397, built between 1405 and 1415 (note the interesting vault), and now featuring the twisted **Cristo de Lepanto** statue that allegedly

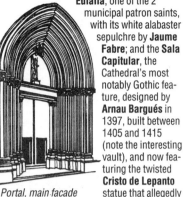

Portal, main facade

Barri Gòtic

became thus contorted while dodging a bullet during its namesake battle when it served as the figurehead of Juan of Austria's flagship. The cloisters, endowed with palm trees, magnolias, geese (said to recall the geese that saved Rome) and a fountain (where an egg also dances on Corpus Christi) topped with an attractive statue of **San Jorge**, patron saint of Catalunya, house the **Museu de la Catedral** and its prized possession, *La Pietat* by **Bartolomé Bermejo**, dating from the end of the 15th century. The entry to the cloisters is distinguished by a door adorned with a carved pieta of the flamenco school. Although remarkably Gothic in appearance, the Cathedral's main facade, like the galleried bridge spanning the C del Bisbe nearby, are of our century. Working from a 15th-century drawing by **Mestre Carlí**, J.O. Mestres and August Font finished the facade and dome in 1913. An especially magical sight is the Cathedral illuminated at night, which usually happens on Thursday, Saturday and Sunday. ◆ Museum daily 10AM-1PM; Cathedral daily 7:30AM-1:30PM, 4-7:30PM. Pl Seu (C Bisbe-C Pietat-C Comtes) 315.35.55

44 L'Almoina Installed in the rear of the Casa Pia Almoina, this shop offers a better brand of souvenir than most and is one of the official outlets for Majorica pearls. ◆ C Tapineria, 39 (Av Catedral-Bda Canonja) 310.16.41

44 Casas de la Canonja y de la Pia Almoina (15th c, Casa de la Canonja; 1546, Casa de la Pia Almoina) The upper wall of the Casa de la Canonja is part of the Roman wall running along C Tapineria. The Gothic Casa de Pia Almoina, restored in 1989, was the former seat of a charitable foundation set up at the beginning of the 11th century that in its heyday fed 100 destitute souls daily. Today it stages diverse cultural exhibitions. ◆ Pl Seu (C Comtes)

45 Museu Frederic Marès A Catalan sculptor in his 90s, Frederic Marès is also a fervent collector who here displays the fruits of the pastime he clearly pursues with great passion. His treasures run the full gamut from Punic arti-

facts to fanciful parasols. The so-called *Museu Sentimental* upstairs reflects the habits and handiwork of daily life from the end of the 15th to the end of the 19th century. Before you enter the museum, look for the remnant of Roman wall to your right. ◆ Admission. Tu-Sa 9AM-2PM, 4-7PM; Su, holidays 9AM-2PM. Pl Sant Iu, 5-6 (C Comtes) 310.58.00

Museu Frederic Marès

Ground Floor

Paleo-Christian sculpture:
1 Sarcophagus, 4th c
Iberian sculpture:
2 5th-1st c BC
Classical sculpture:
3 Nymphs, 2nd-3rd c
4 Roman bronzes, 1st c

Romanesque sculpture:
5 Relief—Vocation of Sant Pere, 12th c
6 Crucifix, 12th c
7 Mare de Déu de Plandogau, 13th c

First Floor

Gothic sculpture:
1 Sant Pere de Cubells, 14th c
2 Funerary relief, 15th c
3 Crucifix, 15th c
4 Relief of Santa Clara, 15th c
5 Mare de Déu de Cuéllar, 15th-16th c
Renaissance sculpture:
6 Relief—Adoration of the shepherds, 16th-17th c
7 Relief—Monastery of la Espina, 16th c
8 Sculptures and reliefs of Nalda, 16th c

Baroque sculpture
9 Sant Pere d'Alcántara, Maria Magdalena, Sant Antoni de Pádua, 17th c
10 Santa Escolàstica, 18th-19th c
11 Cap de Sant Pere martyr, 17th c
12 Mother of God with child, 18th-19th c
19th c sculpture:
13 Clay models
Iberian sculpture:
14 5th-1st c BC

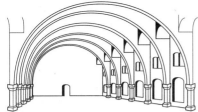

46 Palau Reial Major/Saló del Tinell (1370, **Guillem Carbonell**) In the mid-12th century the residence of the **Comtes de Barcelona** was rebuilt as the Palau Reial Major of **Ramon Berenguer IV**. Still, its current aspect is primarily the result of the transformations undergone during the 14th and 16th centuries, the damage sustained at the beginning of the 19th century, and the various restorations carried out in recent years. Between 1359 and 1370, at the hands of Carbonell, a 10th-century salon was reborn as the grand Saló del Tinell, whose wooden ceiling and 6 semicircular arches anchored in the barrel vaulting of the lateral walls are typical of the Catalan construction of the period. This salon is allegedly where the Catholic Monarchs received Columbus when he returned from his first New-World expedition, although some maintain he was actually received in the **Monasterio de Sant Jeroni de la Murtra**, near Badalona, where the Monarchs occasionally resided. For certain, however, is that in 1479 the body of **King Juan II of Aragon** lay in state here amidst the barking of his hunting dogs. This was especially fitting since it was during a hunting expedition at 70 years of age that he caught the pneumonia that caused his death. This historic hall is now regularly used for exhibitions of all sorts. ♦ Pl Rei

47 Plaça de Ramon Berenguer el Gran The bronze equestrian statue here representing **Ramon Berenguer III** is the work of **Josep Llimona**. Behind it is a cypress-ringed garden and beyond that an important part of the Roman wall, carefully restored.

48 Capilla Real de Santa Agueda (14th c, **Bertran Riquer**, **Jaume del Rei** and **Pere Oliva**) The sacristy and base of the bell tower of this chapel, grafted on to the **Palau Reial Major** in the early 14th century, are installed in a tower of the Roman wall. The chapel's single, narrow nave is crowned by a beautiful coffered wooden ceiling, the apse by ogive vaulting, and the sacristy by barrel vaulting. The notable **Retable de la Epifania** by **Jaume Huguet** dates from the middle of the 15th century. Behind the altar is the **Big Clock of Barcelona** made between 1575 and 1577 by the Flemish clockmakers **Simon Nicolau**. It is the fifth of 6 clocks that have occupied the belfry of the Barcelona Cathedral since 1401. The windows here look out upon fragments of the Roman walls. ♦ Pl Rei

48 Plaça del Rei This square rimmed by Gothic buildings is one of the quarter's premier plazas— or at least it *was* until they allowed the corner bar to expand outdoors and pollute the scene with its flimsy aluminum chairs and tables.

49 L'Anticuary This is the culprit. Though we refuse on principle to sit at its outdoor tables, we do enjoy sipping a drink and nibbling cheese or tapas with the barrio regulars at the indoor bar. ♦ C Veguer, 13 (Bda Santa Clara) 315.31.09

50 Palau del Lloctinent (1557, **Antoni Carbonell**) Since Barcelona suffered a setback in status when the crowns of Catalunya-Aragon and Castilla were united, the aristocratic representative position of *lloctinent* was created to appease bruised sensibilities. Accordingly, the *lloctinent* was built a residence commensurate with his rank annexed to the **Palau Reial Major**. This Gothic building embellished with Renaissance flourishes surrounds a 3-tiered inner courtyard flanked by graceful stairs. Above the stairway to the left is a highly ornamental coffered ceiling well worth a look.

Barri Gòtic

Since 1853 this palau has housed the **Archives of the Crown of Aragon**, but these are now slated to move to the **Plaça de les Arts** when work there is finished. Where the palace meets the **Saló de Tinell** rises a 5-story observation tower. Such towers existed throughout Barcelona from the 12th century on, and most important houses had them to watch the seas and thus avoid surprise attacks. This is the only surviving example of the species in the city. ♦ C Comtes, 2 (Pl Rei-Bda Santa Clara)

51 Casas de Los Canonges (14th-15th c) Upon abandoning the monastic life, the canons set themselves up in private residences skirting the Cathedral. A number of these were concentrated in the Pl de la Pietat behind the basilica. An architecturally heterogeneous group of buildings to begin with, they have been profoundly modified over the centuries. The house at the corner of C del Bisbe was restored by **Rubió i Bellvé** in 1921, when the *sgraffito* decoration was added to the facade. The interior reconstruction and redesign were begun in 1925 by the **Foment de les Arts Decoratives** and finished in 1929 by **Jeroni Martorell**. This building now houses the **Escola Professional Per a La Dona**, devoted to the graphic arts, fashion, tourism and handicrafts. The house at C del Bisbe No. 8 is the little-used official residence of the president of the Catalan Generalitat. ♦ C Pietat, 2-6 (C Bisbe, 4-8)

52 Columnas del Templo de Augusto (1st-2nd c) In the interior patio of this Gothic structure housing the headquarters of the **Centre Excursionist de Catalunya** you'll find a few remaining Corinthian columns from Barcelona's only known Roman temple, the Temple of Augustus. However, it's a question of good timing and luck to find the outer door open. In the **Museu d'Historia de la Ciutat** you'll find a model of the temple. ♦ C Paradís, 10 (C Pietat-C Llibreteria)

53 La Cuineta $$$ Installed in a 17th-century building, this restaurant is more notable for its ambience than its food. Valuable *objets d'art* stud the dining rooms. So do members of the nearby municipal and regional houses of government. At times you'll even find the president of the Generalitat or Barcelona's mayor lunching here. Set lunch menus of varying prices are offered. ◆ Catalan ◆ C Paradís, 4 (C Pietat-C Llibretería) 315.41.56. Also at: La Bona Cuina, C Pietat, 12. 315.41.56

54 Casa Padellàs (15th-16th c) This traditional palacio in the Catalan Gothic style has a few ornamental Renaissance elements, though the Renaissance style never really caught on in Catalonia. Originally built in the C Mercaders, it was moved to this plaza at the beginning of the century when the Via Laietana was con-

structed. Its reconstruction involved some modifications, but none did it any substantial harm. It now contains the **Museu d'Historia de la Ciutat**, whose highlights include some in-situ remains of the Roman and Visigothic incarnations of Barcelona and assorted artifacts from those periods, among them the oldest known inscription giving the complete Roman name of the ancient colony of Barcelona. Uncovered in the excavations of the city's public baths at Plaça de Sant Miquel, it reads: *Colonia Iulia Augusta Faventia Paterna Barcino*. Virtually anything else you want to know about the city can be gleaned from the numerous exhibitions sprawled across the museum's upper floors. ◆ M 3:30-8:30PM; Tu-Sa 9AM-1:30PM, 3:30-8:30PM; Su, holidays 9AM-1:30PM. C Veguer (Pl Rei) 315.11.11

54 Cereria Subirà The longest-standing business in Barcelona, this shop devoted to the making and selling of candles was founded in 1761, although it didn't move into its current quarters until 1909. Except for the sales counter, the interior decor dates from 1847 when a clothing and textile store occupied the premises. ◆ Bda Llibretería, 7 (Pl L'Angel-C Veguer) 315.26.06

55 Hotel Suizo $$ Of the 3 Gargallo group hotels in this area (the Suizo, Rialto and Gòtico), this is the second best of the lot. Its 48 air-conditioned rooms feature televisions, telephones and small balconies. We love the charming cafetería/bar on the ground floor. ◆ Pl L'Angel, 12 (C Llibretería-C Jaume I) 315.41.11; fax 315.38.19

55 Gelateria Italiana Pagliotta One of the best bets for ice cream. It's all homemade, including the sugarless *light* version if you're watching your calorie intake. Also has great *horchata* (a milky drink made from chufa nuts) and cappuccino. ◆ C Jaume I, 15 (C Trompetes-Pl L'Angel) 310.53.24

56 Hotel Gòtico $$ Finishes a close third in the local triad of **Gargallo** hotels with 72 rooms equipped with air conditioning, television and telephone. ◆ C Jaume I, 14 (Pl L'Angel-C Dagueria) 315.22.11; fax 315.38.19

57 Hostal Rey Don Jaime I $ All 30 rooms at this very economical, centrally located hostel have a small balcony and direct-dial telephone and come with varying degrees of bathroom facilities. The furnishings are kept to a bare minimum, but all is clean. The breakfast/TV salon is especially attractive. Half of the 30 rooms are doubles convertible to triples. ◆ C Jaume I, 11 (C Dagueria) No credit cards. 315.41.61

58 Meson del Cafe Founded in 1909, this vest-pocket cafe serves some of the best coffee and cappuccino in town. Great for breakfast. ◆ C Llibertería, 16 (Pl Sant Jaume-C Arlet) 315.07.54

58 Xocolatería Santa Clara A dense, dark hot chocolate is the claim to fame at this popular breakfast and snack place. ♦ C Llibretería, 2 (Pl Sant Jaume) 315.32.08

59 Plaça de Sant Jaume Home of the **Palau de la Generalitat** (seat of the Catalonian government) and the **Casa de La Cuitat** (town hall), this is prime political territory. In Roman days the Cardo and Decumanus roads crossed here, and this was most likely the site of the ancient agora. Until the 14th century there was a cemetery in front of what is now the **Palau de la Generalitat**. The plaza's current aspect dates from 1823.

60 Palau de la Generalitat (Gothic facade and patio on C Bisbe side 1425, **Marc Safont;** Pati dels Tarongers 1536, **Pau Mateu** and **Tomàs Barsa;** facade facing Pl de Sant Jaume 1596, **Pere Blai**) Although the governmental entity known as the Generalitat was created in 1289, it had no headquarters until the end of the 14th century. The Gothic facade facing C Bisbe features a magnificent medallion of **Sant Jordi**, patron saint of Catalunya, by **Pere Johan** and is embellished with a balustrade of pinnacles and gargoyles presided over by a sculpture of the saint killing the dragon to free the princess (so the legend goes). The northern wing of the building is the work of **Pere Ferrer** and dates from 1610. The Neo-Gothic filigree bridge linking the Palau with the **Casa dels Canonges** was built in 1928 by **Rubió i Bellvé.** Pere Blai's facade facing the plaza itself is practically the only example of purely Renaissance architectural styling remaining in the city and recalls the facade of the Farnese Palace in Rome. The equestrian statue of Sant Jordi above the doorway is a 19th-century sculpture by **Andreu Aleu.** For security reasons, it is impossible to visit the interior rooms of the Palau without authoriza-

tion (except on 23 April when the Palace opens its doors, in accordance with medieval custom, to those who come to honor Sant Jordi on his feast day). Most noteworthy among them, however, is the beautiful flamboyant Gothic **Chapel of Sant Jordi** by Marc Safont dating from 1434; and endowed when enlarged in 1620 with vaulting and a cupola framed by 4 hanging capitals, the **Torres García** salon with the newly exposed paintings by that Uruguayan artist; and the **Tàpies** salon inaugurated in 1990 and containing a large work by this contemporary Barcelonan artist. From the end of the 18th century until 1908, the Palau housed the Royal High Court. Ever since it was built it has been a treasured symbol of an enduring Catalan identity. ♦ Pl Sant Jaume (C Bisbe-C Sant Sever-C Sant Honorat)

Barri Gòtic

61 Inma A fine gift shop for decorative items and jewelry. It distinguishes itself from other jewelers in this same street by featuring some very original jewelry designs by local artisans. ♦ C Call, 19 (Pl Sant Jaume) 318.30.33

62 Casa de la Ciutat (Saló de Cent 1373, **Pere Llobet;** Gothic facade facing C Ciutat 1402, **Arnau Bargués;** Neoclassical facade facing the Pl de Sant Jaume 1847, **Josep Mas i Vila;** Saló de Sessions 1860, **Francesc Daniel Molina i Casamajó;** new construction on C Ciutat side 1933, **Antoni de Falguera, Joaquim Vilaseca** and **Adolf Florensa;** 1969, *novísimo* building on Pl Sant Miquel side 1969, **Lorenzo García-Barbón** and **Enric Giralt i Ortet**) The Neoclassical facade fronting the plaza is superimposed on a Gothic one and crowned with a sculptural composition by architect **Daniel Molina** featuring the city's coat of arms surrounded by allegorical tributes.

Palau de la Generalitat

ARXIU ADMINISTRATIU

Casa de la Ciutat

ARXIU ADMINISTRATIU

Barri Gòtic

The lateral Flamboyant Gothic facade facing C Ciutat is more striking and graced by the impressive figure of the **Archangel San Rafael**, one of the most characteristic sculptures in the Catalan Gothic style, whose bronze wings were cast by the sculptor **Pere ça Anglada**. The 19th-century statues of **Jaume I** flanking the main door are by **Josep Bover** and the *conseller* **Joan Fiveller**, a patriot of the 15th century who affirmed the city's municipal freedoms. As with the **Palau de la Generalitat**, public access to the interior rooms is restricted. On entering the building, to the left of the courtyard, is the doorway of the ancient scribes' office flanked by **Josep Clará**'s *La Deesa* (*the Goddess*) and **Frederic Marè**'s *Primavera* (*Spring*). Should you get beyond this point, visit the **Saló de Cróniques** (1929) featuring paintings by **Josep Mª·Sert** and the illustrious **Saló de Cent** built in 3 stages: the Gothic work from 1369 to 1407 (with a continuation to 1525), the Baroque work from 1628 to 1684, and the modern alterations beginning in 1848 and ending in 1929. The current decoration by **Enrique Monserdá** dates from 1925. In 1982, the **Oficina Municipal de Información** opened on the ground floor; its frescoes are by **Ràfols Casamada**. In fact, in the 1980s the building was greatly revitalized with the installation of sculptures by Clarà, Marès, **Gargallo, Subirachs, Rebull, Viladomat, Miró** and others. ◆ Pl Sant Jaume (C Ciutat-Pl Sant Miguel)

63 Herboristería Anormis For generations this aromatic shop has purveyed all manner of salutary herbs and plants both domestic and imported. Also sells a delectable selection of herbal candies. ◆ C Ciutat, 3 (Pl Sant Jaume) 302.30.04

64 Plaça de Sant Just This cozy little plaza is what remained, in the 19th century, of the Sant Just cemetery. It boasts Barcelona's oldest fountain, a Gothic construction by **Joan Fiveller**, subject of one of the town hall statues. Built in 1367 and restored in the 18th

century, it incorporates an image of Sant Just and the coats of arms of the king and the city. Its current state of conservation is fragile.

64 Iglesia de Los Santos Just i Pastor (14th-15th c) The last of a series of churches erected upon the site of the former Roman amphitheater. Work on it began in 1342 under the direction of **Bernat Roca**. The final section of the 5-section nave was completed at the end of the 15th century, and the bell tower, the work of the masters **Pere Blai** and **Joan Safont**, in 1567. The main facade was reconstructed by **J.O. Mesteres** beginning in 1884. Until the 15th century this was the kings' parish church. In its early days it was one of 4 churches in the country endowed with *juradera* (sworn-oath) privileges. Oaths pertaining to 3 situations could be sworn here: 1) when 2 gentlemen were to engage in a duel, they swore here to the truth of their claims and forswore the use of *trick* weapons; 2) when a Jew had to testify in a case between a Christian and a Jew, he would be sworn in here; and 3) when someone died intestate, those persons who had heard his or her last wishes could swear to them before the altar of **San Félix** and thus give them the full legal validity of a written will—a privilege that still exists to this day. The church's resident saint is the venerated black **Virgen de Monserrat**. Artistically noteworthy within is the 16th-century retablo in the San Félix chapel carved by **Juan de Bruselas** and painted by **Pero Nunyes**. ◆ Pl Sant Just, 5-6

65 Café de L'Academia ★★$$$ Hearty Catalan dishes make this place a popular lunch spot for the civil servants who work in the **Palau de la Generalitat** and the **Casa de la Ciutat**. At dinner the crowd is more mixed. ◆ Catalan ◆ C Lledó, 1 (Pl Sant Just) Reservations recommended. 315.00.26

66 Restaurant La Raclette ★★$$$ Offers a 3-course menu and a small selection of à la carte choices in an extremely elegant setting. The tables, edged in ceramic, are tailor-made for the house specialty, raclette, and the dinnerware is choice English china. Tends to fill up for dinner, especially Friday and Saturday. Every Wednesday they feature fondue. ◆ Swiss ◆ C Lledó, 2 (Pl Sant Just) 310.01.17

67 El Paraigua A 2-tiered bar where you can sip exotic cocktails (among them one dedicated to Gloria Swanson)—some of which are made without alcoholic ingredients—in a classy environment further enhanced by classical music. The decor was lifted from the turn-of-the-century **Paraigües Gallés**, an umbrella store, once situated in C Arcs. The downstairs caverns are invitingly intimate and probably formerly served to store wheat. ◆ Pas de l'Ensenyança (Pl Sant Miquel) 302.11.31

68 Hotel Rialto $$ The best and largest of the **Gargallo** hotels in the Gothic Quarter, the Rialto has 129 ample, attractively furnished rooms with air conditioning, televisions, telephones and minibars. ◆ C Ferran, 40-42 (C L'Ensenyança) 318.52.12; fax 315.38.19

69 Passatge del Crédit (1879, **Magí Ruis i Mulet**) With the opening of C Ferran VII, the property occupied by the **Convento de la Enseñanza** was divided in 2. This passage was built on one part linking the new street with the Bda Sant Miquel. One of Barcelona's first endeavors in ironwork architecture, it pre-dates the Eiffel Tower by 10 years and reflects the Parisian influence on the Barcelona of its day. At No. 4 **Joan Miró** was born, lived for many years, and had a studio. A ceramic plaque by **Josep Llorens Artigas** commemorating the artist's 1893 birth was placed at the house's entrance in 1968 on the occasion of Miró's 75th birthday. ◆ Ptge del Crédit (C D'Avinyó-C L'Ensenyança-C Ferran-Bda Sant Miquel)

70 La Manual Alpargatera If it can be woven from reeds, grass, straw or palm, you'll find it here. But the main stock in trade is espadrilles, ready or custom-made. The handiwork goes on in full view at the rear of the store. ◆ C D'Avinyó, 7 (C Lleona-C Ferran) 301.01.72

70 El Gran Café ★$$ The romance of the turn of the last century lives on in the decor of this inviting restaurant which often offers piano accompaniment with meals. Although the menu varies with the market offering, a stable house specialty is the *rape* (angler fish) *al all cremat* (with a creamy garlic sauce). ◆ Catalan ◆ C D'Avinyó, 7 (C Lleona) 318.79.86

71 Agut d'Avignon ★★$$$$ Owner and former chef **Mercedes Giralt Salinas** keeps close watch over the kitchen at this charming, friendly restaurant hidden away at the end of a cul-de-sac. Due to its proximity to the seats of the municipal and regional governments, the lunch crowd is riddled with politicians and businessmen currying their favor. At night things are more intimate and social and the place fills with couples out for a romantic dinner. The menu, based on what's freshest in the market at the time, changes with the sea-

son but caters to the sweet-and-sour preference of the Catalan palate. Divided into multi-level nooks and crannies, the decor exudes an elegant rusticity, a beamed-ceiling charm. Most of the desserts are made here, and the *crema catalana* (the local version of *crème brûlée*) is just as it should be—crisply brown and warm on top and cool and creamy below. The wine list, 99% Spanish, is sprinkled with informative pages on the various wine-producing regions of Spain. Cigars are offered at the end of the meal. ◆ Catalan ◆ C Trinidad, 3 (C Lleona-C Ferran) Reservations recommended. 302.60.34

72 Sombrereria Obach For more than 70 years this store has been purveying all manner of hats and berets. The decoration and furnish-

ings are contemporary with its founding. ◆ C Call, 2 (C Banys Nous) 318.40.94

73 Plaça Reial (1859, **Francesc Daniel Molina i Casamajó**) Inspired by the French plazas of the Napoleonic era, this is the sole plaza of the last century that was completely executed in accordance with its original design. In 1822, the land, which had been occupied by the **Convento de los Capuchinos**, was ceded to the city. In 1848, a decision was made to construct a closed plaza, a design competition was held, Molina's plan won, and the surrounding houses were begun. The gardens and ornamentation, which have been modified over time, owe their current aspect to the recent remodeling by the architects **Correa** and **Milà** who eliminated the central flower beds in favor of an unbroken paved surface but happily retained the **Fuente de las Tres Gracias**, the 2 lamps designed by a young **Gaudí**, and the palm trees. Lined with uniform buildings in faded yellow, this plaza is highly reminiscent of a sultry, southern Spanish plaza. One curious establishment in the square is the **Museu Pedagógico de Ciencia Naturales,** which since 1889 has been among the few places in Barcelona engaged in taxidermy. Since 1880, on Sunday mornings this plaza buzzes with a stamp and coin market. At night the trade more typically turns to drugs.

74 Restaurante Parrilla Grill Room ★$$$ (1902) To a great extent the interior here retains its original turn-of-the-century aspect. Take special note of the sideboard, counters, ironwork ornamentation of the pillars, ceramic appliqués and lamps. Their delicate design and execution make this restaurant's decor a small but valuable work of Modernist art. As the name indicates, grilled meat is the specialty here, especially the lamb. Also try the *paella* and *zarzuela* (the local rendition of bouillabaisse). ◆ Spanish/Grill ◆ C Escudellers, 8 (C Ptge Escudellers) 302.40.10

Restaurants/Nightlife: Red　　**Hotels:** Blue
Shops/Parks: Green　　**Sights/Culture:** Black

75 Los Caracoles ★$$$ Every town has its Tavern on the Green and in Barcelona this is it—a place so famous and renowned one is

Barri Gòtic

embarrassed to say one doesn't know it. In other words, one comes here more for the experience than the food. Established by the **Bofarull** family (who still own it), it gradually transformed itself into a Barcelona tradition noted for its snails (which remain a signature dish), and the spit-roasted chickens that greet passersby in the street. ♦ Spanish ♦ C Escudellers, 14 (C Nou Sant Francesc) 302.31.85

76 Calçats Sole Big-footed men will find a fine selection of sturdy, high-quality, long-lasting footwear here, including cowboy and hiking boots. ♦ C Ample, 7 (C Codols-C Nou Sant Francesc) 301.69.84

77 Plaça de la Mercè (1981, **Rosa M. Clotet, Ramon Sanabria** and **Pere Casajoana**) The demolition of a block of houses cleared the way for this new square that looks old. The main facade of the Baroque church that dominates the square and the Neo-Baroque head offices of the **Official Chamber of Commerce of Barcelona** impart a vintage atmosphere. The sculpture of **Neptune** by the 18th-century sculptor **Adrià Ferran** that graces the tranquil pond next to a flurry of holm oaks was moved here from the port where it served as a fountain supplying water to the ships.

78 Iglesia de la Mercè (1775, **Josep Mas i Dordal** and **Carles Grau**) Superimposed on a church of the 13th century, this one, venerating the **Virgen de la Mercè**, one of the city's 2 patron saints, was part of the **Convento de la Mercèd** established here in the 13th century. One of Barcelona's most interesting examples of the Baroque, its layout is basilican—a central domed nave, a cupola-covered transept, and 2 small lateral naves lined with chapels. The late-Baroque facade is by Grau, who is also responsible for the interior decoration that suffered substantial Civil War damage in 1936. In 1870, a 16th-century portal from the now disappeared Sant Miquel church was installed in the lateral facade. In 1888, the exterior of the cupola was finished by **Joan**

Martorell. Crowning the cupola is an image of the Virgen de la Mercè that is the work of the **Oslé** brothers. ♦ Pl Mercè, 1-3

79 La Plata An outpost of authenticity, this tiny neighborhood bar is full of the coarse flavor of life near the waterfront. Three barrels of wine above the small bar dispense the house favorites in red, white and rosé. There are but a handful of tables and a sprinkling of colorful tiles. The hearty of stomach and soul may want to come here for a fish-based breakfast in the robust tradition of the city's bygone legions of fishermen. ♦ C Mercè, 28 (C Plata) 315.10.09

80 Bar Bodega Las Campanas (Casa Marcos) The name of this hole-in-the-wall bar takes up more space than the galleried taverna itself. Its sepia light is of another era. So is its brief wooden bar backed by a row of cured shanks of horse and veal (not the typical hams) hanging above a handful of small tables. Take away the technological concessions of the day (electric light and a minute, modern kitchen) and we could be back in the days of Cervantes, who praised Barcelona in some of his works. For a taste of the Barcelona lingering beneath the dynamics of progress, stop here for a drink and a special tapa of cheese, ham, *cecina* (one of the cured shanks), *ajo arriero* (a small portion of codfish stew with garlic), *chistorra* (a cold cut of the Navarre region) or *morcilla* (blood sausage). Oft filled with rough-hewn workers, this neighborhood hangout is truly a taste of the past. ♦ C Mercè, 21 (C Marquet) 315.06.09

81 Restaurante Lareira ★$$$ A grace note

of contemporary culinary sophistication in one of Barcelona's oldest and narrowest streets. The cramped spaces typical of these medieval confines have here given way to a couple of spacious dining rooms and an attractive bar. You'll get off to a good start with the special house salad *Lareira* combining baby shrimp, octopus, lettuce, tomato and seafood salad. The fish and seafood, the house specialty, are fresh and delectable. A fine finish to the meal among the ample selection of homemade desserts is the *Tarta de Santiago*, a traditional Galician almond cake. ♦ Galician/Seafood ♦ C Mercè, 13 (C Plata) 315.13.59

82 Palau Sessa-Larrard (1778, **Josep Ribas i Margarit, Joan Soler i Faneca** and **Carles Grau**) Built by the Duke of Sessa and later acquired by the banker Larrard, this is a classic example of late 18th-century Neoclassical Barcelona construction enhanced with decorative Baroque touches on the facade. Note its stylistic similarity to La Rambla's **Palau de la Virreina**. As this palau is now home to the **Col.legi Calasanci** (an elementary school), you might be able to sneak inside for a peek at the central patio and its ample stairway. If not, just admire the wonderful portal, the profuse sculptural decoration, and the balcony by Grau. Like all great houses of the period, it is crowned with a tower. ♦ C Ample, 28 (C Plata)

82 La Dentelliére ★★★$$ A gem of an intimate bistro with only a dozen lace-covered tables, La Dentelliére is owned by Frenchmen and upholds the French tradition of offering daily set menus at lunch and dinner in addition to a fine selection of à la carte choices. The food is prepared with typical French care. Outstanding among the numerous house specialties are the salmon carpaccio, the *solomillo maitre d'hotel* (sirloin steak), and the *confit de pato* (duck). Delicious crepes and homemade desserts make a fine finish. The quality-for-money ratio is very high. ♦ C Ample, 26 (C Simó Oller-C Plata) 319.68.21

83 Hotel Metropol $$ This recently renovated 68-room hotel transformed from a vintage private mansion offers very comfortable accommodations in an area notably lacking in hostelries of this caliber. The rooms have varying layouts but all have telephone, TV and minibar. ♦ C Ample, 31 (C D'Avinyó-C Regomir) 315.40.11; fax 319.12.76

84 El Tunel ★★★$$$$ A sophisticated restaurant tucked away in a cul-de-sac. Founded 1923. Any place that offers goose liver (in season) with Calvados and steak tartare al Armagnac is fine in our book. ♦ Catalan/Seafood ♦ C Ample, 33-35 int. (C D'Avinyó-C Regomir) Reservations recommended. 315.27.59

85 Agut ★★$$$ An inviting restaurant that serves solid fare at fair prices. Try the *brandada de bacalao* (codfish mousse). Homemade desserts. ♦ Catalan ♦ C Gignàs, 16 (C Riudarenes) 315.17.09

86 Pitarra Restaurant ★★$$$ This highly commendable restaurant occupies the former house and watch shop of **Federico Soler Hubert** (aka **Serafí Pitarra** because the son of a carpenter was not taken seriously as a writer). Pitarra, who lived in the second half of the 19th century, was a prized and prolific Catalan playwright and poet who is considered to be the father of Catalan theater. His monument stands in the Pla del Teatre. The restaurant's upstairs dining room contains the complete leather-bound collection of his plays, biographies and verse. The restaurant, over 100 years old, is run by the **Roig** brothers, who consider the memory of Soler sacred and continue to collect the memorabilia of his life. The clocks on the wall, many of them antique, recall the days when this was his clock shop. Today's restaurant patrons include the mighty politicians of the nearby municipal and regional government offices and plain folk like us. Every Wednesday at lunch the upstairs dining room is reserved for **Subirachs** and his team of collaborators, whose goal is the controversial completion of **Gaudí**'s **Sagrada Familia**. The menu is market-driven and thus seasonal. Watch for game and wild mushrooms in the fall. Any time of year order the Olivé Batllor Brut *house cava*—it's crisp and

dry and goes with most things on the menu. ♦ Catalan ♦ C D'Avinyó, 56 (C Gignàs) 301.16.47

87 Tasca La Musiqueta A funky, after-5 dive with medieval cachet. Hanging hams and picture-plastered walls impart a rugged rusticity. Boisterous when in full swing. Specializes in sangrias, wines and tapas. ♦ C D'Avinyó, 31 (C Milans) 315.23.59

88 Harlem Jazz Club A hint of New Orleans in one of the Barri Gòtic's prettier streets. This small, smoky place has no pretensions. It simply serves simple sandwiches and on Sunday and Thursday (sometimes other days of the week too) fine, live jazz. Other nights there's a wonderful selection of jazz and jazz-funky recordings. The melting-pot crowd bonds in its common musical passions. ♦ No admission. C Comtessa Sobradiel, 8 (C D'Avinyó-C D'Ataülf) 310.07.55

89 Taberne Les Tapes A genuine barrio bar ideal for a sip and a snack or an aperitif. ♦ Pl Regomir, 4 (C Cometa-C Calella) 302.48.40

90 Edificio del Bolsín (1883, **Tiberi Sabater**) Former home of the **Casino Mercantil**, a financial trading house that operated until 1915 when the Barcelona Stock Exchange was created. Winner of a municipal architectural prize in its day, it is now home to the **Escuela de Artes Aplicadas y Oficios Artísticos** (School of Applied Arts and Artistic Trades). ♦ C D'Avinyó, 23 (Pl Verónica)

Barcelona's 4th-century city walls were 29.5 feet high, 11.7 feet and 4165.6 feet long. Both strong and beautiful, they defended the city until the 13th century when a new set of city walls was built by **King Jaume I**. It seems certain that Roman Barcino was once larger than its old city walls would have us believe, since these walls stand atop the remains of older Roman buildings, and important Roman remains have been found as far away from the nucleus of the Roman town as today's Sants district.

Restaurants/Nightlife: Red **Hotels:** Blue
Shops/Parks: Green **Sights/Culture:** Black

Montjuïc

Barcelona has long been accused of turning its back to the sea. Nowhere is this clearer than in the case of the steep, southern, seaward slope of the 173-meter-high **Montjuïc**, site of a vast cemetery. Anywhere else in the world this would be prime real estate, a tiered haven of luxury condos with high-priced views of the Mediterranean.

The northern and eastern slopes of the mountain are covered with gardens—the latter effusively planted with the lush tropical vegetation of the **Jardins Mossen Costa i Llobera** named for a Mallorcan poet. Designed by the Frenchman **Jean-Claude Forestier**, these Montjuïc (pronounced mont-zhoo-eek) gardens were physically conjured by the Catalan **Nicolau M. Rubió i Tudurí**. Crowning Montjuïc mountain, which stands between the city and the sea, is a 17th-century castle.

More than any other part of the city, Montjuïc owes its development primarily to the international events that have repeatedly rallied Barcelona's civic pride and spurred its municipal progress. The first plan to use the hill for something other than burials was that of the architect **Josep Amargós** in 1894. After the first International Exhibition held in Barcelona in 1888 (which took place mostly in the **Parc de la Ciutadella**), another, to be held on Montjuïc, was promptly planned for 1914. Though for obvious reasons it was postponed until 1917, **Puig i Cadafalch** drew up a proposed plan for the exhibition in 1915 and in the autumn of that year work began. When the exhibition was further delayed until 1919, Puig i Cadafalch's plan was divided among 3 architectural teams—Puig i Cadafalch and **Guillem Busquets, Lluís Domènech** and **Vega i March**, and **Agustu Font** and **Enric Sagnier**. With the exhibition again on hold, work proceeded slowly and by the late 1920s only the twin **Pavilions Alfonso XIII** and **Victoria Eugenia** had been completed. In 1923, the military dictatorship imposed by **Primo de Rivera** removed Puig i Cadafalch from the project because of his political persuasions. Eventually the majority of the mountain was developed for the 1929 World's Fair according to a plan calling for 3 distinct areas to accommodate exhibitions relating to industry, art and sports.

Still, it has taken over half a century for Montjuïc to become fully integrated into the municipal fabric. The recent revitalization of the **Poble Espanyol**, the installation and expansion of several museums, and the construction of the Olympic installations and landscaping of the surrounding

Parc del Migdia have transformed this southwestern corner of the city into prime leisure territory for residents and visitors alike.

Spearheading its cultural offering is the **Museu d'Art de Catalunya**. Spearheading its conference and convention offering is the **Fira (Feria) de Barcelona**. Spearheading its entertainment offering are the **Poble Espanyol** and the **Parc D'Atraccions**, an amusement park with a view.

Speculations abound about the origin of the name *Montjuïc*. Some say it derives from *Mons Jovis* (Montaña de Júpiter), but *hill of the Jews* (there used to be a Jewish cemetery here) seems the most likely candidate. Written documents indicate that Jewish settlement of the hill dates back to at least 1079. It is likely that the segregation of the Jews to Montjuïc at that time stemmed from the period of Spain's Moorish occupation, there never being much love lost between Jews and Muslims. Later, when the kings of Catalunya-Aragó held sway, the Jews moved back into the city, establishing themselves in the section of the Barri Gòtic known as the *Call*, where they remained until 1492 when the Inquisition expelled all Jews from the country. When they abandoned Montjuïc as their

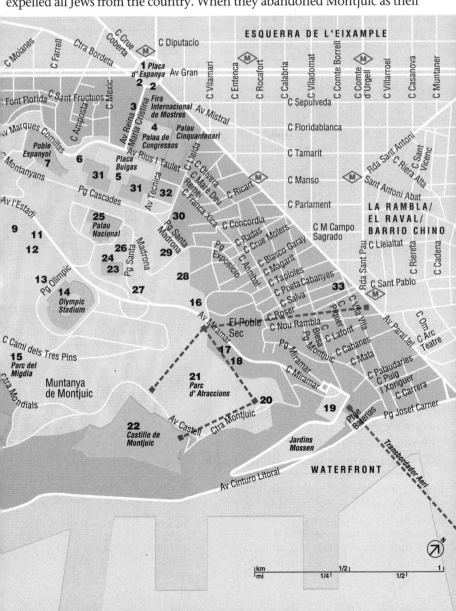

residence, however, they still continued to use it as their burial ground because the mountain's situation and elevation made it a privileged site from which to look toward Jerusalem, and the Jewish tombs were oriented accordingly.

Dubbed by some the city's *acropolis*, Montjuïc appears also to have harbored pre-Roman settlements which continued to be inhabited throughout Roman times. In any event, it seems certain that a settlement called *Laie*, which in the proto-Iberian vernacular means *land of vineyards*, once existed here. Also, in ancient times there was a tower on the mountaintop that in the 15th century served to signal passing boats, using sails during the day and fires by night. Later this tower gave way to the **Castillo de Montjuïc**.

Though it is possible to cover a number of Montjuïc's attractions on foot, it is best to do so by car. If you insist on walking, at least take the funicular and cable cars to the top and walk down. Or, if you prefer, you can hop on and off of Bus No. 61, which makes the circuit of the hill. Originating at the **Plaça D'Espanya**, it continues along the **Avinguda Reina María Cristina** and **Avinguda Marqués de Comillas** to the Poble Espanyol, **Plaça St. Jordi**, **Anella Olímpica** (Olympic Ring), **Fundació Miró** and **Plaça Dante** where the amusement park is.

Montjuïc

1 Plaça D'Espanya (1930) Once upon a time this space was ringed with windmills, and people were hanged here up until 1715 when that particular activity was moved to the Ciutadella. From 1808 to 1813, Napoleon's forces established a fortification here. In 1821, during an outbreak of yellow fever, 400 barracks were put up to house 4000 refugees. In the master plan that **Ildefons Cerdà** drew up in the mid-18th century for the orderly layout and development of the Eixample, this plaza was seen as a point of transition between that new area of the city and Montjuïc. The plaza's first designs were drawn up by **Josep Amargós** in 1915, the same year that **Puig i Cadafalch** presented his design for the proposed 1917 Barcelona Universal Exhibition, which included plans for a large plaza serving as the sole entryway to the Exhibition area and, of course, Montjuïc. In successive plans he proposed a completely circular plaza ringed by a monumental colonnade. As happened with all the works projected for the Exhibition, everything came to a halt in 1920. In 1926, however, the opening of the metro station here virtually forced construction of the plaza. A certain degree of improvisation along the way resulted in the circular plaza you see today. The commemorative fountain at the center, built in 1928-29, is the joint effort of **Josep M. Jujol i Gibert**, a disciple of Gaudí, and the sculptor **Miquel Blay i Fábregas**. In 1969 the subterranean passage was built, and in 1982 the architects **Lluís Cantallops** and **Miquel Simón** added a network of corridors accessing the **Fira (Feria) de Barcelona** and the Avinguda Reina María Cristina.

2 Torres (1927, **Ramon Reventós i Farrarons**) Commonly known as the Venetian Towers, these twin brick beacons boldly marked the entrance to the 1929 World's Fair.
♦ Pl D'Espanya (Av Reina María Cristina)

3 Avinguda de la Reina María Cristina (reconstruction 1989, **Lluís Cantallops**) This stately urban space stretching from the **Pl D'Espanya** to the **Palau Nacional** is one of Barcelona's most prominent features. Dating from 1929 (of course), it is a dynamic space designed to soften the transition from the plaza to the Palau. The original 1929 design elements included circular facades in the Pl D'Espanya, the Venetian Towers, *asparagus-like* light beams, tall columns and **Buigas'** famous fountains. By 1981, much of this had disappeared, and the avenue was little more than a vast parking lot. To recapture the spirit of the original design without sacrificing the subsequent functional utility of this space, the balustrade and flower gardens of the Pl D'Espanya were replaced by a large, circular staircase and 44 20-foot-high fountains were built along the avenue in a 1980s interpretation of the 1929 *asparagus* light beams.

4 Fira de Barcelona (Feria de Barcelona)

Convention and trade-fair traffic is a bread-and-butter industry in Barcelona, and most of the exhibitions and networking goes on at this attractive complex of a dozen structures offering over 2 million square feet of floor space and high-tech infrastructure. Barcelona hosted its first international trade fair in 1888. The embryo of today's *fira* was the *Feria de Muestras* (textile fair) held in 1920 in the Parc de la Ciutadella. In 1924, it moved to Montjuïc. After suffering setbacks during the Spanish Civil War and, to a certain extent, WWII, the *Feria de Muestras* was revived in 1943. An increasingly important commercial platform for both local and national industries, the Fira in 1963 inaugurated its centerpiece **Palau de Congressos**. The Fira now annually hosts some 40 international shows and fairs each year attended by 3 million visitors. In July 1992 the communications network of the 1992 Olympic Games will be headquartered here. The **Palau de las Comunicaciones** was constructed for the 1929 World's Fair by the architects **Adolfo Floresa** and **Félix Azúa**. Built on a pentagonal plan, its most outstanding architectural feature are the high lateral columns designed by **Puig i Cadafalch** in 1917. The **Palau del Cincuentenario** was built 1969-70 and designed by the architects **Manuel Torres Minguez, Enrique Hernández de Avilés** and **Joaquín de Ros y de Ramis**. The **Plaça Univers** was built in 1985 by the architect **Pep Bonet** and consists of a U-shaped building linking the Cincuentenario, Ferial and Congress Halls through an upper-story. An allegorical sculpture by **Llimona** stands in the middle of the plaza. The **Palau Ferial** was built between 1961-63 by architects Joaquín de Ros i de Ramis, **Juan Puigdengolas** and **Antonio Lozoya**. The Palau de Congresos was also built in 1961-63 and is the work of the same 3 architects. The **Pabellón INI** is an incredibly ugly structure considered architecturally daring when built in 1972-73 by **Juan Paradinas Riestra, Luís García Germán** and **Ignacio Casanova Fernández**; it now houses some Olympic offices. The **Palau de la Metalurgia** was known as the Metallurgy, Electricity and Drive Power Hall at the 1929 World's Fair. Laid out longitudinally along Av Reina María Cristina, it was designed by **Alexandre Soler** and **Amadeu Llopart**. Although its facade has undergone significant alterations, its most notable enduring structural features are its reinforced concrete construction and linteled arcades. ♦ Av Reina María Cristina-Av Paral.lel-C Lleida-Av Rius i Taulet. 223.99.00; fax 223.86.51

5 Fuentes de Montjuïc (aka Font Màgica) (1929, **Carles Buigas**) These elaborate fountains are one of Barcelona's most unique spectacles, especially when illuminated and accompanied by music, which they are from October to May on Saturday and Sunday from 8-11PM (9-10PM with music) and June to September on Thursday, Saturday and Sunday from 9PM-midnight (10-11PM with music). This was one of the last works undertaken to complete the 1929 World's Fair offering. Buigas, an engineer, was in charge of the electro-mechanical Fair installations. In 1928 it was decided that the central avenue of the Fair should be endowed with spectacular lighting—clearly a task for Buigas. Not only would this extraordinary project entail colored-glass lamps in the form of Art Deco obelisks suffused with lights of changing color, but it also called for cascades, fountains and incense burners to be scattered about. A fundamental element of this ambitious outdoor stage set

was this fountain built on an elevated platform at the end of the Av Reina María Cristina. An engineering wonder, these dancing fountains boast a repertoire of 50 different combinations of water and colored lights. Make an effort to see the display with musical accompaniment—it makes all the difference. ♦ Pl Carles Buigas (Av Marqués Comillas-Pl Marqués Foronda)

6 Pabellon Mies van der Rohe (aka the Barcelona Pavilion) (1929, **Ludwig Mies van der Rohe**; reconstruction 1985, **Cristià Cirici i Alomar, Ferran Ramos i Galino** and **Ignasi de Solà-Morales i Rubió**) Next door to the **Pabellón INI**, this pavilion was Germany's entry to the 1929 World's Fair. An influential architectural masterpiece touted for its spatial fluidity, it was a paradigm of modern architec-

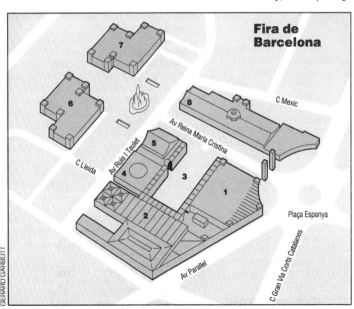

Fira de Barcelona

1 Fira Internacional de Mostres
2 Palau del Cinquantenario
3 Plaça Univers
4 Palau Ferial
5 Palau de Congressos
6 Palau D'Alfons XIII
7 Palau de Victoria Eugenia
8 Palau de Metalurgia

C Mexic
Av Reina Maria Cristina
C Lleida
Av Ruis I Taulet
Plaça Espanya
Av Parallel
C Gran Via Corts Catalanes

GEHARD GARBUTT

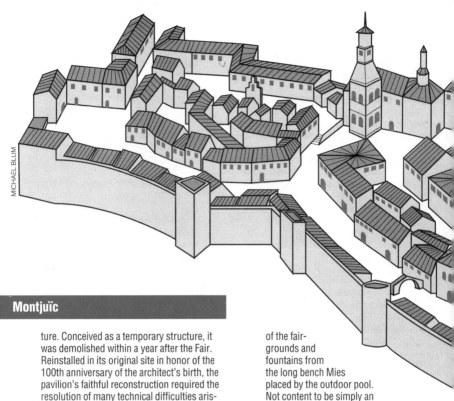

Montjuïc

ture. Conceived as a temporary structure, it was demolished within a year after the Fair. Reinstalled in its original site in honor of the 100th anniversary of the architect's birth, the pavilion's faithful reconstruction required the resolution of many technical difficulties arising from the permanent installation of a structure originally meant to be temporary. Invisible systems for rain drainage and heating were incorporated, and stainless steel rather than chrome plating was used on the 8 X-shaped beams supporting the roof. These beams, separate from the walls that define the building's boundaries, are one of the building's revolutionary features. Traditionally, wall and support were one, but by separating them and creating walls of glass, Mies blurred the distinction between interior and exterior space. Critics of the period lauded his design as a pioneer work of the International Style that ultimately decreed *less is more*. Gracing the pavilion's interior reflecting pool is a beautiful bronze sculpture of a standing nude woman by **Georg Kolbe** entitled *Morning*. We should all be grateful for the pavilion's reconstruction, as its spare, pristine, interlocking rectangular lines, its stark linear planes of glossy green marble, golden onyx and tinted glass, and the ebb and flow of reflections in its 2 decorative pools comprise a delightful and daring display of architectural imagination. During the World's Fair the original pavilion was the site of a reception held for Spain's **King Don Alfonso XIII** and **Queen Victoria Eugenia**; Mies' well-known and highly uncomfortable leather-and-chrome Barcelona chairs (which are again part of the pavilion) were meant to serve as modern thrones for the monarchs. Though the pavilion's immediate surroundings have changed little since the days of the 1929 Fair, the posterior construction of the Pabellón INI blocks what was once a fine view

of the fair-grounds and fountains from the long bench Mies placed by the outdoor pool. Not content to be simply an architectural milestone, the pavilion houses a cultural center with an architectural library and museum. ◆ Free. Daily 10AM-6PM. Av Marqués Comillas (next to Pabellón INI) 423.40.16

7 Poble Espanyol (1929, **Francesc Folguera i Grassi, Ramon Reventós i Farrarons, Xavier Nogués i Cases** and **Miquel Utrillo i Morlius**) This 1929 World's Fair attraction, a scaled-down assemblage of representative regional architectural styles from across Spain, was inaugurated on 21 May 1929 by Spain's king and queen and has recently come into its own as a distinctively dynamic Barcelona *barrio* devoted to merriment. Originally slated for destruction after the year-long fair, most of its construction is actually of simulated stone, wood or brick. But its immense popularity argued strongly against its demise, and after several decades spent in languorous obscurity as strictly a tourist sight, its operation was entrusted in 1986 to **Poble Espanyol de Montjuïc, S.A. (PEMSA)** a private company that has a 30-year concession from the city to run the place. The company's aggressive and progressive management strategies have more than doubled the number of annual visitors, which now run to over one million. Much of the increased traffic is pointedly drawn from city dwellers who now consider its 50 shops, 33 bars, restaurants and night spots, and 15 cultural attractions an important leisure offering, especially on a summer night when the cool breezes seem to blow only on Montjuïc. The **Galeria Artesanal** is a 1988 addition by architects **José Mo Sen Tato** and **Enrique**

Chateau devoted to handicraft and cultural displays. The original architectural overview of Spain that the Poble Espanyol continues to provide comprises 104 structures offering stylistic examples from the 11th to the 20th centuries. They occupy 8 squares, 3 patios, a garden with a Romanesque church, and 18 streets. ♦ Admission. Daily 9AM-4AM. Av Marqués Comillas, s/n (C Mexic-Pg Simon Bolívar) 325.78.66; fax 325.11.98

Within the Poble Espanyol:

Barcelona Experience
An audiovisual presentation, complete with olfactory stimulation, that summarizes the charms of the city. ♦ Admission. Plazuela Iglesia. 325.78.66

Sam's One of the Poble's most elegant and refined night spots, this music bar has comfortable chairs arranged in intimate conversational groupings. The caliber of the performances is volatile, however. ♦ Pl Aragonesa, 4. 426.38.45

Sotavento Good music and a wonderful upstairs cocktail bar in a setting whose patio, cloister and chapel suggest a convent. ♦ C Levante, 2 (C Buen Aire) 423.14.28

El Tablao de Carmen
Offers the finest flamenco entertainment in Barcelona in a casual, intimate setting. ♦ Cover; reduced admission for afternoon shows Su and holidays ♦ C Arcos, 9 (Pl Carmen-Pl Peñaflor) 325.68.95

La Disco del Poble A fun night spot where you can dance to high-volume music or escape for conversation to the upstairs salon where the music is muted. ♦ Cover. Pl Peñaflor, 1. 325.76.72

Las Torres de Avila By far our favorite place in the Poble for the sheer whimsy of it. These towers flanking the entrance portal were transformed into a fascinating, multi-level bar by none other than designer-of-the-moment **Xavier Mariscal** (author of the Olympic Mascot *Cobi*) and **Alfredo Arribas**. One tower is dedicated to the sun and the other to the moon. As so often happens

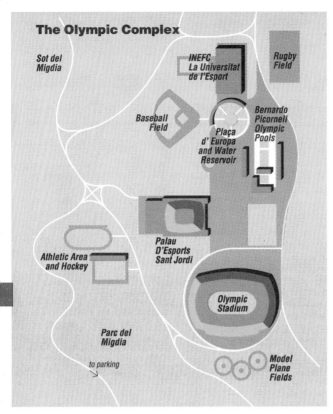

The Olympic Complex

- Sot del Migdia
- INEFC La Universitat de l'Esport
- Rugby Field
- Baseball Field
- Plaça d' Europa and Water Reservoir
- Bernardo Picornell Olympic Pools
- Palau D'Esports Sant Jordi
- Athletic Area and Hockey
- Olympic Stadium
- Parc del Migdia
- to parking
- Model Plane Fields

in today's trendy Barcelona clubs, the bathrooms constitute an attraction in their own right. Here the men's room contains a round pool table. But the best spot of all to be on a summer night is the roof-top bar commanding a knockout view of the entire city. Selective doormen and high-priced libations. ♦ No cover. Puerta de Avila. 424.93.09

8 Plaça Sant Jordi At the center of this plaza stands the 18th-century fountain of **Santa Madrona**. Gracing the nearby lookout point that surveys the Llobregat River is **Josep Llimona**'s bronze sculpture of **Sant Jordi** (St. George), Catalunya's patron saint, who is here represented in a more human mode, looking every bit the valiant but battle-weary soldier.

9 The Olympic Complex (1992) The impetus of the 1992 Summer Olympic Games will finally bring about the full development of Montjuïc first envisioned back in the 1920s. Here is where most of the attention will be focused during the Games, but afterwards the installations will serve as both ongoing tourist attractions and venues for all manner of sports and entertainment activities. In all, the Montjuïc area contains 8 sports centers and 3 circuits.

L'Anella Olímpica (Anillo Olímpico, Olympic Ring), surrounded by parks, overlooks the Mediterranean and includes the structures that will host the main sporting events of the Games. A team of architects—**Frederic Correa, Alfons Milà, Joan Margarit**and **Carles**

Buxadé—produced the design that won the international competition. Their proposal, aimed at bringing together the historical trends of prior plans for Montjuïc's development, calls for a central Olympic esplanade and a 3-tiered terrace that provides access to the buildings in the Ring, regally presided over by the **Olympic Stadium**. The first terrace leads to the **Palau D'Esports Sant Jordi** (Sports Hall) through a square plaza surrounded by waterfalls and flights of steps and containing a lawn traversed in the center by a stream. The second terrace, also in the shape of a square, is similar to the first and leads to the **Bernardo Picornell Olympic Pools** through a monumental arcade. South of it, set amidst gardens, is the **Camp de Beisbol** (Baseball Field) with natural grass and bleachers accommodating 850. The third terrace is the circular **Plaça d'Europa** built over the new water tank (which supplies water to 500,000 Barcelonans) at the lower end of the esplanade and leading through another arcade to the **INEFC (La Universitat de l'Esport)** building. All of the venues detailed below will be linked by the broad **Av del Estadi**, the large **Plaça d'Europa**, and abutted by the **Parc del Migdia**. ♦ Av L'Estadi-Camí dels Tres Pins

10 INEFC (La Universitat de l'Esport) (1992, **Ricardo Bofill**) Work on this Beaux Arts style structure at the western end of the Olympic Ring began in 1988. It will house the future Catalan sports university known as the **Institut Nacional d'Educació Física de Catalunya (INEFC)** with a capacity of 1000 students. The complex will comprise 2 roofed cloisters with a central nave between them that will serve as a reception area and exhibition hall. Surrounding the cloisters will be classrooms, offices, library and dressing rooms directly connected to the open-air sports areas that include a volleyball court, hockey field and large multipurpose field of natural grass. The roof is a metallic structure and the facades are of prefabricated concrete panels incorporating the windows, pilasters, columns and architraves. ♦ Olympic Ring

Barcelona's sports teams, when they win a championship, traditionally sing a *salve* of thanks to the **Virgen de la Mercè**, one of the city's 2 patron saints.

The Olympic Games

Though the mythical origins of the first Olympic Games are legion, it was most likely **King Ifito** of Hellade who got things rolling back in 776 BC. One hundred years later, the games, then held every 5 years, had achieved Panhellenic stature, hosting more than 300 athletes from all of the independent city-states of ancient Greece. At the end of the 4th year of the Olympic cycle, messengers were dispatched from Olympia to announce the forthcoming event; at this point, all conflicts and wars were suspended to ensure the athletes safe passage to Olympia.

Along with the athletes came merchants, musicians, politicians, artists, writers, orators and philosophers, for the games were also a forum for touting political and philosophical theories, new books and new artists.

Always held during the full moon in July or August, the games originally lasted a single day and featured only one competition—the 200-meter dash. During the 1169 years that they were celebrated regularly, additional competitions were added that ultimately dictated a 5-day program. In time, literary and artistic competitions became part of the event as well and, under the eccentric emperor **Nero**, even a singing competition. The prizes were simple crowns of laurel or olive branches—no medals of precious metals.

Not surprisingly, only men competed in the Olympics, and to make absolutely sure of this, they competed in the nude. The spectators, too, were solely male, except for the time when one woman dressed up as a man to see her son compete. He won and, in her jubilation, her tousled tunic revealed her gender. From then on, spectators were also required to attend in the nude.

Olympic controversy seems to be almost as old as the games themselves. When Nero scored a decisive victory in the chariot race, there were those who thought it somewhat unfair given that his team was comprised of 10 horses, while all the others had only 4. But you know what they say—never argue with the Emperor.

It was yet another emperor, **Theodosius I,** a Christian, who proclaimed the games a pagan festival and abolished them. Fifteen centuries later, in 1896, they were revived in Athens thanks to the efforts of **Baron Pierre de Coubertin**, who, according to his wishes, was buried amongst the ruins of Olympia. With the exception of 1916, 1940 and 1944, the games have been held every 4 years since 1896. In 1924 the Winter Games were launched in Chamonix, France.

Of even more recent vintage is the custom of carrying the Olympic flame from Olympia to the current site of the games. Ironically, this custom began with **Hitler**, who initiated the tradition during the Berlin Games of 1936 in an attempt to demonstrate the superiority of the Aryan race. In 1932, during the depths of the Depression when most governments lacked the funds to finance their athletes, Los Angeles miraculously staged one of the most successful Olympiads of modern times. Something of the original spirit of the ancient games surfaced, and the

athletes arrived by hook or by crook. Cuba, for example, sent its team in a boat loaded with tobacco, which was sold along the way to defray expenses. Meanwhile, back in Los Angeles, the Olympic Committee built the first Olympic Village to help keep food and lodging costs down—a practice that has since become custom.

The 1992 Barcelona Summer games (running from 25 July-9 August) will encompass 25 competitions and 3 demonstration events to be spread across 4 geographical areas—**Montjuïc, Diagonal, Vall d'Hebron** and **Parc de Mar**—within a 5-mile radius in the nucleus of the city. Additional sub-sites outside the city were selected for their tradition in a particular sport. The games will comprise 526 sessions or events held at 44 competition sites. More than 167 countries will take part, meaning that accommodation and transportation must be provided for an immediate Olympic Family of 40,000.

---

11 Piscines Bernardo Picornell (Franc Fernández and Moisés Gallego) Located on the second terrace, these already existing pools (named for a famed Catalan swimmer) were remodelled for the swimming events of the Games and will serve city residents well for many years to come. ♦ Olympic Ring

12 Torre de Calatrava (1992, Santiago Calatrava) At this writing, **Telefónica**, Spain's telephone monopoly, has unleashed a good deal of controversy with its decision to build this communications tower in the midst of the Olympic Ring. Its design and construction were vehemently repudiated not only by the 4 architects of the Olymic Ring—**Frederic Correa, Alfons Milà, Joan Margarit**and **Carles Buxadé**—but by 58 professionals and intellectuals rallied by the esteemed local architect **Oriol Bohigas**. The proposed tower measures more than 616 feet (about twice the height of the Columbus Monument), and

those opposed to it deem it not only unnecessary but unsightly, something that will stick out like a sore thumb in the midst of the Olympic Ring project that did not foresee its intrusion. Once finished (if it is finished), you can judge for yourself. ♦ Olympic Ring

---

Before I came to Barcelona, I didn't know what a sporting city was.... Those words were written on 7 November 1926 by **Baron Pierre de Coubertin**, the father of the modern Olympic movement, after his stay in the Catalan capital. Barcelona is a city with a long sporting tradition, as shown by the large number of sport facilities—more than 1300. There are 250 grounds where people can play sports and games and 2000 sporting organizations, outstanding among them the **Barcelona Football** (Soccer) **Club**, founded by **Joan Gamper** in 1897 and the **Barcelona Swimming Club**, established in 1907. The Spanish Olympic Committee was founded in Barcelona.

Palau D'Esports San Jordi

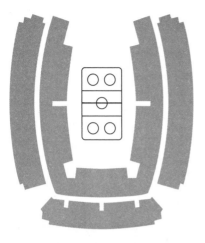

13 Palau D'Esports Sant Jordi (1990, **Arata Isozaki**) Raise high the roof beams Isozaki and company! Besides being a beautiful piece of architecture, the Palau Sant Jordi represents a tour de force of engineering technology. The 10-day roof-raising for this stadium was an event of worldwide interest. Built on the ground, the 525-foot long/360-foot-wide, 110-meter-wide metallic meshwork roof was raised in one piece 148 feet in the air by 12 hydraulic pistons, which were stopped every 8 inches along the way to check that the structure was being raised levelly. This is the third and, to date, largest roof raised by this method, known as the *Pantadome system*, designed by the engineer **Mamoru Kawaguchi**. The roof, covered with gray ceramic tiles, recalls the contours of a Japanese temple. As in the cathedral of Florence, the roof is supported at the perimeter, so there are no interior columns to obstruct vision. As the Olympic Stadium was the architectural symbol of the 1929 World's Fair, so the Palau Sant Jordi will undoubtedly be the design emblem of the 1992 Summer Olympic Games. After the Games, this technically complex and sophisticated construct will be used for all types of indoor sporting competitions as well as all manner of cultural, artistic and popular events. Its acoustics and large access doors permitting the entry of trucks were designed for the many concerts expected to be held here. The complex itself consists of a principal arena and a multipurpose adjoining pavilion. The facilities are impressive for the precision and thoroughness of their high-tech design and construction and for their versatility. In the words of the architect himself: *Its visibility from a distance and its plastic and technical innovation make the Palau Sant Jordi different. The parabolic dome is a reference to Gaudí, and the undulating surfaces are a specific reference to the mountain of Montjuïc.* Other notable Isozaki buildings around the world include the **Los Angeles Museum of Contemporary Art** and the **Palladium** in New York. The 4 large murals in the Palau's main vestibules titled *Flors pels campions* (Flowers for the Champions), *Terra* (Earth), and *Mar* (Sea) are by the painters **Hernández Pijoan** and **Ràfols Casamada**. The sculpture *Change* in the plaza in front of the Palau Sant Jordi is by **Aiko Miyawaki**. ♦ Seats 13,000-15,000. Olympic Ring

14 The Olympic Stadium (1929, **Pere Domènech i Roura**; conversion 1989, **Vittorio Gregotti, Frederic Correa, Alfons Milà, Joan Margarit** and **Carles Buxadé**) Built in a Neoclassical vein for the 1929 World's Fair, this stadium had to undergo a complete interior conversion not only to accommodate an Olympic-sized contingent of spectators in July 1992 but because after the second Mediterranean Games were held here in 1955 the structure had gradually fallen into ruin. The conversion works began in 1984 and were finished in July 1989. To increase the stadium's capacity, the playing field was lowered 36 feet. The facade was conserved, however (some contend almost too well since its pristine perfection makes it look like a woman wearing too much make-up), and **Pau Gargallo**'s famous *Els Aurigues* sculpture of a charioteer once again presides out front. On 8 September 1989 Spain's **King Juan Carlos** inaugurated the reincarnated stadium along with the celebration of the Fifth World Athletics Cup competition. The Barcelona team of the European League of American Football has signed on

Palau D'Esports San Jordi

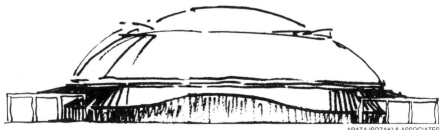

ARATA ISOZAKI & ASSOCIATES

The Olympic Stadium

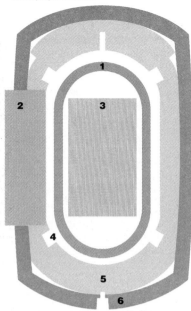

1 9-lane track   **4** Marathon entrance
2 Canopied gallery   **5** Lower tier
3 Central field   **6** Upper tier

as the stadium's first regular user. Besides hosting many of the competitions of the 1992 Summer Games, this stadium will be the site of the opening and closing ceremonies.
♦ Seats 55,000-70,000. Olympic Ring

15 Parc del Migdia Covering some 128 acres, this park occupies the part of Montjuïc left undeveloped after the 1929 World's Fair. Bounded by the Castillo de Montjuïc, the Cementiri del Sud-Oest, the Fossar de la Pedrera, the Port and Can Clos districts, the Olympic Ring and the new Tres Pins municipal plant nursery, it comprises large planted areas and a network of pedestrian walks, stairs, fountains and strategically located vantage points with views of the Olympic Ring and the city. Thirteen thousand trees and 5000 bushes of Mediterranean species have been planted and more than 484,000 square feet have been covered with grass, ivy and other greenery. Within the park is the so-called **Sot del Migdia**, which consists of a large open-air arena with a capacity for 100,000 persons that can be used for concerts or other large-audience events. The park also contains the new **Pau Negre Sports Complex** designed by architects **Pere Pujol, J. Zapata** and **Muntanyola**, and consisting of a regulation natural-grass hockey field, a 6-lane athletic track made of the same material as that of the stadium, outdoor bleachers accommodating 1200, and a building housing services for athletes, press and the public. At this writing the **Jardí Botànic** (Botanical Gardens), transferred from the **Parc de la Ciutadella** to their

current home behind the **Palau Nacional** in 1931, are slated to be installed here between the Olympic Stadium and Montjuïc Castle by 1992. The architects of this project are **Bet Figueras, Josep Lluís Canosa** and **Carles Ferrater**. The gardens will be arranged in split levels forming an amphitheater facing southeast over the Llobregat Valley. The plants will be grouped according to geographical origin and ecological tendencies. Three levels of water, in the form of natural ponds, will contain aquatic vegetation.

16 Fundació Miró (1974, **Sert, Jackson & Associates**; expansion 1986, **Jaume Freixa**) Set in the upper reaches of the **Parc de Montjuïc**, this museum, opened in 1975, was designed by **Josep Lluís Sert**, a personal friend of **Joan Miró**, and stands in homage to the vast body of work by that 20th-century Catalan abstractionist. Its bright, ordered spaces evoking traditional elements of Span-

ish architecture are suffused with light. Skylights in the exhibition areas and large openings linking the interior and exterior maximize the daylight flooding into the great white spaces and foster a sense of communication with the outside world. The outdoor patios and terraces are also used for displays, so as you stroll through the museum, works of art pop up unexpectedly through the windows and doors. Jaume Freixa, who expanded the building in 1986, worked closely with Sert on its original design. One of the buidling's most distinctive features is the octagonal tower housing the library, the room exhibiting Miro's works on paper, and the auditorium. Created by Miró himself in 1971, the Fundació Joan Miró, Center of Contemporary Art Studies, is a private cultural foundation closely linked with the Barcelona City Council and the Autonomous Regional Government of Catalonia. Its objectives are twofold: to study and disseminate the work of Miró and to promote and publicize contemporary art in general. The core of the Foundation's collection, largely donated by the artist himself, comprises 217 paintings on canvas, paper, wood and other supports dating from 1917 to the 1970s, 153 sculptures, 9 textile creations, Miró's complete graphic works, and a collection of almost 5000 drawings that illustrate his artistic development from the first sketches of childhood made in 1901 to his final works. An additional collection entitled *To Joan Miró* contains tributes of friendship and admiration for Miró's work by artists from many countries. On the ground floor you'll find 2 impressive Miró tapestries (one incorporating 8 umbrellas) and the large, kinetic **Fountain of Mercury** by **Alexander Calder**, which was created for the Spanish Pavilion of the 1937 Paris International Exhibition and subsequently warehoused for years due to a lack of mercury

49

Joan Miró sketches

(it requires about 5.5 tons of this expensive commodity to fill the fountain's circular pool, which is over 6.5 feet in both diameter and depth). Recently a mine in La Mancha provided the mercury, and the fountain was per-

Montjuïc

manently installed here in June 1990. The museum regularly holds temporary art exhibitions from around the world, as well as showings of films and videos, recitals of contemporary music, and lectures and seminars. It also offers a fine view of the city from the roof. The large sculpture on the front lawn is by **Eduardo Chillida**. ♦ Admission; students with ID half price. Tu-W, F-Sa 10AM-7PM; Th 10AM-9:30PM; Su and holidays 10:30AM-2:30PM. Pl Neptú, Av Miramar (Pg Santa Madrona-C Poeta Cabanyes) 329.19.08; fax 329.86.09

Within the Fundació Miró:

Bar Restaurant Fundació Miró ★★$$
The bar-restaurant here, which features an outdoor terrace, offers one of the best abbreviated menus in town. The dishes are original, ample and reasonably priced. Try the *salmón ahumado con tortita de patatas y salsa de rábanos picante* (smoked salmon with a potato tortilla and a radish sauce), *la terrina de berenjenas y pimientos con comino y queso de Burgos* (eggplant-and-red pepper terrine with cumin and cheese from Burgos), or the spaghetti with *caviar*. The desserts are among Barcelona's best. Try the chocolate cake with *salsa de café, el crumble caliente de frutas del tiempo con salsa de vainilla* (a fresh-fruit cobbler with vanilla sauce), or the *crema de limón con pastelitos de plátano* (lemon cream with banana cookies). Also offers a selection of excellent sandwiches. ♦ Ground floor. No credit cards

17 Plaça Dante Glimpsed through the trees of the gardens adjoining this plaza are wonderful views of the city and port. Beyond the entrance to the **Parc Laribal**, you'll find the funicular station, this plaza, and the municipal swimming pool, originally built in 1929, but now being reconstructed by designer **Antoni Moragas i Spa** for Olympic Game use.

18 Bali $$$ Located near the entrance to the Parc d'Atraccions (amusement park), this restaurant serves *rijsttafel*, an Indonesian smorgasbord comprised here of either 15, 20 or 26 different *flavors* or dishes. The Balinese decor appropriately sets the stage for the evening folklore presentations. ♦ Indonesian ♦ Av Miramar, s/n (Pl Dante-Pl Torreforta) 241.36.09

19 Plaça Armada This esplanade offers a magnificent view of the port and the sea. ♦ Av Miramar-Ctra Miramar

20 Plaça Sardana Situated along the Ctra de Montjuïc, this plaza with its famed *Monumento a la Sardana*, the folk dance that has become a symbol of enduring Catalan culture, is a quintessential photo opportunity. ♦ Ctra Montjuïc (Av Miramar-Pl Mirador)

21 Parc d'Atraccions Stretching from the outskirts of Montjuïc Castle to the edge of Parc Laribal, this amusement park rimmed by gardens offers a selection of some 40 rides and several fine views. The funicular that scales Montjuïc from the Paral.lel metro stop leaves you near the entrance gate. Hours are very erratic and vary greatly throughout the year, so check if it's open before you make any promises to the kids. ♦ Admission. Av Miramar-Camí Baix Castell-Ctra Montjuïc. 242.31.75

22 Castillo de Montjuïc (17th c; reconstruction 1779, **Juan Martín de Cermeño**) A stone lookout tower was known to occupy the peak of Montjuïc as early as the 11th century, and in 1607 a road leading to it was first built. The first castle on this site was built (in a mere 30 days) in 1640 in response to the revolt of Catalunya against **Felipe IV**. On 26 January the Catalans won the celebrated battle against Felipe IV's forces. In 1652 that castle reverted from the city to the Spanish State, and in 1694 it was converted into a great fortress. After being taken by the **Prince of Hesse-Darmstadt** during the War of the Spanish Succession (1702-14), Bourbon troops destroyed it in 1706. In 1751 the Bourbons themselves rebuilt a pentagonal, star-shaped fortress on the spot designed by Juan Martín de Cermeño in a French Neoclassical vein. In the 18th century, the Bourbon kings modified and expanded it to its current aspect. In 1842 the castle turned on the city that theoretically was its duty to defend when **General Esparterto** ordered a 12-hour bombing of Barcelona to suppress a popular uprising. A similar event occurred in 1843 ordered by the provisional president of the government **Joaquín María López**. At the end of the 19th century, the castle served as a military prison and was the site of several legendary political executions. In 1960 it once again became municipal property when **General Francisco Franco** ceded it for conversion to a military museum (an enormous monolith within the fortress commemorates that *generous* decision, but the equestrian statue of the late General Franco himself is now gone). The military still has a great deal of say in its administration, however, and a detachment of soldiers is still quartered within. At one point in this castle's convoluted history it housed 120 pieces of artillery; today it houses the **Museu de L'Exercit** (Military Museum), 4 cannons dating from 1898, 4 cannons of more recent vintage, and an architecturally jarring restaurant-cafe situated along its walls that serves an expansive view of the city and port. ♦ Admission to museum. Daily 10AM-2PM, 4-7PM, winter; daily 10AM-2PM, 4-8PM, summer. Montaña de Montjuïc (C Cartoixa-Av Castell-Ctra Montjuic) 329.86.13

23 Pavelló Albéniz y Jardins Joan Maragall (1929) Built as the **Pavelló Reial** for the World's Fair, this palatial structure once housed a music museum and later some of the city's more illustrious citizens. Substantially enlarged in 1970, it was then endowed with a **Dalí** mural. Used for gala municipal receptions, it is closed to the public and may be viewed with special municipal permission only. The surrounding gardens stretch up to the edge of the Olympic Stadium. ♦ Pg Pavelló Albeniz (Av L'Estadi-Pg Santa Madrona)

24 Parc de Montjuïc (Original plan for park development 1892, **Josep Amargós i Samaranch**; final plan for gardens 1922, **Jean C.N. Forestier** and **Nicolau M. Rubió i Tudurí**;

Parc Laribal 1916, Jean C.N. Forestier) When Amargós was charged by the city with drawing up plans for this park, it was with an eye toward developing the area destined to stage a second International Exhibition in 1914. It was his idea to transform the entire northern slope of Montjuïc into a park, and he mapped out the road leading from the Plaça d'Espanya to Miramar. With the world at war and municipal finances tight, work didn't begin until 1915. Called in to help with the project was the prestigious French designer of gardens Jean-Claude N. Forestier, caretaker of the Paris parks, who was then working in the south of Spain. Under his guidance, and in close collaboration with local architect Nicolau M. Rubió i Tudurí, several diverse scenic environments were designed and landscaped, most notable among them the gardens of **Miramar**, **la Font del Gat**, **la Plaça del Polvorí**, **Parc Laribal** and **la Rosaleda**. ♦ Northern slope of Montjuïc

Montjuïc

25 Palau Nacional (1929, **Enric Catà i Catà**, **Pere Cendoya i Oscoz**, and **Pere Domènech i Roura**) **Puig i Cadafalch**'s general plan for the World's Fair grounds called for a broad avenue rising from the Pl D'Espanya to a monumental structure with prominent cupolas presiding from a perch halfway up Montjuïc. Despite modification of the plan over time and the removal of Puig from the project with the commencement of the dictatorship of **Primo de Rivera**, the concept of the structure as a focal point of the fair remained a constant, although its intended function varied. Ultimately, the building was devoted to displaying Spanish art. Its exterior styling is a synthesis of diverse Spanish architectural modes, and its interior layout is a network of vast spaces now being recomposed (and not without some controversy) by **Gae Aulenti**, redesigner of Paris' **Musée d'Orsay**. ♦ Pl Mirador (Pg Cascades-Av L'Estadi)

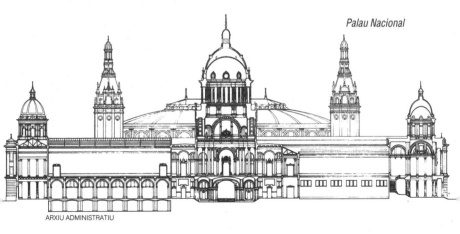

Palau Nacional

ARXIU ADMINISTRATIU

Within the Palau Nacional:

Museu d'Art de Catalunya In 1934 the collection of Barcelona's first art museum, housed in the **Arsenal de la Ciutadella**, was moved to the Palau Nacional. The artistic apple of both Barcelona's and Catalunya's eye, the collection derives its singular importance from the historic depth and broad scope of Catalan artistic expression it conveys. In the world-class category is the collection of 10th-12th-century Romanesque paintings, statues, carvings, sculptures, frescoes and murals, many of which were extracted from Catalan churches in the Pyrenees and added to the collection in 1919. Another of the museum's strong suits is its Gothic collection (12th-15th century) falling chronologically into 3 distinct stylistic eras—the Franco-Gothic, Italian-Gothic and International-Gothic—and including important works from around the country. Especially notable are

the works of **Soriguerola**. The third artistic pillar upon which the museum's reputation rests is the Renaissance, Baroque and Neo-classical collection comprising representative works of the Flemish, Italian and Spanish schools dating from the 16th to 19th centuries. You'll also find here a few creative efforts by **El Greco, Tintoretto, Zurbarán**and **Velázquez**. ♦ Admission. Closed for renovation at this writing. 423.71.99

26 Museu Etnològic Set within the **Rosaleda Gardens**, this modern building adorned with reliefs by **Eudald Serra** harbors objects of art and artifacts garnered from the peoples and cultures of 5 continents. Of especial interest are the pre-Columbian objects from Ecuador and Peru, the refined artistry of Japan, and the carved creations from Cameroon and the Ivory Coast. ♦ Admission. Tu-Su 9AM-8:30PM; M and holidays 9AM-2PM. Pg Santa Madrona, s/n. 424.64.02

27 Restaurant Font del Gat ★$$$ For centuries the fountain here has been a popular destination for Sunday daytrippers. Installed in gardens by the same name, this restaurant was designed just about a century ago by **Puig i Cadafalch**. You can't go wrong with the zarzuela (local bouillabaisse) or sole. If you find rabbit on the menu, dare to be different. ♦ Catalan/International ♦ Pg Santa Madrona, s/n. 424.02.24

28 Teatre Grec (1929, Jean C. N. Forestier, Nicolau M. Rubió i Tudurí, and Ramon Reventós i Farrarons) Situated within the **Rosaleda Gardens** that form part of the greater **Parc de Montjuïc**, this open-air theater is rendered in the ancient Greek tradition of that at Epidaurus. The rock wall of an old quarry forms the background to the stage that offers performances all summer and is a prime venue for the city's annual theater

festival. ♦ Seats 2000. Parc de Montjuïc (Pg Santa Madrona-Av Miramar) 301.77.75; fax 317.12.40

29 Museu Arqueològic (1929, Pelagi Martínez i Paricio) Originally built as the **Palau de les Arts Gràfiques** (Palace of Graphic Arts) for the 1929 World's Fair, this structure was subsequently adapted to the requisites of the Archaeological Museum. Rooted in the spirit of the Italian Renaissance and the masters of the *Quattrocento*, it is a stylistic example of *Noucentisme*, a local, post-Modernist architectural vernacular. Most important among its prehistoric collection of artifacts from the Iberian Peninsula and the Balearic Islands (Mallorca, Minorca and Ibiza) of the Mediterranean are the Carthaginian sculptures from Ibiza, the Greek findings from Empúries, and the Iberian ceramics. Don't miss the Roman house outfitted with authentic objects of the period. ♦ Admission. Tu-Sa 9:30AM-1PM, 4-7PM; Su 9:30AM-2PM. Pg Santa Madrona (C Lleida) 423.21.49

30 Mercat de les Flors (1929, José M^a. Ribas y Casa and Manuel M^a. Mayol y Ferrer) Erected as the Agricultural House for the World's Fair, the main section of the Mercat de les Flors was first used as a theater by **Peter Brook** to stage *Carmen* in 1983. This auditorium seating 999 continues to stage cutting-edge theater, dance and musical events. The paintings on the hallway dome are by **Miquel Barceló**. Before, during and after performances patrons can enjoy the pretty lobby, the bar, and the restaurant surveying the rooftops of the city. An adjoining building, once a flower market (hence the theater's name) houses a theater space that can accommodate 4000 and is dedicated to more experimental fare. ♦ C Lleida, 59 (Pg Santa Madrona) 325.06.75

31 Palaus de Alfonso XIII y de Victoria Eugenia (1928, Josep Piug i Cadafalch) Situated between the Fuentes de Montjuïc and the Palau Nacional, these massive, symmetrical, twin structures are hollow shells outfitted within for heavy-duty industrial and trade fair exhibitions. The severity of their solid-block construction is mitigated by some external ornamentation recalling Viennese Secessionist influences and a bit of Baroque inspiration. ♦ Pl Marqués de Foronda (Pl Carles Buigas-Pg Cascades)

In 1929 the **Estadio de Montjuïc** was inaugurated by **King Alfonso XIII**. Seventy years later his grandson, **King Juan Carlos I**, inaugurated the new **Olympic Stadium** that preserves the facade of the 1929 stadium.

In the 2nd century AD at the CCXVII Olympiad, **Lucius Minicius Natalis Quadronius Verus** brought to the then **Barcino** its first Olympic triumph. A general born in Barcelona, he earned the laurel wreath as victor in the chariot race. A frieze was dedicated to his victory in 129.

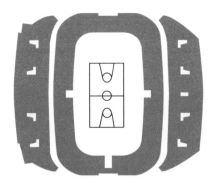

32 Palau Municipal d'Esports (1955, **Josep Soteras** and **Lorenzo García Borbón**) Built for the Second Mediterranean Games in 1955, this was Barcelona's first multipurpose facility. In the world of sports it has hosted the 1973 European Basketball Championship, the 1979 Hockey Championship, the 1986 World Basketball Championship, the 1987 Taekwondo World Championship, and the 1984 Pre-Olympic Volleyball Tournaments. In the world of entertainment it has staged concerts by **Bob Dylan, Elton John, Leonard Cohen, Miles Davis, Chick Corea** and more. ♦ Seats 6500-8000 ♦ C Lleida (C Jocs Mediterranis-C Joaquim Blume)

33 El Molino (1913, **Manuel-Joaquim Raspall i Mayol**) This long-standing landmark in the Barcelona nightscape began life in 1916 as the Moulin Rouge, an outpost of burlesque when that was still a risqué business. Baptized *El Molino* in 1939, the windmill that echoes its name tops a kitschy, columned entranceway that is in keeping with the tone of the spectacle that awaits within. Feathers, bangles, sequins, beads, and bare bottoms and breasts constitute the once scandalously scanty underpinnings of the entertainment offering. A vaudeville-style variety show fleshes out the program with a contingent of singers, acrobats, jugglers, comedians and magicians. Matinee audiences swell with old-timers, many from the Catalan countryside, amused but still somewhat agog at the licentiousness of city life. Evening audiences typically comprise a cosmopolitan cross-section of the populace come for a nostalgic night of piquant fun. You don't really have to understand Spanish to appreciate the broad humor and good-natured, playful nudity. ♦ Admission. C Vila i Vilà, 99 (C Roser) 241.63.83

NBC paid a total of $416 million ($401 million in cash and $15 million in advertising) for the television rights to the Barcelona Summer Olympic Games. Channel 7 in Australia paid $33.75 million; the Canadian network CTV, $16.5 million; the European Broadcast Union (EBU) $90 million; and New Zealand Television (TVNZ) and its associate Sky Network Television $5.9 million for exclusive rights for their country. A pool of Japanese television networks (led by NHK) paid $62.5 million for the exclusive rights for Japan.

Luis Marcó
General Manager, Ramada Renaissance Hotel

A leisurely walk down **La Rambla** to the **Gothic Quarter**. Look for the bird vendors, flower stalls and street artists on your way to the **Cathedral** in this 1000-year-old Gothic city.

Stroll through the **Antiquaire's Mall**, in Passeig de Gràcia, and shop for bargain antiques.

A night at the **Gran Teatro del Liceo**, one of the oldest and best opera theaters in the world.

An evening at fun-filled, fashionable **Club Up & Down**. Watch the local jet set on their own turf. Good food and drinks and great music.

Sunday at **Tibidabo Mountain** overlooking Barcelona, with its amusement park, beautiful gardens, and great panoramic views of the city and the Mediterranean Sea.

Montjuïc

Eliseo Gretz
Director, Hotel Colón

Picasso Museum

Fundació Miró

Sagrada Família

La Pedrera

La Casa Milà

El Parc Güell

The **Gothic Quarter**, home to the **Cathedral**.

Jordi Romea
President, Guide's Association of Barcelona

A walk along **La Rambla** to the water, where you can stroll along the **Moll de la Fusta**, a seaside promenade.

The gorgeous Modernist buildings by **Gaudí** and the fashionable shops along **Passeig de Gràcia**, the longest street in the city.

Montjuïc, Tibidabo and **Parc Güell** are the ideal places for good views of the city.

The **Picasso, Miró** and **Tàpies** museums.

The **Hilton** (Av Diagonal, 589, 419.22.33), **Princesa Sofia** (Pl Pius XII, 4, 330.71.11) and **Ritz** (Gran Via, 668, 318.52.00) hotels.

Botafumerio (Gran de Gràcia, 81, 218.42.30) for seafood; and **El Petit Dorado** (Dolors Monserdà, 51, 204.51.53) for International/North Catalonia cuisine.

Boulevard Rosa (Passeig de Gràcia, 55, 309.06.50) and **Corte Inglés** (Plaça Catalunya, 14, 302.12.12), which are shopping malls.

Loewe (Passeig de Gràcia, 35, 216.04.00) and **Gonzalo Comella** (Passeig de Gràcia, 16, 218.35.16) for clothes.

Unión Suiza (Av Diagonal, 482, 237.62.23) and **Tomás Colomer** (Portal del Angel, 7, 301.55.22) for jewelry.

Waterfront

In the 4th century, Barcelona straddled ponds and salt marshes by the **Waterfront** (then basically a beach). Gradually the city expanded, but it didn't hit its stride until the 13th and 14th centuries when the populace began to spread out to surrounding *vilanoves* (the medieval equivalent of the *burbs*). The new city called for new walls, which were built by **Jaume I** in the 13th century but left the maritime face of the city unprotected.

Properly speaking, there was no port here then. Until the 16th century the bulk of the boat traffic used the **Farga Port** on the far side of **Montjuïc**. Although there were always a certain number of boats that put in at Barcelona's beach, the first stone of the port area we know today was not laid until 1474. The first major fleet to anchor here was that of **Carlos V** (1516-56), which set off from here to take Tunisia.

This signaled the dawn of a new era for the city's coastal edge. During Carlos V's reign, Barcelona's waterfront became the most prominent barrio in town. A new **Carrer Ample** became the fashionable seaside artery where the bulk of Barcelona's viceroys took up residence—not to mention Carlos V himself—and where, in the following century, the order of **Our Lady of Mercy** built its sizeable convent. Aware of the area's vulnerability, the Emperor Carlos ordered the construction of the **Muralla del Mar**, a wall protecting the waterfront area.

Not until 1755 were the first provisional docks of the port built. In 1834 the Muralla del Mar was transformed into an elegant, elevated promenade overlook-

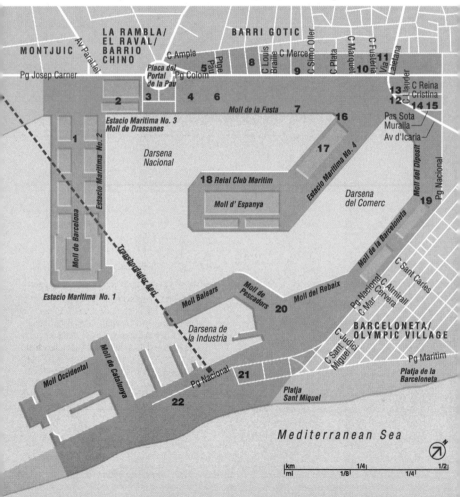

ing the port. Between 1878 and 1881 the wall was torn down, and 7 years later, in its place, they built the palm-lined **Passeig de Colom**, which served as a main artery accessing the 1888 International Exhibition headquartered in the **Parc de la Ciutadella**.

In those days the seafaring folk and fishermen made their home in the **Barceloneta** section of the city, and the seedy side of port life was relegated to the **Barrio Chino**, several blocks from the port itself. Meanwhile, the waterfront stretch from the **Plaça Portal de la Pau** to the **Plaça d'Antoni López** was, until the end of the 19th century, Barcelona's most bourgeois barrio, and it retains to this day, despite the departure of its fashionable residents, not only a number of important public buildings, but a clean, upstanding demeanor.

It was 20th-century Barcelona that turned its back on the waterfront, and with good reason. In our century the port became the province of cargo ships, stevedores, hydraulic lifts, winches and the unsightly industrial infrastructure that make ports the world over rather unpleasant and often unsavory places. And as if that weren't visual pollution enough, an iron rail separating the dock from the broad, heavily trafficked Passeig de Colom posed, if not a strictly physical barrier between Barcelona and the sea, certainly an important psychological one.

In a major municipal effort to get the city to turn full face to the sea once again, the **Redevelopment Project of the Port Vell** is investing an estimated 30 billion *pesetas* (over two-thirds from private investors) in upgrading and revitalizing the old port under the architectural auspices of the Technical Services of the Authority of the Autonomous Port of Barcelona. The plan embraces the following 6 areas: **Barcelona Quay, Espanya Quay, Diposit and Barceloneta Quays, Rellotge** and **Pescadors Quays, Nou Quay** and **Plaça del Mar**. Work began in 1989 and is scheduled to be completed in 1992.

But we suspect that beyond 1992 much of this area will likely remain in a state of flux as merchants bid for positions along the new promenades and entrepreneurs of varying stripe try to determine how best to profit from a reclaimed civic interest in the new port-turned-playground.

---

1 Barcelona Quay About halfway down this pier you'll find a station of the **Transbordador Aéreo del Puerto** that runs from the **Sant Sebastià Tower** in Barceloneta to the **Miramar Esplanade** on Montjuïc with an interim stop here, where the larger of the 2 Transbordador towers, known as *Jaume I*, measures 351 feet. Projected by **Carles Buigas** (author of the *Fuentes de Montjuïc)*, **Ramón Calzada** and **Josep Rodríguez Rodá** in 1926 to connect the World's Fair facilities of Montjuïc with the bathing areas of Barceloneta, it was not built until 1930 and suspended service from 1936 to 1963. By 1992, you'll also find on this quay the new **International Trade Centre**, to be located at the end of the quay, which will consist of 3 office buildings with an additional building serving as the new headquarters of the **Autonomous Port of Barcelona**. The Centre will be 131 feet high and cover a surface area of 860,670 square feet. All 4 buildings will share both a central patio adorned with fountains and outfitted with shopping arcades and an upper-level patio. A pedestrian walkway, lined with pine and palm trees, will run the length of the quay.

On either side of the walkway will be two 2-story buildings housing ferry terminals. Their lower floors will be devoted to services and administration, their upper floors to lounges and cafeterias. A new square will also be built on **Drassanes Quay** providing access to the southern edge of the **Ciutat Vella**; the north side of this square will feature a new hotel. Barcelona Quay will also have an underground car park with a capacity for 2500 vehicles.

2 Duana (Aduana) (1902, **Pere García Faria** and **Enric Sagnier**) A not terribly interesting structure, the **Customs House** continues about its duty-levying business here, though on the face of things the place looks all but deserted and its great winged sphinxes seem formidable sentinels guarding an empty nest. Characterized in local architectural circles as *colosalista* in styling (and just a tad Viennese), it has been acknowledged by some as a Modernist structure—more for the timing of its construction than its tenor. ◆ Pg Josep Carner (Av Paral.lel-Pl Portal Pau)

Restaurants/Nightlife: Red   Hotels: Blue

Shops/Parks: Green   Sights/Culture: Black

3 Monumento a Cristobal Colón (1886, **Gaietà Buigas i Monravà**; restoration 1929, 1965; restoration 1982, **Joan Margarit** and **Carles Buxadé**) Barcelona's most popular monument reminds us that upon successfully completing his first New-World mission Columbus returned to Barcelona where he was debriefed by Queen Isabella. The design competition for the monument was won by the engineer Gaietà Buigas i Monravà, and the first stone was laid in 1882. Financial difficulties delayed the inauguration until 1888, thus making it coincide with the celebration of the Universal Exhibition. The monument comprises 3 distinct sections. The first is an elevated circular base garlanded by 8 iron lions designed by **Agapit Vallmitjana** and fabricated by

Waterfront

Josep Carcassó. On the plinth are 8 bronze bas-reliefs depicting the principal accomplishments of Columbus. The originals were the work of **Josep Llimona** and **Antoní Vilnova**, but these were destroyed and replaced by the present ones by **Manuel Fuxà, Pere Carbonell** and **Josep Tenas** during the 1929 restoration. The second section is the base of the column, which is an 8-sided polygon, 4 of which serve as buttresses with statuary corresponding to the kingdoms of Catalunya, Aragon, Castilla and León. Their respective sculptors are Pere Carbonell, Josep Carcassó, **Josep Gamot** and **Rafael Atché**. The sculptures gracing the other 4 sides are of **Fray Bernardo Boïl** (by Manuel Fuxà), a Catalan monk from the Montserrat Monastery who did missionary work in India; **Captain Pere Margarit** (by **Eduardo Batista**), a symbol of Spain's American empire; **Jaime Ferrer de Blanes** (by **Francésc Pagès**), a celebrated astronomer; and

CHRIS MIDDOUR

Luis de Santángel (by Josep Gamot), who helped secure the provisions and materials Columbus needed to pursue his dream. The third section is a Corinthian column measuring 168 feet. Represented on its capital are the continents of Europe, Asia, Africa and the Americas. Lastly, atop a prince's crown and a semisphere symbolizing his newly discovered part of the globe, stands the 25-foot bronze statue of Columbus himself by Rafael Atché, scheduled to be married to the Statue of Liberty in 1992 as part of the quincentenary celebrations marking the explorer's New World discoveries. Inside the column a claustrophobia-inducing elevator (7½-feet in diameter) carries visitors to a severly hindered view.
♦ Admission. Daily 9AM-9PM, 24 July-24 Sep; Tu-Sa 10AM-2PM, 3:30-6:30PM, Su, holidays 10AM-7PM, rest of the year. Pl Portal Pau. 302.52.24

4 Puerto Autónomo de Barcelona (1905) Until it relocates to its new headquarters on **Barcelona Quay**, the Autonomous Port of Barcelona's administration of the port and customs activities will continue to be carried out in this rather attractive building. What happens to the building after the move is anybody's guess. ♦ Moll de les Drassanes (Pl Portal Pau)

5 Passeig de Colom Like the monument commemorating the same man, this broad, seaside boulevard dates from 1888. It's 2000 feet long and 138 feet wide, and occupies the site of the 16th-century **Muralla del Mar** torn down in 1881. In recent years its aspect has been radically transformed by the changes made in the **Moll de la Fusta** (below) and the construction of the **Cinturó Litoral** (Coastal Ring Road).

6 Moll de la Fusta (aka Moll de Bosch i Alsina) (1988, **Manuel de Solá-Morales**) Commonly known as *Moll de la Fusta* (Wooden Dock) because until 1982 this stretch of waterfront dock area paralleling the Pg Colom served as a depository for wood. In that year the Autonomous Port of Barcelona ceased to use it as wharf space and ceded it to the city for development as a communal urban space. The first of several projects aimed at opening Barcelona to the sea, the development of the Moll de la Fusta has thus far fallen short of the hype touting it as a shining example of the city's seaside renaissance. Its development to date has also proved shortsighted, since apparently this stretch of reclaimed leisure land had to be at least partially uprooted within 2 years of the project's completion because the clearance for trucks passing beneath it on the new **Cinturó Litoral** (Coastal Ring Road) had been miscalculated. At this writing, the *adjustment* work was about to begin. We only hope that those in charge will take advantage of this opportunity to improve some of the glaring flaws inherent in the project's original conception. To be fair, the new promenade skirting the sea is not half bad, its stone walkways pleasingly laced with tropical palms. It's the upper portion between the Pg Colom and the seaside promenade that we find most unpleasant. Within months of its construction, its bland, boxy fixtures already looked old and weathered. It's been said that architect **Manuel de Solá-Morales** wanted to make it appear as if this promenade had always been here. (A stab at retroactive face-saving?) All we can say is he got his wish. Some attempt at attractiveness is made with the tilework adorning the underpasses, but there is an abundance of unsightly construction all around. A second problem here is the high level of traffic noise that severely hampers conversation and relaxation at the string of upscale, *al fresco* restaurants and cafes, which are situated at quite a remove from the brisk sting of the sea air. Linking them with the seaside promenade below are several hideous footbridges. Since the Moll de la Fusta's inauguration, it has also been chided by its critics for the stylistic diversity of its fixtures and for the planting of palm trees instead of the traditional Mediterranean pine. The criticisms have not kept the public away, however, and summer nights find the Moll de la Fusta brimming with Barcelonans having a marvelous time. Among those involved in the design of its bars and restaurants are such leading names as **Mariscal, Cortés** and **Arribas**. On a positive note, bravo for the Moll de la Fusta's attractive use of 3 types of wrought-metal street lamps based on models prevalent in the Barcelona of the late 1800s. Plans also call for the installation of a large sculpture group by **Francisco López** near the stairs connecting the dock with the sea. His *Homage to the Catalan Mediterranean* will incorporate some of master sculptor **Miquel Blai**'s extant plans for figures that he himself never carried out. Additional sculptures paying tribute to illustrious Barcelona citizens who, through their positions and/or works, have made patent the marine character of the city, will also enhance the city's new waterfront facade. Architect and sculptor **Rob Krier** is working on the first 3 sculptures dedicated to the poet **Salvat Papasseit, Bosch i Alsina** (mayor and directing engineer of the port) and **J. Cermeño** (the original designer of the **Barceloneta Quarter**). Each of these bronze

sculptures will be approximately 13 feet high. Perhaps these and more things to come will redeem this area conceived to be an exemplary case study in urban development. By all rights the Moll de la Fusta *should* be a municipal showcase, a decisively aesthetic exploitation of one of the city's most compelling assets, the Mediterranean Sea. We hope that once all the work is done, it will be.

Along the upper level of the Moll de la Fusta:

Distrito $ A casual snack bar serving pizzas and a variety of croissants located at the western end of the Moll. ♦ Snacks

Blau Mari ★★$$$ As with most places along the Moll, seafood is the starring attraction. Co-starring here, next door to Distrito, are a selection of rice dishes and 3 types of bouillabaisse. If you've got room left after *tapas* and a main course, try the apple tart or chocolate cake. ♦ Seafood/Catalan ♦ 310.10.15

Gambrinus ★★$$$$ At the eastern end of the Moll, this restaurant stands out from the crowd thanks to the giant, roof-top prawn (looks more like lobster to us) conceived by Barcelona's designer of the moment, **Xavier Mariscal**. Its decor is further distinguished by the hand-painted umbrellas of the outdoor terrace and an indoor bar in the shape of a ship's prow. The traditional Catalan toasted bread with tomato and cured ham is good here, as are the various seafood salads. ♦ Seafood/Catalan ♦ 310.55.77

The Columbus Monument weighs more than 513,000 pounds.

The construction of Barcelona's port began in 1474; the first fleet to harbor there was that of **Charles V** as it prepared to set out and conquer Tunisia.

7 Las Golondrinas Since 1888 the golondrinas fleet has ferried sightseers between the port and the *Rompeolas* (breakwater). Barcelonans have always regarded the breakwater as a place of recreational pilgrimage. Built between 1905 and 1926, it was extended in 1959. Upon docking here, you are greeted by **Salvador Aulèstia**'s curious abstract sculpture *Sideroploide*, dating from 1963 and fashioned of bits of iron recovered from the sea. Often too, you'll find hobby fishermen perched patiently amidst the Rompeolas' rocks. The round-trip run from the Moll de la Fusta takes about 30 minutes. ♦ Fee. Moll de la Fusta. 310.03.82

8 Plaça Duc de Medinaceli (1844, Francesc Daniel Molina) From 1276 to 1822, the vast **Convento de Sant Francesc** complex extended from here to La Rambla. Its demolition was completed in 1835, and in 1844 the **Pl de Sant Francesc** was constructed. After reclaiming title to the monastery's land by virtue of being a descendant of the longstanding, noble Catalan family that had first ceded the ground for its construction, the **Duke of Medinaceli** then ingratiated himself

Waterfront

with his fellow citizens by receding part of it for the construction of the larger plaza that now bears his name.

Within the Plaça Duc de Medinaceli:

Monumento a Galceran Marquet (1851, Francesc Daniel Molina i Casamajó; sculptor, **Josep Anicet Santigosa i Vestraten**; 1929, restoration) When Francesc Daniel Molina enlarged his own **Pl de Sant Francesc** in 1849, he envisioned adorning it with a grand fountain that, given its proximity to the port, would recall some episode in Barcelona's maritime history. The design was done by **Lluís Rigalt** and carried out by Molina and sculptor Santigosa, who fashioned the allegorical figures and attendant accouterments that detail their maritime significance. The fountain comprises a circular stone basin from whose center rises a fragmented column sustaining 4 smaller, angular basins that catch the water from the marine horns sounded by 4 Tritons. Above this rises a cast iron column that represents the first use of this type of construction in Barcelona. Although initially the forms and composition of the monument were agreed upon, there was no agreement as to who would be honored atop the column—Columbus or Blasco de Garay. Ultimately, a Solomonic decision of sorts was reached: enshrined atop the column in the company of tall palm trees is the figure of **Vice Admiral Galceran Marquet**, who in 1331 led the Catalan fleet in the war against the Genoese.

Plaça Duc de Medinaceli, 7 A fine example of Romantic architecture whose decorative flourishes are fashioned of baked earth.

Casa Girona A bit of architectural trivia: this house sports the oldest balcony with marble balustrades to be found among Barcelona's privately owned buildings. ♦ Pl Duc de Medinaceli, 8 (C Josep Anselm Clavé)

9 Antiguo Convento de la Mercè (1642, **Hermanos Santacana**; new facade on Pg Colom 1847; another new facade on Pg Colom 1928, **Adolf Florensa i Ferrer**) Originally part of the convent complex from which the **Iglesia de la Mercè** behind it broke off during the last century, this massive, block-long structure was 5 years in the building. With the secularization of the order of **Our Lady of Mercy** in 1846, it came to house the **Capitanía General** (a military headquarters) and has since undergone numerous modifications, most notably the new facade acquired for the 1929 World's Fair (some maintain that the 1847 facade with its baked-earth reliefs and distinctive galleries was more attractive). By far the building's most interesting feature now are the polychromatic mosaics of the interior patio, but you'll have to get special permission to get in and see them. ♦ Pg Colom, 14-16 (C Boltres-C Simó Oller)

10 Restaurante Mediterraneo ★★$$ Although on the face of it this looks like just another plain-Jane outdoor cafe, the indoor dining areas become progressively pretty and inviting. The house specializes in *paella* and *arroz negro* (rice with seafood in squid ink). Also serves a smattering of fine pasta dishes. ♦ Catalan ♦ Pg Colom, 4 (C Fusteria-C Marquet) 315.17.55

10 La Brasserie del Moll ★★$$$ Offers a menu similar to that of its parent restaurant, the **Brasserie Fló**, in the Ribera section of town. The indoor dining is pleasant and comfortable; the outdoor dining is regrettably underscored by traffic noise. Some highlights among the fresh, seasonal fare are the mussels, *arroz negro* (black rice), the fish and shellfish platters, and the *solomillo* shish kebab. The daily specials are moderately priced, and the desserts are delicious. ♦ Seafood/International ♦ Pg Colom, 3 (C Fusteria-C Marquet) 310.32.68

10 Casa de Cervantes Despite this building's 20th-century remodelling, its facade retains sculptural mementos (most likely 16th century) from the transitional period between the Flamboyant Gothic and Renaissance architectural styles. Of particular interest, however, is the baseless George-Washington-slept-here-type legend that claims Cervantes, who praised Barcelona in his writings, once stayed here. ♦ Pg Colom, 2 (C Fusteria-C Marquet)

CIUTAT VELLA, LA ISLA DE LOS TESOROS

11 Correos y Telegrafos (1927, **Josep Goday i Casals** and **Jaume Torres i Grau**) When this building was put up, it was the policy of the Spanish postal service to erect monumental post offices in the country's principal cities. As grandiose within as without, its central vestibule is adorned with notable paintings by such characteristically Catalan *noucentista* artists as **Alexandre Galí, Josep Obiols** and **Labarta i Canyelles**. The 4 sculptures on the facade are the work of **Manuel Fuxà**; the ducal coat of arms on the lateral facade is by **Arnau**. ♦ Via Laietana, 1 (Pl d'Antoni López) 302.75.63

12 Carrer Reina Cristina/Carrer Llauder These perpendical streets between **Pl d'Antoni López** and **Pl Palau** bustle with duty-free shops selling all manner of electronic and audiovisual equipment and other imported items at attractive prices. ♦ Pg D'Isabel II-Pas Sota Muralla

13 Carballeira ★$$ A down-home restaurant that has earned a reputation for serving fine fish. ♦ Seafood ♦ C Reina Cristina, 3 (C Llauder)

14 Pascual A bar that claims to serve *el mejor café del distrito* (the best coffee in the district). OK, they do serve a fine coffee, but—even better—they serve *churros*, fried strips of donut-like dough commonly found in Madrid but hard to come by in Barcelona. They're a favorite of ours at breakfast. Those in the know dunk them in their coffee. ♦ Pas Sota Muralla, 7 (C Llauder)

15 Casa Carbonell-Collasso (Rovira i Riera) An illustrative example of Neoclassical architecture fronted by Doric portals. ♦ Pl Palau (Pas Sota Muralla-C Reina Cristina)

16 Monumento al Deportistas del Mar This little-known 1969 sculpture by **Ros Sabaté** pays homage to water sports. ♦ Espanya Quay (Moll de la Fusta)

17 Espanya Quay (1992) As part of the port redevelopment project, this dock will be equipped with recreational, cultural, sports and commercial installations, all located on a platform about 15 feet above the level of the quay and accessed by a ramp. Among these installations will be an **IMAX** panoramic cinema accommodating 700 to 800 spectators,

a large amphitheater, dance halls, restaurants, bars, regular cinemas, shops and the highly touted **Centre del Mar**, which will include an aquarium, a marine museum, and various leisure, experimental and educational facilities. Plans call for a plaza to be built at the far end of the quay (facing **Barcelona Quay**) that will be linked to **Pl Portal Pau** via tunnel or walkway. Espanya Quay will also offer underground parking spaces for 2000 vehicles.

18 Reial Club Marítim de Barcelona ★★★$$$ The only public restaurant in town that offers a view of Barcelona from the water, it is located just beyond the private **Club Náutico** at the far end of Espanya Quay. Its wonderful view and mouth-watering selection of daily, market-fresh specials are 2 compelling reasons to come all the way out here (we suggest you catch a cab). The chef has developed his own version of Mediterranean cuisine characterized by light sauces, innovative flavor blends and nouvellesque artistry. Try the wonderul *arroz conpulpo* (rice with octopus), the salmon-stuffed pasta rolls topped with a vinaigrette-and-tomato sauce, the *butifarras*

Waterfront

de Camprodón con judías (Catalan sausages with beans), the *parrillada de pescado* (platter of grilled fish) or *la dorada* (a local fish) *con salsa de cigalas* (with prawn sauce). Also commendable are the homemade desserts (especially the *crema catalana*), the selection of aromatic coffees and teas, and the wine list. All in all, a good value for the money. ♦ Mediterranean ♦ Moll D'Espanya, s/n. Reservations advised. 315.02.56

19 Diposit and Barceloneta Quays (1992) Plans are to renovate the existing warehouse here and build a new seafront promenade and a sports marina that will accommodate 700 vessels.

20 Rellotge and Pescadors Quays (1992) Projected site of a new market and installations complementing the adjoining sports marina. It's not clear whether the pyramid (1751) crowned with a lantern and bearing a clock (*rellotge*) with 4 dials will be left standing on Rellotge Quay or not.

21 Plaça de Mar (1992) This new cultural and recreational space looking out to sea will replace the aquarium and San Sebastián baths now located here.

22 Nou Quay (1992) Founded in 1836, the current *La Vulcano* workshops (which built Spain's first steamship, the *Delfin*, and, in 1864, built and launched—or rather, immersed—the copper-lined *Ictineo*, the world's first submarine) will move to the other side of the port and Nou Quay will be devoted to repairing and launching all manner of marine sports and leisure craft. The 2 existing breakwaters will be joined to form a quay with an area of more than 9600 square feet. The **Club Natació** (Swimming Club) will be renovated and used as an Olympic training facility.

La Ribera/Parc de la Ciutadella

This is the oldest section of Barcelona, Adelaide told us as we sifted through the appealing curiosities in her **Les Liles** antique shop.

Everybody always talks about the Barri Gòtic, but this is really where the city began.

In this city with at least 2000 years of history under its belt, barrio allegiances run strong, and the lovely, loquacious Adelaide is not alone in feeling that her barrio has been short-shrifted in the attention it is given.

Barcelona's oldest barrio? In aspect assuredly, if not in age. The Roman remains of the adjoining **Barri Gòtic** argue strongly for its seniority. But even if **La Ribera** is not Barcelona's oldest barrio, it might be fair to say that it is the oldest in *authentic* medieval flavor. Still, except for a few must-see sights—the **Museu Picasso**, **Palau de la Música** and **Iglesia de Santa María del Mar**—its dense network of streets is largely ignored by tourists.

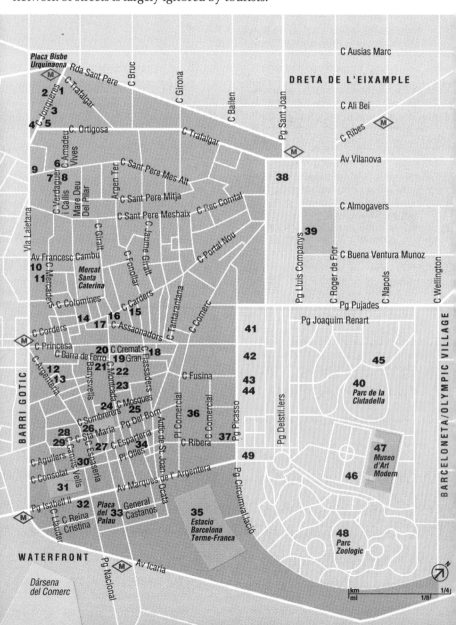

Actually, La Ribera's origins appear to revert to the 9th century when history has it that along the road that linked Barcelona with the rest of Europe, **Luis el Piadoso**—during a siege of the city then under Moorish rule—dedicated a temple to the martyr **San Saturnino** in 801. Around this temple gathered a settlement known as **Vilar de Sant Pere** that was later incorporated into the city with the construction of new municipal walls in the 13th century.

In the Middle Ages La Ribera was the city's commercial and social nerve center, the home of its sailors, seamen and fishermen. Later it became the enclave of the city's earliest industrial enterprises, with the area above the **Avinguda de la Catedral** (now technically known as the **Barrio de Sant Pere**) housing the city's first textile factories. In the 19th century the barrio peaked in riches and prominence on the strength of this textile trade. At the beginning of the 20th century the great textile factories fled the barrio, although to this day you'll find many of their commercial offices here.

The area below the Avinguda de la Catedral is commonly known as the **Barrio de Santa Maria** for its historically significant church. Before that it was known as the **Vilanova de la Mar**. Here you'll find Barcelona's narrowest street and the museums and mansions of **Carrer de Montcada**, whose construction marked the union of the maritime and commercial sections of La Ribera, a marriage that made this the vital nucleus of Catalunya's maritime expansion throughout the Mediterranean area from the time of **Jaume I** (13th century) to that of **Carles V** (16th century). When the commercial focus shifted from the Mediterranean to the Atlantic in succeeding centuries, Barcelona's—and more especially, La Ribera's—fortunes declined. In the late 18th century the city's maritime activities were based primarily in the Barri

Gòtic, and the **Iglesia de la Mercè** and the **Carrer Ample** supplanted the **Iglesia de Santa María del Mar** and the **Carrer de Montcada** as the spiritual and aristocratic hubs of the city.

Since its diminished importance did not require the massive renovation of streets and buildings that ultimately took place along **La Rambla** and in the Barri Gòtic, La Ribera fortuitously preserved many of its vintage structures. Now largely the province of small businesses and independent merchants, it exudes a decidedly provincial, medieval air wholly in tune with its narrow, cobblestoned streets. By the same token its charms are more quotidian, a blue-collar barometer of Barcelona life. At the height of the tourist season, this is one place to escape the hordes.

So is the **Parc de la Ciutadella** at the southeastern edge of La Ribera, conjured in the 1880s on terrain formerly occupied by the much-hated fortress built by the troops of **Felipe V** in the early 18th century. The park's master plan was the work of **Josep Fontseré**. Assisting him with some of the details was a young **Antoni Gaudí**.

Just a few years earlier Barcelona had torn down its city walls and embarked on a cosmopolitan course of expansion. The main impulse for completing the park was the International Exhibition of 1888 to be held here. In the 1920s improvements were made in the park under the direction of the master French landscaper **Forestier**, who simultaneously participated in the development of Montjuïc for the 1929 World's Fair.

Though Barcelona has blossomed with many municipal parks in recent years, la Ciutadella remains *the* city park—perhaps because for many years it was the *only* one. To us it has always been most remarkable for the wealth of structures, sculptures and assorted curiosities (among them Gaudí's grandiose fountain, the **Museu d'Art Modern**, the **Museu de Geología** and the **Parlament**) it packs into a rather small area without upstaging the *natural* charms that make it an urban oasis, a green breathing space between the concrete demands of city life. And still its ranks of busts of illustrious Catalan cultural figures grows—every May since 1908 a new one has been added.

Nevertheless, the park's abundant, varied, and at times singular, vegetation remains a prime attraction. Between the Parlament and Gaudí's cascade you'll find several species of palm trees, an orange tree from Louisiana, a Chinese poplar and a Mexican oak. On the other side of the lake beside a monumental cypress rooted in the water stands an authentic fir tree from the Himalayas.

Though La Ribera has been down on its luck for quite a while now, it could erupt with trendiness at anytime, as it did several years ago when a flurry of new bars, restaurants and nightclubs channeled a fashionable, late-night crowd into its tangle of tiny streets. In the interim, however, don't overlook its more enduring enchantments.

---

1 Gratacels Urquinaona (1942, Luis Gutiérrez Soto) Actually designed before the Civil War began in 1936, this highly functional, triangular structure reflects the Central European architectural trends of that period and is somewhat politically significant in that its Madrid architect later authored the Spanish capital's most representative State structure of the Franco era, the **Ministerio del Aire**. This earlier, 15-story building earned its nickname *Gratacels* (skyscraper) by being the first building to exceed the traditional height of Barcelona's buildings. ◆ C Jonqueres, 18 (C Trafalgar)

La Ribera/Parc de la Ciutadella

2 Hostal Alhambra $ Cheap, basic accommodations near the **Palau de la Música**. The 36 rooms come with telephones. All doubles have baths, but some singles have in-room sinks only. ◆ C Jonqueres, 13 (Pl Bisbe Urquinaona-C D'Ortigosa) 317.19.24; fax 241.22.04

3 Brasserie Flo Restaurante ★★$$$ Parent restaurant to the **Moll de la Fusta**'s **La Brasserie del Moll**, this Parisian-style bistro tempts passersby with an appetizing assortment of fresh seafood displayed in the attractively tiled passageway leading up to its front door. House specialties include choucroute, châteaubriand with Béarnaise sauce, and duck pâté. ◆ French/Catalan ◆ C Jonqueres, 10 (Pl Bisbe Urquinaona-C D'Ortigosa) 317.80.37

4 Edificio Caixa de Pensions (1918, Enric Sagnier Villavecchia) Sagnier simultaneously built this office building and the following one with the same name for the Caixa de Pensions, a savings bank. As this one was the bank headquarters, we wonder if its Gothic Revivalist styling and the cathedral overtones of its spire and ogival front window were not a tongue-in-cheek comment on the growing worship of Mammon. The lateral facades are in the local *noucentiste* vein that reached its apex in some of the structures built for the 1929 World's Fair. The sculptural groupings are the work of **Manuel Fuxà**. ◆ Via Laietana, 56-58 (C Jonqueres)

5 Edificio Caixa de Pensions (1918, Enric Sagnier Villavecchia) This convex structure built at the same time as the one cited above has more of a modern flavor to it until one reaches the crowning finials and crenellated tower that echo the Gothic allusions of its sibling structure. The sculptural groupings here have been attributed to **Eusebi Arnau**. ◆ C Jonqueres, 2 (C D'Ortigosa-C Ramon Mas Sant Francesc de Paula)

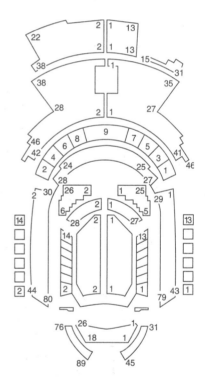

6 Palau de la Música Catalana (1908, Lluís Domènech i Montaner; remodelling and expansion 1989, **Oscar Tusquets** and **Lluís Clotet**) A sumptuously exotic summation of the Catalan Modernist tradition at its most elegantly effusive, this tour de force concert hall, considered among the finest in the world, was built by the **Orfeó Català** (largely by popular

subscription) between 1905 and 1908 as a social headquarters and auditorium. The irregularly shaped plot of land posed a special challenge, but Domènech rose to the occasion and fashioned what is arguably his most important creation. Its explosion of domes, striking mosaics and stained-glass flights of fancy are an example of the Modernist imagination at its most fecund and sensuous, but by no means frivolous. Everywhere images of Sant Jordi, patron saint of the region, and red-and-yellow-stained-glass allusions to the Catalan flag root the loquacious ornamentation in references to religion and the homeland—although the building is not without its Moorish allusions, especially in the facade. Conceived as an intelligent set of spaces, it makes optimum use of the *double facade* and maximizes the use of natural light (try to see it at least once by day). The floral, stained-glass windows and skylight are especially whimsical. The lateral lamps are a Gaudí echo. Completing the extravagant decoration are dynamic sculptures by **Pau Gargallo, Eusebi Arnau** and **Miquel Blay**; numerous ceramic flowers, fruits and vegetables; mosaics (those on the facade and stage are by **Lluís Bru**); busts of leading composers; and ceilings vaulted in the Catalan style. To top it all off, the place boasts fine acoustics. The unusual pipe organ on the stage is in need of repair, however. Also by the stage are large, striking **Gargallo** sculptures including a bust of **Clavé**, father of Catalan choral music; a bust of **Beethoven**; and a depiction of the procession of **Wagner's Valkyries**. Of special interest on the outside of the building is the large corner sculptural grouping by Miquel Blay entitled *Cançó popular*. On the whole, this building corresponds to the Wagnerian ideal—characteristic of Catalan Modernism—of the integration of the arts. Unfortunately, the rich, full complexity of the Palau's (as it is commonly called) original external and internal decoration has been, like that of other Modernist structures in the city, *simplified* over time. To improve deteriorating conditions and enhance the Palau's use, the Orfeó Català recently undertook a profound program of renovation, restoration and remodelling not only of the building itself but of the block it occupies. The work entailed the addition of administrative space at the expense of eliminating part of the neighboring **Sant Francesc de Paula** church, which for years had obscured one wall of the Palau that is now again visible; the addition of dressing rooms, rehearsal space and lounges; installation of a grand vestibule bar; adaptation of the stage to accommodate orchestras and choirs; the installation of air-conditioning; and the restoration or many original structural and decorative elements. All manner of musical performances are held here throughout the year.
♦ Seats 2000. C D'Amadeu Vives, 1 (C Sant Pere Més Alt, 11) 301.11.04; ticket reservations 268.10.00

7 El Tropezon This vintage, neighborhood *tasca* (tavern) regularly buzzes with Palau de la Música patrons before performances. Judging from the autographed photos on the wall, it's a favorite with the performers too. ♦ C Verdaguer i Callís, 9 (C Sant Pere Més Alt) 268.07.21

8 La Cava del Palau This is where everybody comes *after* performances at the Palau. A very sophisticated *champañería*, it offers dozens of regional *cavas* (Spanish vintners are prohibited from calling their sparkling wines *champagne*), dozens of French champagnes, and hundreds of appellation wines—some from beyond Spain's borders. The bubbly is served with flair in fine, fluted glasses. You can also

La Ribera/Parc de la Ciutadella

choose from among a selection of snacks, including imported and domestic cheeses, pâtés, and, yes, caviar. Although the space is large, it is divvied up into multilevel sections that permit a bit of privacy. The place is at its liveliest after 11PM. Starting at 11:30PM, a pianist often entertains the crowds. ♦ C Verdaguer i Callís, 10 (C Sant Pere Més Alt-C Sant Pere Mitja) 310.09.38

8 Sopeta Una ★★$$ A diamond in the rough, this small restaurant serves very fine fare at reasonable prices in a coarsely rustic setting. The *Cuina i Vins de Catalunya* plaque out front proclaims that quality awaits within. Although the standard menu is limited, there are typically at least half a dozen market-fresh specials of the day. ♦ International ♦ C Verdaguer i Callís, 6 (C Sant Pere Més Alt-C Sant Pere Mitja) 319.61.31

8 Bodega Carlos This authentic, low-ceilinged *tasca* (tavern) is a favorite breakfast and snack spot for students at the music school across the way and the nearby Institut de Teatre.
♦ C Verdaguer i Callís, 4 (C Sant Pere Més Alt-C Sant Pere Mitja) 319.10.26

Deep within the 16 miles of caves under the **Cordorníu Winery** in Sant Sadurní d'Anoia lies the tomb of **Don Manuel Raventos**, the man who made Catalunya's *cava* internationally renowned.

Restaurants/Nightlife: Red   Hotels: Blue
Shops/Parks: Green   **Sights/Culture: Black**

CIUTAT VELLA, LA ISLA DE LOS TESOROS

9 Casa Gremial dels Velers o de la Seda (1763, **Joan Garrido**; restoration and expansion 1931, **Jeroni Martorell**) The *sgraffiti*-covered facades of this structure are possibly

La Ribera/Parc de la Ciutadella

the city's most vivid illustration of this local decorative tradition. The building was almost torn down in 1913 to make way for the Via Laietana, but it was rescued in 1916 upon being declared a national monument. Nevertheless, the adaptations required by the reconfiguration of the surrounding streets resulted in substantial alterations to the building, and the *sgraffito* decoration of the facade facing the Pl Mestre Lluís Millet is a 1931 imitation of the original. It was originally built as the headquarters of the sailmakers' guild, which was founded in 1533. ♦ Via Laietana, 50 (Pl Mestre Lluís Millet)

10 La Perla Nera $$ The trattoria decor here runs to murals depicting houses festooned with drying laundry—a bit kitschy but pleasant. The lasagna bolognesa, fettuccini, risotto, carpaccio and large pizzas fresh from a wood-burning oven are authentically delightful. ♦ Italian ♦ Via Laietana, 32-34 (Pl Antoni Maura) 310.56.46

11 Carrer dels Mercaders For 500 years beginning in the 15th century, this was the focal point for the grand fortunes of industrial Barcelona. Catalan merchants and entrepreneurs who had branch offices in the capitals of North Africa, the Near East and along the Mediterranean coast of Europe built their stately homes here. ♦ C Sant Pere Mes Baix-C Bòria

Restaurants/Nightlife: Red   Hotels: Blue
Shops/Parks: Green   **Sights/Culture: Black**

12 Carrers Argentería and L'Espasería Once known as the **Camino del Mar** since it led to the sea, this street later housed the workshops of the city's sword, lance and dagger makers and its silversmiths. Thus, the lower end leading to the Pl Palau is still called C L'Espasería (alluding to its sword-forging days), and its upper end is called C Argentería (or Platería) for the silversmithing activities that took place here until the end of the 19th century, when they moved to C Ferran. Until 1823 almost all the buildings along this street featured picturesque wooden projections; in that year they were destroyed by municipal edict. Still, the street preserves a good deal of its historic flavor. Note especially the arches at the entrance to the adjacent streets Giriti, Grunyí and Brosoll. ♦ Via Laietana-Pl Palau

13 Senyor Parellada ★★$$$ An elegant eatery with a loyal following of businesspeople, yuppies and upper-echelon civil servants. The cuisine is classic Catalan embellished with some innovative grace notes. Some dishes to try are the canelones, *caldereta de pescado* (yet another version of bouillabaisse), salmon carpaccio, lamb, *calamarcitos* (squid), and, for dessert, *crema quemada* (basically, *crema catalan*). ♦ Catalan ♦ C Argentería (Platería), 37 (C Giriti-C Grunyí) 315.40.10

14 Krakatoa Beautifully displayed Asian exotica for sale. ♦ Pl Llana, 1 (C Corders) 310.56.59

15 Capilla Marcús (12th c) Now dwarfed by its surrounding edifices, this tenacious chapel is all that remains of a hospital for the poor built here during the second half of the 12th century along the former Roman road and what was then the northeastern road out of town. Its construction was instigated by the merchant **Bernardí Marcús**, who probably had some

Capilla Marcús

CIUTAT VELLA, LA ISLA DE LOS TESOROS

relationship with the *troters*, the medieval mounted mailmen who organized themselves into a guild in this chapel in 1187. Despite the various misguided restorations inflicted upon it, its added upper story, and its unification with a Baroque building from 1787, the chapel retains a good bit of its original Romanesque character. The interior, reflecting 19th-century Neoclassical tastes, was severly damaged by fires in 1909 and 1936. Today the building is a favorite gathering spot for pigeons.
♦ C Carders, 2 (Placeta d'En Marcus)

Palacio Dalmases,
Carrer de Montcada

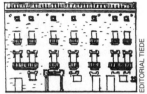

EDITORIAL TIEDE

16 Carrer de Montcada Despite continual remodelling and recent restorations, this street forged in the 12th and 13th centuries at the behest of **Guillem Ramon de Montcada** remains an incomparable example of the civil architecture of medieval Barcelona. It was Montcada's intent to unite the upper **Barrio de Sant Pere** with the lower **Vilanova del Mar**, and as Barcelona was then deriving great economic might from its Mediterranean empire, in no time at all the street was lined with the exuberant mansions of Barcelona's aristocracy. From the 14th to 18th centuries it remained their municipal enclave. In the late 1700s this role was usurped by the **Barri Gòtic**'s **C Ample**. At the end of the 19th century C Montcada's decline was hastened by the construction of the **Eixample**, and many of its spacious mansions were converted into modest rental flats. In 1974 the street was declared a national *Conjunto Monumental Histórico Artístico*, and in 1953 the municipal authorities began restoring its most outstanding structures and adapting them for use as museums and other outlets of culture. Originally a long, uninterrupted street, C Montcada was bisected in 1853 by the new **C Princesa**. The stretch between the **Capilla de Marcús** and C Princesa contains no notable buildings. From **C Cremat Gran** and **C Barra de Ferro** to the end, however, you'll find a succession of architecturally interesting structures, except for the modest house at No. 16 built in 1857. ♦ Placeta d'En Marcus-Pl Montcada

South side of the
Carrer de Montcada

17 Lluna Plena $$ A small, attractive eatery whose largely Catalan menu is supplemented with a selection of pâtés and cheeses.
♦ Catalan ♦ C Montcada, 2 (Placeta d'En Marcus) 310.54.29

18 Les Liles A browser's delight where the owner, sweet **Adelaide**, actually encourages you to have a look—and *feel*—of the antique merchandise, which includes many turn-of-the-century items, Art Deco objects and assorted furniture, feathers, frills and jewelry. She enjoys foreign visitors immensely and offers them maps and lots of genial hospitality. ♦ C Princesa, 40 (C Corretger) 315.16.09

La Ribera/Parc de la Ciutadella

19 Museu Picasso This museum occupying 3 Gothic mansions is cited as Barcelona's most popular attraction—and with good reason. Its collection of works spanning the artist's long, fruitful and multifaceted career from adolescence to the final years, clearly reveals the depth and scope of his prolific accomplishments, which by no means begin or end with Cubism. Typically, the paintings, engravings, drawings and ceramics are displayed chronologically. Notable in the **La Corunya** section (1891-95), which largely contains pencil and charcoal drawings, are 2 evocative portraits— *Hombre con Boina* (Man with Beret) and *Retrato del Viejo* (Portrait of the Old Man),

EDITORIAL TIEDE

both dating from 1895. The **Barcelona** section (1895-97) contains mostly oils and drawings and includes an important series of studies of the human figure. Outstanding in the **Málaga and Barcelona** section (1896) is the *Retrato de la Tía Pepa* (Portrait of Aunt Pepa), a portrayal of the artist's own aunt. *Ciencia y Caridad* (Science and Charity) dating from 1897 is a large, impressive canvas depicting a doctor (modeled on Picasso's own father) at his patient's bedside. Dating from the Madrid period (1897-98) are city scenes and a copy of **Velázquez**'s portrait of **Philip IV**. An interesting memento from the 1899-1900 period is a drawing over the menu from **Els Quatre Gats**, a restaurant that has been reborn in C Montsió and was headquarters at the turn of the century for a group of artists calling themselves *Els Quatre Gats*. In the **Barcelona-Paris** section (1900-01) we begin to see the Picasso most of us have come to know. Note *El Final del Número* (The End of the Number) from 1901 and *La Espera (Margot)* (The Waiting [Margot]) from 1900. During the **Epoca Blava** (1901-04) we see more human studies in pencil and charcoal and portraits in oil. **Barcelona 1917** features the *Caballo Corneado* (The Gored Horse) in charcoal and the clear beginnings of Cubism. Two entire rooms are

La Ribera/Parc de la Ciutadella

devoted to the *Las Meninas* series produced in Cannes in 1957 as a tribute to Velázquez's famous painting. Other individual highlights are sketches of his friends **Sabartés** and **Junyer** and selected works from his Blue period. During your tour of the museum you'll come across 2 salons devoid of Picasso works that are illustrative of the Gothic artistry of the host buildings. One of these is the **Palau Berenguer D'Aguilar** (No. 15), a structure that evinces architectural vestiges of the 13th and 14th centuries, but whose current aspect derives principally from the remodelling undertaken by nobleman **Joan Berenguer d'Aguilar** in the 15th century, possibly with the assistance of **Marc Safont**, designer of the **Palau de la Generalitat**'s Gothic facade. Certainly dating from this renovation is the central patio framed by a series of ogival arches over corbels. Like other buildings in C Montcada, this one has suffered numerous changes and mutilations, the most recent alterations (1960-63) occasioned by its conversion into the Museu Picasso. In 1981 the museum further engulfed the adjoining **Palau del Baró de Castellet** (No. 17) and **Palau Meca** (No. 19), which were both clearly updated in the 18th century. The former housed some beautiful medieval paintings chronicling the conquest of Mallorca which are now in the **Museu d'Art de Catalunya**. ♦ Admission. M 4-8:30PM; Tu-Sa 9AM-2PM, 4-8:30PM; Su 9AM-2PM. C Montcada, 15-19 (C Cremat Gran) 319.63.10

Within the Museu Picasso:

Cafe del Museu $$ The invitingly artistic and cosmopolitan atmosphere might tempt you to eat here, so you should be aware that the quality of the food has fluctuated greatly in the past. It might be wonderful at the time of your visit, it might not. Perhaps you'll want to test the waters with a snack. ♦ International ♦ Tu-Sa 1-4PM. No credit cards

20 Nou Celler $$ A friendly, neighborhood *tasca* (tavern) serving a wide variety of tapas at its bar and rough-hewn wooden tables. You can also have a full-fledged meal here. ♦ Spanish ♦ C Barra de Ferro, 3 (C Banys Vells-C Montcada) 310.47.73

20 Picasso, Miró, Dalí (Galeria Picasso) Sells lithographs, posters, postcards, prints, books and assorted souvenirs pertaining to the trio of its namesake artists and to the city of Barcelona itself. ♦ C Barra de Ferro, 5 (C Banys Vells-C Montcada) 315.38.81. Also at: C Tapinería, 10. 310.49.57

1 Early 20th c
2 16th, 17th and early 18th c; 16th c tapestries
3 Late 19th and early 20th c; Modernist era
4 18th c liveries and coats of arms
5 Royal cloak of the Order of Charles III; early 18th and 19th c men's vests
6 Apparel from the Directory, First Empire, and Romantic periods
7 Isabelline era, Second Empire

21 Museu Textil i d'Indumentària (14th-18th c) It is only fitting that a neighborhood that once thrived on the textile trade should have a museum (established in 1969) devoted to fabrics and fashions ranging from the time of ancient Egypt to our own century. The collection dates back to 1883, a time when collecting textiles, clothing and accessories was a trendy European pastime. Recent additions that have enriched the collection include a group of **Balenciaga** dresses; noteworthy pieces by contemporary designers (mostly Catalan) such as **Margarita Nuez, Carmen Mir, Pierre Cardin, creadores Ad-Lib, Paco Rabanne, Chanel**; and examples of contemporary jewelry. The vintage house that holds all this are the **Palau de los Marqueses de Llió** (No. 12), one of the largest buildings on this street, and the **Palau Nadal** (No. 14), dating from the 15th to 16th centuries. In the 18th century the Marqués de Llió reconstructed the original 14th-century edifice conserving its structure and patio area, whose Gothic elements are accented by Renaissance windows and doors added during a 16th-century renovation. ♦ Admission. Tu-Su 10AM-2PM, 4:30-7PM June-Sep; Tu-Sa 9AM-2PM, 4-7PM, Su 9AM-2PM, Sep-June. C Montcada, 12-14 (C Barra de Ferro-C Sombrerers) 310.45.16

SURREALISTA

22 Galería Surrealista Hello, **Dalí!** This gallery sells the full gamut of the Surrealist master's work—mostly in reproduction. The selection includes drawings, tapestries, ceramics, sculptures, engravings, enameled ware and lithographs...and a sofa in the shape of lips that recalls one of the illusions the artist orchestrated at his outrageous **Teatre-Museu Dalí** in Figueres. Purchases will be shipped if so desired. ♦ M-Sa 10AM-1:30PM, 4-8PM; Su 10AM-1:30PM. C Montcada, 19 (C Cremat Gran-C Arc St. Vicenç) 310.33.11

23 Carrer de Montcada, 23 (14th c) This house also preserves to a great degree the original, opulent character of the 14th-century facades that once flourished along this street. Of further interest is its characteristic square tower terminating in a flat roof. ♦ C Cremat Gran-C Arc St. Vincenç

23 Casa Cervelló-Giudice (15th c) The facade here is perhaps C Montcada's most authentic. Originally of the 15th century, this stately residence underwent some 16th-century changes that integrated elements of the Catalan Gothic within a markedly Renaissance composition. And it is that mix that we still see today. Not easily missed is its tall, gargoyled gallery, but the patio within has been profoundly redone. The house belonged to the family Cervelló but was the 18th-century residence of the Giudices, a family of Genoese merchants. ♦ C Montcada, 25 (C Arc St. Vincenç) 310.42.45

Within Casa Cervelló-Giudice:

Galería Maeght In 1974 the pretigious Parisian Galería Maeght opened this Barcelona outpost that has become one of the city's leading purveyors of contemporary art—both name-brand and up-and-coming. Here you can acquire works by **Bennàssar, Braque, Broto, Calder, Chagall, Giacometti, Leger, Llimós, Miró, Tàpies, Valdés** and many more. Maeght also publishes well-respected books and magazines on art. ♦ Tu-Su 10AM-1:30PM, 4:30-8PM. 310.42.45

23 La Pizza Nostra ★$ The pizzas at this pleasant eatery are as imaginative as they are good, and if you can't quite decide among the tantalizing topping blends, you can straddle the fence and order a pie half topped with one combination and half with another. The desserts are good too. We particularly like the chocolate mousse. ♦ Italian/Pizza ♦ C Montcada (C L'Arc St. Vicenç) 319.90.58

24 Palau Dalmases (17th c) What you see today is the result of a complete renovation carried out in the mid-17th century. Of the pre-existing 15th-century palace only a few grace

La Ribera/Parc de la Ciutadella

notes remain—one of them, a star-shaped vault. But still the structure (one of the largest along this street) is notable for the fluid sculptural ornamentation that alternates with large, smooth stone surfaces—a marriage of formal extravagance and bland austerity representative of Barcelona's architectural preferences of the day. Its interior patio (by far the most interesting one along this street) is endowed with a grand staircase that is considered one of the Baroque masterworks of Barcelona and is further noteworthy for its sculptures. Also preserved within the building is a 15th-century chapel. During the Franco dictatorship this palau housed the **Institut d'Estudis Catalans**. Since 1962 it has been the headquarters of the **Omnium Cultural**, an organization dedicated to promoting Catalan culture. ♦ C Montcada, 20 (C Barra de Ferro-C Sombrerers)

24 El Xampanyet Join the barrio regulars here in a glass of sparkling Xampanyet wine from Girona from which this tapas bar gets its name. Or rather, its nickname. Its real name is **Casa Esteban**—well, no, that's not really true either. When this bar was founded in 1929 by a man named **Esteban**, he chose not to give it a name, saying that all bars eventually come to be known for the special drinks they serve. So to this day, the facade carries no name at all, and no number for that matter. You might also want to try the fresh cider and seafood tapas (though mostly dished up from tins, they are delicious). ♦ C Montcada, 22 (C Barra de Ferro-C Sombrerers) 319.70.03

25 Carrer les Mosques (*Street of the Flies*)
Barcelona's narrowest street. ♦ C Montcada-
C Flassaders

26 Iglesia de Santa María del Mar (1329-84,
Berenguer de Montagut) Affectionately known
as the **Catedral de la Ribera**, this gem of a
church was built during Catalunya's era of
colonial expansion, when the city's economy
basked in its commercial dominance of the
Mediterranean seas and lands. Then situated
at the bustling heart of the vital new capital,
this church stood as a triumphant symbol of
the Catalan maritime empire that came to
include Mallorca, Ibiza, Valencia, Sicily and
part of Greece. However, a document dating
from 998 cites for the first time the existence
of an Iglesia de Santa María del Mar down by
the sea, which came to be the heart of the barrio of shipowners, merchants and stevedores
that worshipped there. The importance of this
seafaring populace to the 13th-century city
resulted in the conversion of the old parish
church into a grand archdiocesan cathedral.
A prime promoter of the conversion was
Canon Bernat Llull, named archdeacon of
Santa María in 1324. The first stone was laid
by **King Alfonso el Benigno** upon his return
from the conquest of Sardinia, the closing
chapter of Catalunya's Mediterranean domination. When **Jaume I** initiated the Catalan colonial quest a century before, he had vowed to
dedicate a cathedral to Santa Maria if he met
with success. From then on whenever Barcelona's warring seafarers engaged in battle they
would cry *Santa María*. No wonder then that
when this church was built, seafarers, stevedores and deck hands all participated in its
construction. This was their expression of
thanks to their elected patron saint, Santa
María. Not surprisingly then, to many Barcelonans (especially residents of La Ribera) this
church has greater historical and sentimental
significance than the Barri Gòtic's Cathedral.
It is also deemed to be the only perfectly completed example of a great Catalan Gothic
church (at least on the outside). Externally,
the predominance of solid mass over empty
spaces, the pronounced horizontality, the vast,
unornamented surfaces, the massive abutments sans flying buttresses, and the octagonal, flat-topped towers are prime features of
Catalan Gothic construction (even though the
northern tower was not completed until 1496
and the southern one not until 1902). The
main door leading onto the Pl Santa María is
flanked by images of **San Pedro** and **San
Pablo** (Sts. Peter and Paul); in the tympanum
San Salvador stands between the **Virgin** and
San Juan. The door leading off the apse and
onto the Pl Born was built in 1542 by **Bernat
Salvador**. Within, the church evidences the
characteristic attempt of Catalan Gothic architecture to conquer space and purify form.
Partially destroyed by fire in 1714, the subsequent restoration work and the Baroque altar
installed afterward were severely damaged
by another fire in 1936. In 1967 the presbytery was built and spectacular interior
and exterior lighting was installed. The
overall impression is one of a soar-
ing space of perfect proportions,
a sense of unity and openness
stemming in part from the elimination of the Classic transept.
Here you'll find a large central
and 2 lateral naves that fuse in
the ambulatory of the apse. The
lofty dimensions of the naves are
strikingly offset by a series of
relatively slim, octangular columns devoid of the typical Gothic
scrimshaw ornamentation. The
semicirle of columns guarding the
main altar is particularly attractive. Now a word about the math-
ematics that give rise to this
beautiful eurhythmy. The central
nave, 42.6 feet wide, is exactly
twice as wide as the lateral naves.
The total width of the structure
equals the combined height of
the shorter lateral naves, and the
width of the lateral naves is equal
to the difference between their
height and that of the central
nave. This church is also singled
out for its 15th-century stained-

CIUTAT VELLA, LA ISLA DE LOS TESOROS

glass finery (recently restored to renewed brilliance) that peaks in the striking rose window (the original 13th-century rose window was destroyed in the earthquake of 1428). Should you visit here when the church's fine acoustics resound with a special operatic performance, a concert of Gregorian chant, or the spiritual strains of the boys' choir (the only active one in the city), you're sure to be memorably moved. A closing bit of trivia: in 711, the body of **Santa Eulàlia** was hidden in a cave on the site of this church and eventually forgotten; 500 years later it was discovered and enshrined in the Barri Gòtic's Cathedral. The marble sepulchre used to bury her in 711 is now the baptismal font of the Iglesia de Santa María del Mar. ◆ Pl Santa María (C Santa María-Pg Born-C Sombrerers)

27 **El Fossar de les Moreres** This area, which took on its current aspect in 1989, was formerly the cemetery of the **Iglesia de Santa María del Mar**, and legend has it that the remains of the defenders of Barcelona against **Felipe V** were buried here. Every 11 September their fighting spirit is echoed in the demonstrations staged here in support of Catalan independence. ◆ C Santa María

28 **Plaça de Santa María** One of those special corners of Barcelona where the passing of time seems to have been effectively held in check. Note the torch holders at the corners of the church and the Gothic fountain dating from 1402. Here you'll also see one shop bearing the sign of a star and another that of a boat—vestiges of a time when most people couldn't read.

29 **Carrer Caputxes** A typical Ribera street of yore, this one preserves yesteryear's porticoes supported by octagonal Gothic columns. Similar porticoes are found in the nearby C Panses and C Consolat Mar. If you look up in these streets and espy the figure of a head sustaining a balcony, you've come upon a former bordello. Centuries ago these porticoes were also used as exhibition space by painters wishing to sell their works.

RESTAURANT PASSADIS DEL PEP

30 **Restaurant Passadis del Pep**
★★★★$$$$ Sure of its well-heeled clientele, this restaurant posts no sign to announce its low-key presence at the end of the hall. Well known as one of the better seafood restaurants around town, it also dispenses with menus and wine lists. Your meal is simply a matter of being apprised of the finest and freshest in fish and seafood available that day and being served accordingly. The choice of wine is similarly open to discussion. ◆ Seafood ◆ Pl Palau, 2 (C Canvis Vells-C L'Espasería) Reservations imperative (sometimes days in advance) 310.10.21

Edificio de la Llotja, 1392

Edificio de la Llotja, 1802

31 **Edificio de la Llotja** (Saló de Contratación 1392, **Pere Arvey**; renovation and expansion 1794, **Joan Soler i Faneca**; construction completed 1802) The fervent commercial activity of the Kingdom of Catalunya-Aragon gave rise to the construction of *llotjas* throughout the realm. Typically, these halls of trade and commerce were the most beautiful and impressive civil structures of the Flamboyant Gothic period during which they were built. Barcelona's first one was built by the architect **Pere Llobet** between 1352 and 1357 and was

merely a simple portico protecting merchants and their merchandise from the harsher elements of wind and weather. Ill treated by the sea and a naval attack by Castilla in 1359, it was replaced by a more substantial, late 14th-century edition comprising a patio and a large salon, the only portions of the construction to survive intact. The salon's wooden ceiling is supported by arches in keeping with the prevailing civil Gothic construction of the day. In the 15th century a portico for customs activities was added on to the side facing the sea. Above it, in 1457-59, a floor was added to house the **Consolat de Mar**, a body concerned with maritime law. In the mid-16th century the facades facing the garden acquired numerous sculptural embellishments. Consequent to **Felipe V**'s occupation of the city, the Llotja was converted into barracks and its surrounding plot of land enlarged. Later this would accommodate a new, enlarged llotja built in the Neoclassical style. The work dragged on until 1802 due to the reconstruction work required in the original salon, which had fallen upon a ruinous state. You'll find Neoclassical sculptures by **Bover** and **Oliver** in the patio and by **Salvador Gurri** alongside the interior staircase. From the late 19th century to the 1960s the **Escuela de Bellas Artes** (School of

La Ribera/Parc de la Ciutadella

Fine Arts) occupied part of the building. Not only did **Picasso** study here, but so did virtually all the important Catalan artists of the first half of the 20th century. Today you'll find here the **Bolsa de Barcelona** (stock exchange) and some elegant old salons that can be rented for conferences, meetings and dinners. Overall, the building's balanced Neoclassical composition and its dovetailing of differing architectural stylings render it a hallmark in the annals of Barcelona architecture. ♦ Pl Palau (Pg d'Isabel II-C Consolat de Mar)

32 Casas d'En Xifré (1840, **Josep Buixareu** and **Francesc Vila**) Xifré was a Spanish emigrant who returned to his homeland a wealthy man. In the middle of the last century he erected this block of buildings opposite the **Llotja** in accordance with the urban development plan for the coastal area drawn up by **José Massanés**. Despite the uniform facade, the block of buildings actually consists of 5 sections. Shops and other businesses occupy the porticoed ground floor; the 3 upper stories are given over to flats. Conspicuous on the spandrels and pilasters are either terracotta medallions by **Damià Campeny** making allegorical reference to commerce and industry or busts of figures associated with the Spanish conquest of America. This was the first building in Barcelona to have running water and also served as the backdrop for the first photograph taken in Spain. It has been declared a national monument. ♦ Pg d'Isabel II, 2-14 (Pl Palau-C Llauder)

32 Restaurant 7 Portes ★★★$$$ Originally called **Cafe de les 7 Portes**, this establishment was founded in 1836 and installed in the **Pórtics d'en Xifré** (ground floor of the Casas d'En Xifré). A Barcelona landmark, it is riddled weekdays at lunch with stockbrokers from the nearby **Llotja** and at lunch on Sunday with families from around the city. Persons of note too numerous to mention have also dined on the various *paellas* and Catalan rice dishes that are the house specialties. High, beamed ceilings, lots of dark wood, and marble-topped tables complete the appealing offering. After 10PM you can often dine to the accompaniment of live piano music. Another plus is that you can eat here anytime between 1PM and 1AM. You'll likely see a line of patrons without reservations out front during the peak lunch and dinner hours, but the restaurant is large and the line moves quickly. ♦ Catalan/Spanish ♦ Pg d'Isabel II, 14 (Pl Palau) 319.30.46

33 Edificio del Gobierno Civil (1792, **Conde de Roncali**) Until 1902, when the Gobierno Civil took up quarters here, this Neoclassical structure was the **Aduana** (Customs House). Its facade is richly adorned with allegorical references to overseas trade. ♦ Pl Palau

34 Patissería Güell La Mallorquina The specialties at this small, delectable sweet shop are *carquinyolis* (crunchy almond confections) and *pals de piñyons* (crunchy pastry squares topped with pine nuts). ♦ Pl Les Olles, 7 (C Vidriera) 319.38.83

In Catalonia a dark day is turned into a holiday. National Day, 11 September, commemorates the people of Barcelona who refused to relinquish their rights when King Felipe V took the city in 1714.

34 Cal Pep ★★$$ It's often difficult to find a stool at the bar or a table in the minuscule dining room of this most agreeable, down-home restaurant. Consistently good are the *fideos con sepia* (noodles with cuttlefish), *paella*, *chopitos* (baby squid), fresh cod with potatoes, and stuffed *calamares*. What's more, the price compares favorably. ♦ Spanish ♦ Pl Les Olles, 8. No credit cards. 315.49.37

35 Estació Barcelona Terme-França (1929) So that visitors to the 1929 World's Fair would be more impressively greeted, work on this station began in 1924, replacing the former station dating from the time of Spain's first railway line (1848). The spectacular metal structures over the platforms were designed by engineer **Andreu Montaner i Serra**. The administration building with its glass roof is the work of engineer **Eduard Perxes**; and the exterior facade is the work of Madrid architect **Pedro de Muguruza**. Now, so that visitors to the 1992 Summer Olympic Games will be more impressively greeted, this station is being renovated, cleaned, repaired, redecorated and outfitted with a garage and possibly a basement discotheque. The street out front (**Av Marqués de la Argentera**) is named after the man who, as director of the MZA Railroad, ordered the station's original construction.
♦ Av Marqués de la Argentera (C Comerç-Parc Ciutadella)

36 Mercat del Born (1876, **Josep Fontseré i Mestres** and **Josep Maria Cornet i Mas**; restoration 1979, **Pere Espinosa**) In 1873 City Hall approved the plans for construction of the **Mercat Central de Barcelona**; the following year work began. All materials used were of Catalan manufacture. Its plain, glass-tile roof rests on iron ribs braced with ties and cast-iron pillars. Within, 2 large aisles are crossed by 4 small ones. Modelled after Les Halles in Paris, it is one of Spain's leading examples of the ironwork architecture so popular in Europe at the time. When the wholesale market it housed for many years moved to the outskirts of the city in 1971, the building was restored for use as an exhibition hall and now regularly presents shows of all types ranging from antiques to automobiles. Plans are afoot to revive it in a Covent Garden vein. In medieval times, the **Pg Born** in front of the market was the stage for all manner of tournaments, and subsequently, the principal venue for Carnival celebrations and guild fairs. ♦ Pl Comercial, 12 (C Fusina-C Comercial-C Ribera)

Picasso thanked the city where he had lived in his youth by donating a generous portion of his work to Barcelona's **Museu Picasso**.

Some claim that **Picasso**'s turning-point painting *Les Demoiselles d'Avignon* was inspired by a brothel in Barcelona's **Carrer D'Avinyó**.

Restaurants/Nightlife: Red   **Hotels:** Blue
Shops/Parks: Green   **Sights/Culture:** Black

37 Homage to Picasso With tributes like this, who needs insults? At the edge of the **Parc de la Ciutadella** stands **Antoni Tàpies'** hideous sculpture honoring **Picasso**. It is a large, transparent cube standing in a pool of neglected water and filled with random pieces of furniture and canvas alluding to Picasso's nonconformity. In theory the water should stream down the inside of the cube, but from time to time faulty technology thwarts the artistic intention, and the cube instead becomes off-puttingly streaked and clouded with condensed water. Quite frankly, it could do with a thorough cleaning both inside and out. Or better still, it could be removed.
♦ Pg Picasso (C Fusina-C Ribera)

38 Arc del Triomf (1888, Josep Vilaseca) Conceived as the monumental portal to the International Exhibition of 1888. Of the same proportions as Classical triumphal arches, it is made of unclad brick with ceramics (figurative scenes and plant motif friezes). The brick construction also employs *Mudéjar* forms and bears several important sculptures. Those of the main facade by **Josep Reynés** depict Barcelona receiving visitors to the Exhibition. Those of the rear facade by **Josep Llimona** illustrate the presentation of awards to those who made a positive contribution to the exhi-

La Ribera/Parc de la Ciutadella

bition. The sculptures on the right side by **Antoni Vilanova** symbolize industry, agriculture and commerce. Those on the left side by **Torcuato Tasso** represent commerce and the arts. If you head toward the park via the **Pg Lluís Companys** (built in 1884 and originally known as the **Saló de Sant Joan**), you'll come to the park gate designed by **Gaudí**. Its two 1888 ornamental sculptures representing industry and commerce are by the brothers **Venanci** and **Agapit Vallmitjana**, who also created the 2 similiar sculptures found on the door of the **Estació Barcelona Terme-França**.
♦ C Trafalgar (Pg Lluís Companys)

39 Palau de Justicia (1911, Enric Sagnier and Lluís Domènech i Estapà) One of the city's first modern public buildings, the Palau de Justicia is imposing and austere as befits its funciton as the **Court of Justice**. The main facade of this massive structure built entirely of stone from Montjuïc is 656 feet long. Although not built until 1911, it was designed in 1887 and therefore stylistically belongs to the early days of Modernism. It comprises 2 buildings with courtyards in the middle and towers at the corners. The main building, with its characteristic porch and interesting gate, contains the grand hall with rose granite columns, a high roof with unclad iron arches, and decorative work by **Josep Maria Sert**. In the **Saló de Pasos Perdidos** are some 16th-century tapestries and murals by Sert.
♦ Pg Lluís Companys (C Almogàvers-C Buenaventura)

*Gazebo at the
Museu de Zoología*

CIUTAT VELLA, LA ISLA DE LOS TESOROS

La Ribera/Parc de la Ciutadella

40 Parc de la Ciutadella (old Ciutadella 1727, **G. Prósper de Werboom**; development of the park 1873, **Josep Fontseré i Mestres**) Dating from the 1880s, this park represents the replacement of a much-hated military symbol with a much-loved municipal sanctuary. The fortress constructed by **Felipe V**'s troops in the 18th century to accommodate 8000 soldiers was so vast and imposing it was quite possibly Europe's largest. In clearing this area for his fortress, Felipe V forced the owners of 1262 Ribera houses to destroy their own dwellings at their own expense. About 40 barrio streets disappeared as well. The demolition took 3 years (1715-18), and in 1716 the fortifications began to take shape. Ultimately the fortress' pentagonal perimeter with a bastion at each vertex presented a star-shaped aspect. In 1718, with the outer walls finished, construction of the interior barracks, arsenal, governor's residence, chapel and so on began. But for all its blustering architectural bravado, the fortress never served its rightful purpose, but ended up instead serving primarily as a civil prison. The French took it by surprise in 1808. The populace, already resentful of the structure's origins, came to despise it even more for the executions the French carried out there and for the atrocities committed there during Spain's barbarous Civil War. Attempts to raze the fortress in 1841 were undone 2 years later by the regional Regency. Finally, in 1869, the fortress became city property, and all but the governor's residence, chapel and

arsenal came tumbling down by 1888. Ever since it has been, for all intents and purposes, Barcelona's equivalent of Central Park, a versatile urban oasis containing several museums, the zoo, the Catalan Parliament, and the lakes, lawns and trees with which city dwellers embroider their pastoral reveries. Its completion was spurred by the International Exhibition of 1888 that took place here. It was also— and quite appropriately, given the barrio's commercial pedigree—the site of Barcelona's first textile trade fairs (**Ferias de Muestras**). In the 1920s the prominent French landscaper **Forestier** delivered a new, improved version of the park. ♦ Pg Picasso-Pg Pujades-C Wellington-Pg Circumval.lació

41 Museu de Zoología (1888, **Lluís Domènech i Montaner**) For reasons unknown to us, this was once popularly known as the **Castell dels Tres Dragons** (Castle of the Three Dragons), which is the title of a celebrated comedy by **Serafí Pitarra**, the father of the Catalan theater. Its intended original function was that of cafe-restaurant for the 1888 Exhibition, but as it was not completed on time, it never fulfilled its ordained role. After the Exhibition, the city and the architect agreed that upon its completion it would house a workshop dedicated to the resuscitation of such moribund industrial arts and handicrafts as decorative ceramics and wrought iron. This in turn spurred a general resurgence of the decorative arts throughout Catalunya. For some time the architect also used part of the building as his studio.

72

In this his most clearly rationalistic work, he experimented with double brick walls, unclad on the outside (a great novelty in non-industrial architecture) and used a sheet-iron structure in the large upper room. Reducing the building to simple geometrical shapes, he concentrated the Gothic-inspired decoration (merlons, shields and tower) in well-defined spaces. The structure's utilization of rolled iron and the new technologies of the day coupled with its plain facades and unified interior space qualify it as but a precursor of Modernism. Interestingly, though, its strictly utilitarian forms, bare brick and unabashed iron structures influenced the design of Amsterdam's **Berlage Stock Exchange** (1898). In fact, the only extravagances this building permits itself are the ceramic *plaques* depicting herbs, animals, portraits, scenes, flowers and more designed in collaboration with the architect **Antoni M. Gallissà**. Since 1917 it has housed the **Museum of Zoology**. In addition to its insect, fish, reptile and mollusk displays, the museum specializes in Mediterranean fauna. It also features a zoological library and *fonoteca* for listening to specialized recordings in the fields. ♦ Admission. Tu-Su 9AM-2PM. ♦ Parc Ciutadella (Pg Picasso at Pg Pujades) 319.69.50

42 Hivernacle (or Invernadero) (1884, **Josep Amargós**) This Modernist greenhouse typical of the iron-and-glass architecture of the Eiffel Tower era has been recently restored. ♦ Parc Ciutadella (Museu de Zoología-Museu de Geología)

43 Museu de Geología (1878, **Antonio Rovira i Trias**) And you thought a rock was just a rock. Step inside and be enlightened. This museum's collection includes 10,000 mineral specimens and Europe's most important fossil display. The 2 sculptures by **Eduard Alentorn** at the door depict the naturalists **Jaume Salvador** and **Félix de Azara**. This was the first building in Barcelona to be built expressly as a museum. ♦ Admission. Tu-Su 9AM-2PM. Parc Ciutadella (Hivernacle-Umbracle) 319.93.12

44 Umbracle (1884, **Josep Fontseré i Mestres**; remodelling 1888, **Jaume Gustá**; restoration, **Josep Amargós**) Noted for its cast-iron columns, curved metallic profiles, wooden louvers and lobe-shaped construction, this building was remodelled for use as a pavilion in the 1888 Exhibition. Restored to its original form and function by Amargós, it is once again a botanical garden devoted to plants that require shade. Especially attractive are its Modernist ironwork benches. ♦ Parc Ciutadella (near Museu de Geología)

45 Cascada y Lago Artificial (1881, **Josep Fontseré i Mestres** and **Antoni Gaudí i Cornet**) A concatenation of stylistic currents and ornamental excesses, this colossal cascade-fountain-lake is primarily Neoclassical in con-

La Ribera/Parc de la Ciutadella

ception with hints of Classicism and a goodly portion of naturalistic decoration strongly pointing to Gaudí's participation in the design.

Hivernacle

A student of architecture at the time, Gaudí was an assiduous collaborator of Fontseré's. Specific elements attributed to Gaudí are the sculpted rocks of the cascade and the iron masts. Among the robust sculptures are excellent pieces by **Venanci Vallmitjana**—note the **Venus** centered in the large arch. The *Carro de l'Aurora* sculpture crowning this monumental construct is by **Rosend Nobas**. All has been recently restored. In the plaza fronting the cascade is a gazebo dating from 1881 that is one of the oldest elements of the park. In another corner of the plaza you'll find the concrete mammoth installed in 1906 at the instigation of the naturalist **Font i Sagué**. You can take a spin in a rowboat in the lake nearby or take the kids to the neighboring playground added in 1961. ♦ NE corner Parc Ciutadella

46 La Plaça de les Armes (1917; garden, Jean C.N. Forestier, sculpture, Josep Llimona) This rectangular space, formerly the arms plaza of the Ciutadella, is flanked on 2 sides by the only remaining vestiges of the vanished fortress: to the east, the old Arsenal, now home to the Museu D'Art Modern and the Parlament de Catalunya; to the west, the Palau del Gobernardor (now home to the Institut Verdaguer, a secondary school), and the chapel. The layout of the gardens

La Ribera/Parc de la Ciutadella

is the work of Forestier and dates from the 1920s. In the middle of the lake is the graceful and evocative 1903 marble sculpture *El Desconsol* (Disconsolation) by Llimona, the most important Catalan sculpture of the time.

47 Arsenal de la Ciutadella (1718, G. Prósper de Werboom) Conceived in the French Classicist style imposed by the Bourbon rulers when they acceded to the Spanish throne, the fortress' lingering arsenal was adapted by architect **Pere Falqués** (in collaboration with **Gallissà**) at the end of the 19th century to serve as the **Palau Real** (Royal Palace). They added the upper part of the central pavilion, decorated the facade with *sgraffiti*, conceived the notable wood-and wrought-iron door, and crowned the interior rooms with highly original ceilings. In 1902 the building was again adapted to house the **Museu de Bellas Artes** and **Museu Arqueológic** (both of which moved to Montjuïc in the 1930s). After further adaptations and decorative changes were made by **Santiago Marco**, the **Parlament de Catalunya** moved here in 1932. It stayed 7 years (through the Civil War) after which the facilities were converted into barracks. In 1945 it became the **Museu D'Art Modern**. Since 1980, it is again home to the Parlament de Catalunya, which appropriated part of the building from the museum.

Within the Arsenal de la Ciutadella:

Museu D'Art Modern Although it contains works from the 18th century to the present, this museum essentially chronicles Catalunya's

artistic accomplishments of the 19th and early 20th centuries. **Marià Fortuny, Nonell, Gargallo, Rusiñol, Casas** and **Llimona** are among the featured artists. Overall, the collection underscores Modernism and *Noucentisme*, including some fine examples of Modernist furniture (especially those by **Puig i Cadafalch**). Its selection of contemporary pieces, on the other hand, is very limited. Our favorite is the courtyard conglomeration of wooden poles and mobiles by **Josep Guinovart i Bertran**. Recent rumor has it that this museum may be moving into the **Palau Nacional** when work there is finished. ♦ Admission. M 3-7:30PM; Tu-Sa 9AM-7:30PM; Su and holidays 9AM-2PM. 319.57.28

47 Parlament de Catalunya Cynics take note! The Catalan Parliament is right next door to the municipal zoo. ♦ Parc Ciutadella (Pl Arnes)

48 Zoo (1902; enlarged 1927 and 1957) To a great degree the installation of this zoo disfigured the original configuration of the park that hosted the 1888 Exhibition. The zoo's starring attractions are the world's only captive albino gorilla, Copito de Nieve (now getting on in years), and the trained-dolphin show. The deer statues by **Núria Tortras** were installed near the ticket windows in 1969 as a tribute to **Walt Disney**. Inside stands the famous *Senyoreta del paraigua* (*Dama del paraguas* or Lady with Umbrella) statue by **Roig i Solé** (who used his niece as the model) dating from 1885. Sporting the bustle so fashionable at the time and holding an umbrella shielding her from the shower ingenuously engineered to permanently rain down upon her, she has been an enduring symbol of the city and of the romantic spirit of her age. In the flower beds bordering the zoo's fence you'll find what many consider to be the park's most artistically noteworthy sculpture. The work of **Josep Clarà**, it depicts a naked man with arms raised and is a tribute to the Catalan volunteers that took part in WWI. ♦ Admission. Daily 9AM-sundown, summer; 10AM-sundown, winter. SE corner Parc Ciutadella. 309.25.00

49 Capilla de la Ciutadella (18th c, Alejandro de Rez) Along with the **Palau del Gobernador** and the old **Arsenal**, this is one of the first buildings in the city evincing French Classicism. Of simple construction, the church has a single nave with chapels installed between the abutments. Its singular, central cupola, covered with decorative majolica tiles, is edged with geometric borders. Both within and without, the church is almost completely devoid of sculptural ornamentation. ♦ SW corner Parc Ciutadella

Santa Eulàlia was Barcelona's only patron saint until the monks of the **Convento de la Mercè** managed to get their **Virgen de la Mercè** declared municipal–patron saint as well. According to legend, Santa Eulàlia got so angry that since then it almost always rains on the festivities of 24 September, the feast day of the second patron.

Bests

Diego Piedra
Director General, Diagonal Hotels

Museums: **Picasso**; **Miró**; **Romanesque**

Architecture: **Gaudí**

Bars: **Nick Havanna**; **Partycular**; **Zsa-Zsa**; **Universal**

After-hours Discos: **Otto Zutz**; **KGB**; **Zeleste**; **Salsa Latina**

Joseph Rojas
Promotions Manager, Barcelona Patronat de Turisme

An aerial overview of Barcelona's harbor and La Rambla, from the top of **Columbus Monument**. An elevator will take you up there.

A walk through **La Rambla**, the main street through the old city to the sea, lined with newsstands and flower and bird stalls. It's also great for people-watching—especially in front of the **Gran Teatro del Liceu** on a gala evening.

Getting lost in **Montjuïc**, the hill that dominates the city, with a huge park with gardens, sports facilities, amusements and a castle on top. In the **Olympic Ring**, look for the **Palau D'Esports Sant Jordi** by the Japanese architect **Arata Isozaki** and the **Olympic Stadium**.

Tibadabo, the other mountain in the city, with a 100-year-old amusement park (don't miss the robot museum). To get there, take the blue tram and then the cable car to the top.

A sea trip in the harbor on board a *golondrinia*, a popular passenger boat. These boats have been sailing in the port for more than 100 years; they depart from the dock in front of the **Columbus Monument**.

Take a leisurely walk through **La Ribera**, a section of the city with the **Santa María del Mar** (14th c) and other buildings dating from the middle ages to the Renaissance.

Get lost for a while around the cloisters: the **Cathedral Cloister** (Gothic Quarter), with its geese, or the **Pedralbes Monastery Cloister** (14th c), considered one of the most accomplished of Gothic buildings.

See the Roman remains in the underground of the **Gothic Quarter**. The entrance is at the **Museum of History of the City**.

Spend a whole day at **Ciutadella Park Zoo** with the only albino gorilla in the world, dolphins and a killer whale.

José María Luna
Owner, Orotava Restaurant

Orotava Restaurant. The oldest first-class restaurant in Barcelona, with signed paintings by Miró.

Gothic Quarter. The most romantic and oldest area of the city.

La Rambla for a walk.

Parc Güell. A masterpiece by Gaudí.

Rambla de Cataluñya. Wonderful shops, cafes, etc.

TOCS. Books, records and so on.

Angela Mojica Soto
Manager, Asociación Barcelona Centro Medico

Beltxenea, at C Mallorca, 275, for classy, expensive, old-style Catalan food. Use the garden terrace in good weather.

El Dorado Petit, at C Dolors Monserda, 51, for its excellent—if expensive—food.

Senyor de Parellada, at C Plateria, 17, for excellent food at good prices. It's popular, so make reservations a couple of days in advance. The owners don't speak English—let them surprise you with a dish!

Poble Espanyol, with its small-scale reproductions of most of Spain's significant old buildings. Inside are restaurants, shops, etc. Located on Montjuïc Hill, it's a cool respite in the summer.

A stroll up and down fun, colorful **La Rambla**, ending at the seaside.

The **Picasso Museum**, set in a gorgeous house within the Gothic Quarter. After the visit have lunch at **Senyor de Parellada**.

Shopping on **El Bulevard Rosa** in Passeig de Gràcia. Stop to see the **Pedrera** and the **Quadrat d'Or** (the square with many Modernist houses).

On Sunday around 11AM at the **Plaça de la Catedral**, do not miss the congregation of people of all ages dancing the *Sardanas*, a Catalan dance. Some

La Ribera/Parc de la Ciutadella

people come with a group of friends, but others come alone and join in.

Vilanova i la Geltru, a small fishing town outside of Barcelona. In June, the town organizes a lovely festival in honor of the Virgen del Carmen. To get to the village take a train (1½ hours) or rent a car.

Tourist information and leaflets in all languages at the **Tourism Board** at Passeig de Gràcia, 35.

Sardanas

A prim, Catalonian folk dance, the *sardanas* are a symbol of renewed Catalonian patriotism. Participants join hands, form a circle and are accompanied by a *Cobla*—a band comprised of diverse wind instruments and a double-bass. Prohibited during the Franco years, the sardana is now danced regularly wherever there are enough Catalonians to care. Barcelona *hoofers* indulge themselves in front of the Cathedral Saturday at 6:30PM and Sunday at noon; at the Plaça Sant Jaume on Sunday and holidays in summer at 7PM, in winter at 6:30PM; at Plaça Eivissa Sunday at noon; at Plaça Sant Felip Neri at 6PM the first Saturday of the month; and at Parc de l'Escorxador and Parc de la Guineueta Sunday at noon.

Fiesta Fever

Bullfights are not indigenous to this part of Spain, but Barcelona has its share of aficionados. During the March to September season bullfights take place Sundays at 5:30PM at the Plaça de Toros Monumental, Gran Via de les Corts Catalanes, 743 (245.58.04). You can pick up tickets in advance at Carrer Muntaner, 24 (253.38.21).

Barceloneta/ Olympic Village

Barceloneta was spawned by regal vengeance. In 1714, after an 11-month siege, **Felipe V** finally vanquished the Catalan resistance centered in Barcelona. He subsequently *punished* the city for its role in the uprising by demolishing the heavily populated **Ribera** barrio, inhabited mostly by seamen and fishermen, to erect a colossal **Ciutadella** (fortress). Some of the displaced citizens were compensated with lots by the beach where they built shacks of wood and brick in accordance with guidelines established by the military engineer **Próspero de Werboom**. These shoddy, dilapidated dwellings swelled in number until 1749, when the **Marqués de la Mina**, the new *Capitán General*, decided to clear the beach of them and build a more respectable barrio for Barcelona's seafaring citizenry. The proposal drawn up by the military engineers **Juan Martín de Cermeño** (author of the **Castillo de Montjuïc**) and **Francisco de Paredes** called for a grid of 15 streets perpendicularly intersected by another 15 streets to form narrow, rectangular blocks aligned with the Ciutadella and thus easily subject to military control.

Beginning in 1753, the new barrio took shape. All the buildings were to be the same height (2 stories) and to have virtually identical facades. The height restriction not only ensured strategic visibility from the Ciutadella (the barrio remained under military jurisdiction until 1858), but also permitted sunlight to penetrate into the neighborhood's slim streets. In 1839 the height restriction was lifted, but not until around 1868 did residents begin grafting additional stories onto their homes, shops and factories.

Given the chronic shortage of housing in the city, Barceloneta, originally projected to have a square configuration, gradually grew to become the wedge-shaped, working-class barrio we see today, its small, rectilinear streets occupying a kind of mini-peninsula between the old port and the open sea.

WATERFRONT

Darsena del Comerc

Av Icaria

LA RIBERA

Ptge Cadena

C Ginebra

C Balboa

C Gasometre

2

C Maquinista

C Mariners

C Atlantida

1

C Portal de Don-Carlos

C Don Carlos

3

La Placa de Sant Miquel

C Cermeno

C Torrevella

Moll de la Barceloneta

4 Placa de la Font

Barceloneta

Pg Maritim

C Andrea Doria

14

Pg Salvut Papasseit

Bioparc Mediterrània

5

Placa del Poeta Bosca

6

C Pescadors

C Sant Carles

C Alcana

Platja del Somorrostro

7

C Nacional

C Mar

C Sant Miquel

C Santa Clara

C Barcelo

C Baluard

C Almirall Aixada

C Meer

C Almirall Cervera

C Vinarós

13 Pg Maritim

C Judici

8

10 11

12

Platja de la Barceloneta

9

Platja Sant Miquel

Espigo Ginebra

C Drassana

Mediterranean Sea

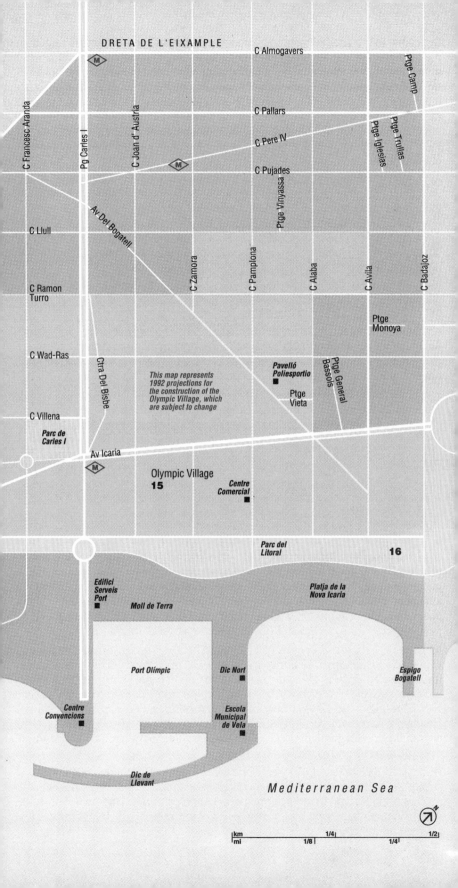

Beginning in the late 19th century, successive ordinances permitting buildings to rise to greater and greater heights at times resulted in structures that are out of proportion with the narrow streets. Notable examples of this are found in the **Carrer de Sant Elm**. At the same time, beginning about the middle of the 19th century, Barceloneta, like many other working-class barrios, became a hub of important political, cultural and workers' movements that gave rise to numerous social clubs, political associations, cooperatives and choral groups. Though few of these survived the Civil War, their existence is evidenced still by a sprinkling of architectural vestiges and obsolete signs.

At the far end of Barceloneta is the municipal beach that fills up on summer weekends with row upon row of sun- and sea-bathers. Naturally these people have to be fed, so Barceloneta accommodates them with numerous restaurants (some of them spilling right out onto the beach) that over the years have become destinations in their own right, especially for the traditional family Sunday lunch. You'll also find a string of restaurants along the **Passeig Nacional**. With respect to the barrio's abundant restaurants, choose with care, for the quality of their fare varies widely.

Its legion of seafood restaurants aside, Barceloneta's peculiar charm resides in its jaunty, nautical swagger. Many of the city's seamen and fishermen continue to live here, and the barrio is riddled with shops selling sails, navigational equipment, marine ropes and enamel paints. Many of the houses are painted with leftover ship's paint. And many of their balconies, adorned with flowers and in bright curtains, harbor caged canaries and goldfinches. In summer, family discussions, rock music and TV news pour through the houses' wide-open doors and windows to underscore the animated seafaring activities going on in the narrow streets.

But what will become of all this in the future is not completely clear. More than anywhere else in the city, we're dealing here and in the adjoining **Vila Olímpica** (Olympic Village) with the Barcelona of tomorrow. Plans call for a complete revamping of these areas by 1992. Naturally, all the

Barceloneta/Olympic Village

projected tearing down and putting up has met with its share of controversy, not the least of which swirls around the long-standing, beach-side restaurants of the Barceloneta where proprietors and their habitual Sunday-lunch patrons alike feel strongly about the impending demise of a mutually satisfying tradition. By the time this book sees print, however, those establishments may well be history. Those who considered them an eyesore all along (as many did) will rejoice in the new, sophisticated seaside promenade scheduled to supersede them. Those who didn't will surely lament their passing for years to come—very likely over meals in the very same restaurants that, after being demolished here, will re-surface elsewhere. If you find that some of the places mentioned in this chapter are no longer around when you get here or that they deviate greatly from our descriptions, forgive the lack of clairvoyance.

Meanwhile, we see in our crystal ball that the area from the edge of the **Parc de la Ciutadella** to the **Carrer de Badajoz** will, by 1992, present a completely new face to the sea, something along the lines of a Catalan Copacabana. Replacing this former industrial area of **Poble Nou** will be **Nova Icària**, aka the Vila Olímpica. At the seaside end of **Passeig de Carles I** will be a small port harboring a large convention center. Hotels, shops and office buildings lining the new pedestrian **Passeig Marítim** at the edge of the sea will give Barcelona a brand new skyline. In the center of the **Avinguda del Litoral** you'll find a large, new park.

Fortunately, before tearing down the vintage structures of Poble Nou, the municipal authorities had the foresight to document their historical, social and architectural significance on film, and in models, photographs and paintings. These will likely be on view in a museum around here somewhere. But to speak of these things before 1992 is largely an exercise in speculation.

1 El Eixample de la Barceloneta Where once the fields and orchards of the **Marqués de la Quadra** stood, these large, square blocks similar to those of the city's Eixample district, emerged at the end of the last century. The Marqués' memory lives on in one of the street names. Participating in the development of this area of Barceloneta, as well as in the design of some of its individual edifices, were such name-brand Modernist architects as **Josep Amargós** and **Enric Sagnier**. Nevertheless, the area is largely devoid of interest except for a few buildings like the one at C Mediterrani, 4, which features some relatively interesting Modernist decoration. There are, however, some notable restaurants and bars in the area serving delicious fish specialties. Among them are **Cheriff** (★$$), **Jaica** (★$$) and the more sophisticated **Aitor** (★★★$$$) and **Vaso de Oro** (★★$$$). Just ask someone to point them out. ♦ Pg Nacional-C Balboa-Pg Salvat Papasseit-C Andrea Doria

2 Casa Tipa ★★$$ Among the legion of restaurants along the Pg Nacional, this one rises well above the mediocre gastronomic mean. Since 1886, its cozy confines fronting the harbor have been offering such specialties as *paella, frituras* (fried fish), *parrilladas* (assorted fish platters) and *zarzuela* (bouillabaisse). But perhaps it reaches its culinary apogee in the *suquillo*, which is similar to the *zarzuela* only better—it contains potatoes, more fish and is more savory. ♦ Seafood/Catalan ♦ Pg Nacional, 6 (C Ginebra-C Maquinista) Reservations recommended for Su lunch. 319.70.32

3 La Plaça de Sant Miquel The **Iglesia de Sant Miquel del Port** presiding over this plaza dates from the time of the original construction of the barrio. The work of military engineers **Pedro Martín de Cermeño** and **Francisco Paredes** and architect **Damià Ribas**, it took only 28 months to build between 1753 and 1755. Its facade recalls a Roman Baroque styling. Enlarged in 1863, its interior comprises 3 naves separated by Tuscan columns. On the terra-cotta facade of the building to the right of the church is a plaque commemorating the fact that in 1858 **Fernando de Lesseps**, builder of the Suez Canal, spent some time in Barceloneta. At the other end of the plaza another inscription alludes to the fact that in 1850 the first choral concert in Spain was given here by the Coral Euterpe.

4 Plaça de la Font Since 1882 this has been the site of the Barceloneta market. Two buildings at its western end (C Baluard, 30-32)

illustrate the typical barrio construction of the 1700s. Now the property of the **Banco de Sabadell**, they were, in the last century, the site of factories making rigging and sails. Quite possibly the fountain you see on one of their facades gave rise to the plaza's name.

5 Carrer Sant Carles, 6 One of the few examples of a traditional, 18th-century Barceloneta house that has survived unmodified. A 2-story, one-family structure, it features segmented arches adorned with small volutes and a pediment in the section of the cornice. For the more than 100 years that the barrio remained under military jurisdiction, this was the prescribed styling of barrio dwellings, although beginning in 1839 it was permitted to add an additional story and a small side door leading to the upper stories. ♦ C Pescadors-C Sant Miquel

6 Edificio de la Cooperative La Fraternitat (1914) Founded in 1874, the La Fraternitat cooperative decided in 1914 to build a headquarters commensurate with its considerable economic and social standing in the community (it then had 300 members and carried a lot of weight in the neighborhood). A brick structure in a Modernist vein, it occupies half the block. ♦ C Sant Carles (C Pescadors-C Santa Clara)

7 Passeig Nacional, 42-43 (1955, **J.A. Coderch de Sentmenat** and **Manuel Valls**) This apartment building is considered a representative example of Barcelona's post-war architecture. ♦ C Almirall Cervera

Barceloneta/Olympic Village

8 Evocación Marinera (1960, **Josep Maria Subirachs**) This abstract sculpture on the lawn at the end of the Pg Nacional was one of the first non-figurative sculptures to be installed in a public space in Barcelona. ♦ Pg Nacional (C Drassana)

9 Cal Pinxo ★★$$$ The long, narrow dining room here culminates in a sea view and, weather permitting, open-air, seaside dining. But this won't be the case for long if the municipal authorities have their way. Plans call for tearing down the beach-front restaurants to make way for a pedestrian promenade. The family **Ribera Vellbe** owns this and the following 2 restaurants that are only a matter of feet away. All offer similar menus, similar quality and similar prices. Seafood is, of course, their specialty, and within that gastronomic genre the house specialty here is *rape* (angler fish)

al Pinxo, prepared with shrimp or *langostinos* in a sauce topped with *ali oli* (garlic mayonnaise). Another house favorite is *arroz pelado*, a local version of *paella* in which the shellfish has already been divested of its shells and extraneous appendages. ◆ Seafood/Catalan ◆ Platja Sant Miquel, 10 (C Baluard) Reservations required at lunch, especially Su. 310.45.13

10 Casa Costa ★★$$$ A sister establishment to **Cal Pinxo** that offers 3 floors of dining; the upper 2 are prettier and more pleasant (the top one was recently renovated). All look out to sea, though the upper ones naturally have the better views. ◆ Seafood/Catalan ◆ C Baluard, 124 (Platja Sant Miquel) Reservations required at lunch, especially Su. 319.50.28

11 El Merendero de la Mari ★★$$$ The third of the **Ribera Vellbe** family restaurants by the beach, this one has the most distinctive decor. Also a cut above is its very authentic cuisine, including such favorites as *pescaditos fritos* (small fried fish), *esqueixada* (an eggplant salad of sorts), *chipirones* (baby squid), the traditional fish and shellfish platters, and the *zarzuela*. ◆ Seafood/Catalan ◆ Platja Sant Miquel, 20 (C Meer) Reservations required at lunch, especially Su. 319.14.25

12 El Salmonete ★★$$$ *Paella, suquillo* (a mixed fish casserole) and shellfish are the specialties here, where in fine weather you can also dine outdoors. For some reason the indoor dining room has an unsightly screen at

Barceloneta/Olympic Village

the seaside end that detracts substantially from the view. Nevertheless, of all the restaurants along the **Platja Sant Miquel**, this once seems to attract the most amusing and heterogeneous crowd. On summer nights diners range from actors and artists to yuppies and tourists. ◆ Platja Sant Miquel, 34 (C Vinaròs) Reservations recommended. 319.50.32

13 Fuente de Carmen Amaya This fountain pays tribute to the legendary flamenco dancer of the 1950s who was born and lived in the ramshackle gypsy *ghetto* that existed in this area until 1966. ◆ Pg Marítim at end of C Conreria

The **Olympic Village** is called **Icària** in commemoration of the first settlements in this area by the working class of Poble Nou, who, in the middle of the last century, chose the name in honor of the community that **Etienne Cabet**, a utopian socialist, founded in the US during the same period.

Restaurants/Nightlife: Red **Hotels:** Blue
Shops/Parks: Green **Sights/Culture:** Black

14 Fábrica la Catalana de Gas y Electricidad Installed in 1843, this gas and electricity facility was Spain's first and continued in operation until not too long ago. At this writing the office building and water towers designed by **Josep Domènech i Estapà** in 1905 remain standing. A large park is planned along the perimeter of the facility. ◆ C Ginebra-Pg Salvat Papasseit-Pg Marítim

15 Vila Olímpica (Olympic Village) (1992) The Vila Olímpica is a highly ambitious project that essentially amounts to the creation of a new neighborhood. Formerly, this was an area of obsolete factories, old warehouses and rundown residences. But the railway lines that once cut the city off from the sea have been directed underground, and some 183 acres of commercial, recreational and living space are being fashioned anew, along with 2½ miles of new beaches and 4 parks. Some 63 acres of land will be reclaimed from the sea, and in all there will be 140,000 square feet of commercial and recreational space replacing the old **Poble Nou**. Intended to be an extension of the city, the new area next to the **Hospital del Mar** (built in 1930 on part of what had been the maritime section of the 1888 International Exhibition) will contain a hotel, restaurants, shops, banks, office buildings and a leisure harbor. The new **Cinturó Litoral** (Coastal Ring Road) will run partially underground through the parks. In general terms, the district has been designed in line with **Cerdà**'s **Eixample** and with an eye toward maximizing open-air spaces and exposure to sunlight.

Two nearly 450-feet-high skyscrapers built by the sea will be Barcelona's tallest buildings. Sponsored by the Spanish insurance company Mapfre and the American Travelstead Group, they are of different architectural designs, but will be the same height. The **Mapfre Tower** will accommodate offices, and the other will house a 42-story, 5-star hotel that will be part of Atlanta's **Ritz-Carlton** chain and offer over 450 rooms; adjoining apartments will be an integral part of the hotel complex. The hotel's design is the collaborative effort of **Skidmore, Owings & Merril** and the **Society of Construction and Architecture of Barcelona**. Its most distinctive element will be an exterior steel structure completely surrounding the inner body of the building, which will be covered in natural stone and mosaics. At the base of the skyscraper will be a complementary service complex, whose design is in part the work of architect **Frank Gehry**.

The Olympics provided a convenient excuse for this much-needed urban renovation, which further entails the reorganization of the road network and the improvement of water drainage in the area. Built for the Olympic athletes, **Nova Icària**, a complex of approximately 2000 apartments, has already been put on the market for post-Olympic occupancy.

The nearby **Olympic Harbor**, designed for both sailing competition and recreational yachting, will enclose more than 17 acres of sea, comprise more than 3½ miles of wharves, and accommodate 300 boats.

The dossier of the Vila Olímpica is sprinkled with the names of Barcelona's leading architects of the moment, among them **Taller d'Arquitectura (Ricardo Bofill), Correa, Milá, Clotet, Bonell, Rius, Gil, Viaplana, Piñón, Domènech, Amadó** and **Tusquets**.

The **Conference Centre** designed by **Miguel Usandizaga Caproro** will be located in the **Parc de Mar de Poble Nou** at the end of Pg Carles I on a platform built on reclaimed land. It will contain an auditorium accommodating 1500 persons and 2 more seating 350 persons each, which can be combined into one large hall with a total seating capacity of 2200. ♦ Av D'Icària-Pg Carles I-C Badajoz-Mediterranean Sea

16 **Los Parques del Mar** These parks, extending from the **Vila Olímpica** to the **Río Besós**, will round out Barcelona's new coastal offering with a series of beaches including those of **Barceloneta, Somorrostro, Icària, Bogatel** and **Mar Bella**. Those who don't have a car will be able to take advantage of the recreational delights of the new **Parc del Litoral del Poble Nou**, **Parc Esportiu** and **Parc Marí** via a network of express buses.

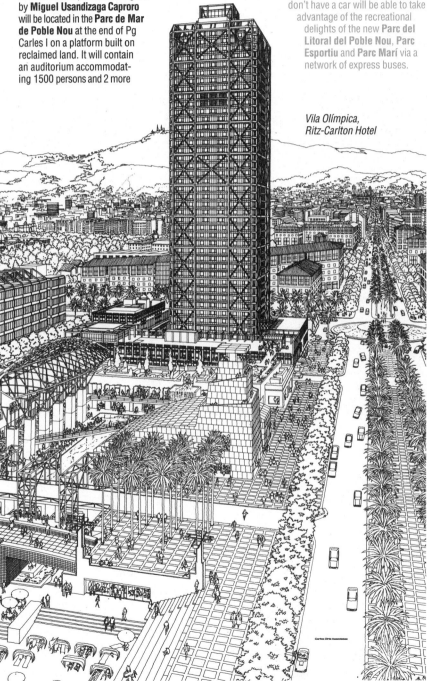

*Vila Olímpica,
Ritz-Carlton Hotel*

Carlos Diniz Associates

Pedralbes/ Sarrià/Sants

Map labels:

C Angli
C Iradier
C Escolespies
C Marquesa Vilallonga
Pg Bonanova
C Dalmases

TIBIDABO/GRACIA

C Pau Alcover
C Doctor Carulla
51
C Vergos
C Calatrava
C Escoles Pies
C D'Alacant
C Mandri
C Balaguer
Via Augusta
6
50
Rda General Mitre
C Doctor Roux
C Vico
C Modolell
C Vallmajor
C Jacinto Benavente
49
48 47
C Sta. Fe
C Ganduxer
C Calvet
Via Augusta
Dr Fleming
Nou Mèxic
C J.S. Bach
C Rector
46
C Calaf
Parc del Poeta Eduard Marquina
C Tenor Vinas
C Ganduxer
C Bori Fontesta
45
42
44
31 32 33 34
Av Diagonal
43
C Mestre Nicolau
AV Pau Casals
41
40
C Amigo
C Santalo
C Muntaner
38
39
Plaça Francesc Macià
35
C Loreto
36 37
C Rta Bonnat
C Bordeus
C Buenos Aires
Av Sarrià
C Londres
C Paris

ESQUERRA DE EIXAMPLE

C Corsega
C Rosello
C Provenca
C Mallorca
C Comte Urgell
C Villarroel
C Casanova
C Muntaner
C Calabria
C Viladomat
C Comte Borrell
Av Roma
C Valencia
C Arago
C Consell de Cent

In the northern reaches of Barcelona, the neighborhoods become nebulous, their distinct boundaries of old blurred by the progress that binds yesterday's suburbs to today's city proper. Once upon a time, **Pedralbes** and **Sarrià** were satellite villages in their own right. Then when the **Eixample** was finished and shortly before the outbreak of the Civil War, the city's elite looked beyond Barcelona's newly expanded borders to establish new, improved residential areas for themselves. They followed the **Avinguda de la Diagonal** toward Pedralbes and the **Vía Augusta** toward Sarrià.

Now Pedralbes, in the northwestern corner of the city, is an upper-echelon residential area, a kind of intra-city bedroom community where you'll find posh apartment buildings, private schools, BMWs, Mercedes, the occasional Jaguar, tennis and polo clubs and little else except the occasional fancy restaurant or shop. At the northern edge of this high-rent district is the old **Royal Monastery of Santa Maria de Pedralbes**, one of Catalunya's most beautiful medieval structures. At the southern edge, along the very broad Avinguda de la Diagonal, is the **Palau Real** and its soothing gardens. Just across the way is the **Ciutat Universitaria**.

Today's Sarrià has reached well beyond the borders of the former *pueblo de Sarrià* (which sprang up around the year AD 1000 at the foot of a church) to conceptually annex portions of **Sant Gervasi**, Pedralbes, and the **Serra de Collcerola**, which includes **Tibidabo** and **Vallvidrera** (though to many Barcelonans these still remain a concept apart). Sarrià residents are predominantly from the upper crust and include numerous artisans. Whatever their socio-economic status, they are uniformly proud to state that they are from Sarrià, and when they head down into the center of town, they tend to say they are going to Barcelona, as if

Sarrià were still a separate world untainted by the afflictions of modern city life. In some areas this is still true; in others it isn't.

In 1835 Sarrià was linked to the then distant city of Barcelona via carriage service—the trip required 75 minutes of travel on a bad road. In 1850 a road was built, and in 1858 train service was implemented. A horse-drawn tram began operating in 1878 and an electric one in 1900. In those days the city's upper-class citizens built their palatial summer homes—known as *torres* for their distinctive towers—in Sant Gervasi, Pedralbes and at the foot of **Tibidabo Mountain**. Today those graceful, rambling, breezy old structures often contrast sharply with our own century's high-rise apartment blocks.

The barrio **Sants** (formerly **Santa Maria dels Sants**) on the eastern edge of the city joined the municipal ranks somewhat earlier than the northern burbs. Sants was largely an agricultural enclave until the construction of its first factories in the 18th century set it on an industrial course that hastened its fusion with the city. Home to one of Barcelona's busiest railway stations, the **Estació Central-Sants**, it was in this barrio that last century's immigrants (both from within Spain and beyond) tended to settle.

Nowadays Sants boasts several new hotels, a revamped railway station, and the showpiece **Parc de L'Espanya Industrial**, all harbingers of a new era, a neighborhood image reflecting a shift in demeanor from a blue-collar industrial persona to a white-collar commercial one.

1 Museu-Monestir Pedralbes (14th-15th c)
The **Royal Monastery of Santa Maria de Pedralbes** was founded in the year 1326 by **Elisenda de Montcada i de Pinós, Queen of Aragon** and 4th wife of **Jaume II el Just**. After the king's death in 1327 she lived out the rest of the king's death in 1327 she lived out the rest of her 37 years here. In 1357 she petitioned the Consell de Cent de Barcelona for protection of the monastery, and ever since it has

been overseen by the municipal government. In 1931 the complex was declared a national historic and artistic monument. Its name comes from *pedres albes* (white stones), and it was formerly a completely walled complex with 2 portals defended by towers. The wall you see today dates from the 14th century, but was partly reconstructed and repaired in the 15th and 17th centuries. The first stone of the church was laid in March 1326; May of the following year it was consecrated and dedicated by royal decree to the Virgin Mary. Subsequently the cloister was built and, at the end of 1419, the **Sala Capitular** and the cloister's 2nd story. The architects of all this are unknown, but the directors and administrators of the construction work were **Ferrer Payró** and **Domènec Granyer**. From the **Pl Monestir**, which is surrounded by gardens dominated by cypresses, we see the lateral facade of the church in all its grand simplicity. On the door is Queen Elisenda's coat of arms. The stairs to the right lead to a fortified gate whose tower was the convent's prison (the mind boggles). The church itself has a single nave comprised of 7 sections covered with

ogival vaulting and terminates in a heptagonal apse. On either side are 6 barren lateral chapels. The absence of ornamentation both within and without makes the 14th-century stained-glass windows of the apse and the 3 choirs stand out more than they would in typically more effusive surroundings. The marble sepulchre of the monastery's founding queen is located next to the presbytery. It bears the reclining figure of Her Majesty dressed in crown and royal regalia. The monastery's 3-storied, square cloisters are one of the most spacious and harmonic Gothic cloisters in the world. The first 2 galleries date from the 14th century and the third from the 15th. In the southwestern wing, the small chapel dedicated to **Sant Miquel** is entirely covered with mid 14th-century murals done by **Ferrer Bassa**, who injected an Italian spirit into the Catalan Gothic painting style of the day. The cloisters are now an unusual and captivating museum. The refectory, dating from the 15th century, incorporates 16th-century modifications and owes its current aspect to a restoration done at the beginning of this century by **J. Martorell**. Along the cloister's periphery you'll find re-enactments of a medieval herbal apothecary, several monks' cells, a collection of crèches dating back to the 15th century, an impressive kitchen with an assortment of stoves from different centuries, and the 16th-century sick room built in 1568 with funds supplied by **Philip II** (a magnificent example of the hospital architecture of the period). Between the sick room and Sala Capitular is a 14th-century room called **L'abadia** decorated with murals in a Gothic style. Additional rooms house assorted paintings and sacred objects from across the centuries. In brief, what you'll glimpse here is a slice of long-ago monastic life, its simplicity matched throughout with an architectural austerity purged of all pretense. Currently, **Ricardo Bofill** is modifying part of the monastery in preparation for the installation of over 50 works from the famed collection of **Baron Hans Heinrich Thyssen-Bornemisza**, which are scheduled to come here prior to the 1992 Olympic Games. The small gateway leading to the street alongside the monastery complex was once an entrance to the adjoining village of Pedralbes; it was locked at night, presumably to keep the villagers in and the riffraff and marauders out. ◆ Admission. Tu-Su 10AM-1PM. Pl Monestir (Bda Monestir) 203.92.82

2 **El Mato de Pedralbes** ★$$ Ever popular at lunch and dinner, El Mato offers an atmosphere of seasoned rusticity not found among the city's newer restaurants. But as often happens, the cuisine at this long-time classic is becoming a bit uneven. Avoid the *esqueixada de bacalao* (codfish salad), *escalibada* (eggplant and pepper salad), *calamares rellenos* (stuffed squid), *butifarra con judías* (sausage with beans) and *entrecôte*. Go for the *anchoas con pan con tomate* (anchovies with tomato bread), *sobrasada* (another Catalan sausage), *jamón del país* (cured, country ham), *conejo* (rabbit) *a la brasa, el mató de Pedralbes* (the eponymous house speciality, a local rendition of cottage cheese), and the *crema catalana*. With the exception of such out-of-place dishes as carpaccio (a concession to culinary trendiness), the menu is Catalan through and through. ◆ Catalan ◆ C Bisbe Català, 10 (Bda Monestir-Av D'Espasa) No credit cards. 204.79.62

3 **Nuevo Monasterio Benedictino de La Mare de Déu de Montserrat, Parroquia de María Reina** (1936, **Nicolau Maria Rubió i Tudurí**; completion of project around 1940, **Raimon Duran i Reynals**) The architect himself acknowledges this structure's debt to Brunelleschi. An outgrowth of the 1930s exuberant *noucentista* movement, its styling can perhaps best be characterized as *streamlined Renaissance*. The octagonal cupola recalls the baptistry of Florence's San Juan and the nave is a literal interpretation of Brunelleschi's Pazzi chapel. The stone and polychromatic marbles employed throughout are top quality. Because Rubió i Tudurí was exiled after the Civil War, work on the monastery was completed under the direction of Duran i Reynals, who put the finishing touches on certain elements, the bell tower among them. ◆ Ctra d'Esplugues, 101 (C L'Abadessa Olzet)

4 **Conjunto Residencial Les Escales Park** (1973, **Sert, Jackson & Associates**) Many feel that the considerable amount of time Sert spent in the US is reflected in this building and accounts for the lack of enthusiasm with which it was greeted locally. Despite his attempts to plug into the local architectural vernacular with the use of small-slatted shutters, glazed

ceramics, and scaled-down, wrought-iron vaulting, his use of American-style prefab concrete construction was out of sync with the prevailing Catalan architectural icons of the day. ◆ C Sor Eulàlia d'Anzizu, 46 (Av Pedralbes)

5 **Hotel Pedralbes** $$$ This small, intimate hotel is one of the several reliable, business hotels of the NH chain to be found mostly in Barcelona's newer districts. Though a bit far afield from the city's tourist and commercial hubs, the Pedralbes offers parking facilities and 28 well-equipped rooms nestled in a pleasant residential setting. ◆ C Fontcoberta, 4 (C Santa Amèlia) 203.71.12; fax 205.70.65

6 **Azulete** ★★★$$$$ One of Barcelona's most elegant and expensive restaurants, Azulete has earned one Michelin star and the favor of Spain's **King Juan Carlos**. A woman of eclectic tastes, chef **Victoria Roqué** mixes and matches French, Chinese and Catalan influences on her surprising menu (which she likes to change about 3 times a year), but always includes a selection of traditional Catalan favorites. The lush, enclosed garden provides an airy setting for dining, and the restored Beaux Arts house an elegant one for drinks. ◆ Nouvelle International ◆ Via Augusta, 281 (C Doctor Roux) Reservations essential. 203.59.43

7 **Casa Ramon** ★★★$$ The place in Pedralbes for sausages, cheeses and grilled meats. Its savory fare coupled with attractive prices has generated a loyal following among the local citizenry. The aroma of the grilling *butifarras, chorizos,* rabbits, steaks and chops that greets you at the door immediately inspires an appetite that one happily indulges

around a marble table in any of the restaurant's 3 intimately rustic dining rooms. The wine list reaches beyond Spain's borders to Portugal and Italy. ◆ Delicatessen/Grill ◆ Pg Sant Joan Bosco, 47 (C Manuel de Falla) 205.75.56

8 **L'Occelletto** ★★$$ The young owner here bases his solid, satisfying menu on fresh pastas (appropriately cooked al dente and teamed with anchovies, garlic, salmon, etc.) and on some highly flavorful and personal dishes such as rabbit with tarragon and *choucroute,* cuttlefish with noodles, and grilled meats served with various exotic sauces. The 3-course *menu del día* at lunch is an exceptional bargain. ◆ Mostly Italian ◆ Pg Sant Joan Bosco, 34 (C Maria Auxiliadora-C Buïgas) No credit cards. 204.92.55

The bonfires of the **Verbena de Sant Joan** light up the night of 23 June. Tradition calls for consuming *coca,* a confection of fruit and pine nuts, and watching the fireworks.

Restaurants/Nightlife: Red   Hotels: Blue
Shops/Parks: Green   Sights/Culture: Black

9 Gate of the Finca Miralles (1902, **Antoni Gaudí i Cornet**) After **Hermenegild Miralles Anglés** bought some land in Sarrià, he called on Gaudí to design a distinctive fence for his refuge. Gaudí came up with a masonry fence of warped shapes and a wavy top and a stone gate with a double canopy topped by an iron cross. The canopy you see today is a 1960 restoration and projects out less than the original one, which collapsed many years ago. ◆ Pg Manuel Girona, 53 (C Capità Arenas)

10 Paradis Barcelona ★★$$$ Patrons here can choose between cafeteria-style buffet dining or à la carte service in a more posh, private setting. The buffet is not your run-of-the-mill buffet dining experience, but rather a lavish smorgasbord of deliciously fresh, quality fare beginning with numerous salads, continuing with the meat of your choice grilled before your eyes as you choose it, and ending with scrumptious desserts. Understandably, it is popular with well-heeled executives in a hurry. Those with more time to spare prefer the more leisurely à la carte restaurant. There is now also a Paradis Barcelona in New York at 145 E 50th St; 212/754.3333. ◆ Catalan/International ◆ Pg Manuel Girona, 7 (C Marqués Mulhacén) 203.76.37

11 Puerta y Pabellones de Entrada a La Finca Güell (1887, **Antoni Gaudí i Cornet**) This remarkable gate sporting, among many other things, a wide-mouthed, stylized serpent (a representation of Ladon, the guardian dragon of the garden of the Hesperides, known among the cognoscenti as the *Drac de Pedralbes*), was the entrance to the summer house of Gaudí's prime patron, **Eusebi Güell**.

Pedralbes/Sarrià/Sants

The adjoining building, once a stable for horses, now houses the **Catedra Gaudí** (Gaudí Chair) of the **Universitat Politécnica de Barcelona**, where the Modernist master's life and works and the evolution of Modernism in general are meticulously studied and chronicled for the world's edification. Both that gate and pavilion are contemporary with the **Palau Güell** off La Rambla and illustrate Gaudí's fascination at

the time with Moorish-influenced ornamentation. His alternating use of colored ceramics and brick contributes to the rich, polychromatic texture that consistently emerges in his work. For a look inside the Catedra Gaudí, just ring the bell at the gate. The only other thing to see on the abandoned, overgrown grounds is a small Gaudí fountain that once graced the garden of **Casa Vicens** and was reconstructed here. ◆ Av Pedralbes, 7 (Pg Manuel Girona) 204.52.50

12 Tilos A great place for drinks on a pleasant summer night. It actually feels more like a garden party than a bar since the mixing and mingling takes place within an old mansion and on its surrounding grounds. The crowd is usually mixed and the music not too loud. ◆ Pg Tillers, 1 (Av Pedralbes) 203.75.46

13 Palau de Pedralbes (1929, **Eusebi Bona i Puig** and **Francesc de P. Nebot i Torrens**; gardens 1925, **Nicolau Maria Rubió i Tudurí**) After the **Count de Güell** donated the property, his *torre*-mansion **Can Feliu** was transformed into the Palau, a residence fit for the royal family during their visits to Barcelona. The first plans were by the architect Bona i Puig, but the work was later continued by Nebot i Torrens. Although some attribute the gardens to **Jean-Claude Forestier**, Rubió i Tudurí is typically given credit for them. The 3-story, Italianate Palau was inaugurated with the royal visit of **Alfonso XIII** in the mid-1920s, although the building wasn't completely finished until 1929. In those days the ground floor contained the dining room, library, several salons, a music room, meeting rooms and the throne room. The first (our 2nd) floor contained the bedrooms, and the upper floor the servants' quarters. Until 1930 the royal family stayed here several times. When the Second Spanish Republic was proclaimed in 1931, the palace became city rather than state property and the **Museu de les Arts Decoratives** (Decorative Arts Museum) was installed in 1932 (in recent years it has rarely been open, and its fate at this writing is uncertain). In 1936 the Palau was again used as a residence, this time by the President of the Spanish Republic, **Manuel Azaña**. In 1937 the International Brigade was

Puerta y Pabellones de Entrada a La Finca Güell

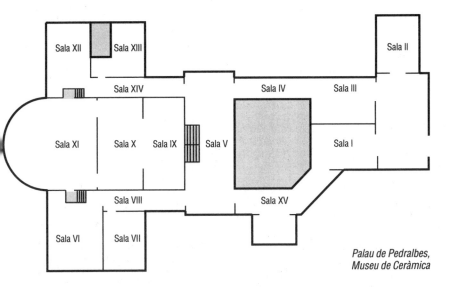

*Palau de Pedralbes,
Museu de Ceràmica*

bid a grateful farewell here. After the Civil War, Franco reinstated it as a residence for Spain's head of state and as a guest house for visiting dignitaries. Still today it hosts the occasional municipal function or reception, and there is talk of preparing part of the palace for use by the royal family again. In addition to the virtually defunct Decorative Arts Museum, you'll also find here the **Museu-Gabinet Postal**; the **Cambó Collection** of paintings including works by **Raphael, Botticelli, Tintoretto, Titian, Tiepolo, Fragonard, Rubens, Van Dyck, Goya** and **Zurbarán**; and the **Museu de Ceràmica**, which moved here in 1990 from the **Palau Nacional** when remodelling work began there. Its collection (arguably the most important collection of medieval ceramics in Europe) begins with the 13th century and traces in ample detail the history of Spain's diversely colorful ceramic tradition. The first-floor collections span from the 13th to the late-19th century. **Sala I** is devoted to Islamic ceramics; **Salas II-V** to medieval ceramics from Valencia; **Sala VI** to ceramics from Talavera de la Reina and Puente del Arzobispo; **Salas VII-VIII** to ceramics from Aragon; **Salas IX-XI** to Catalan ceramics; **Sala XII** to ceramics from Seville; **Salas XIII-XIV** to the work of L'Alcora; **Sala XV** to 19th-century Valencian ceramics. On the floor above is a collection of contemporary ceramics reflecting the turn-of-the-century transition from utilitarian to artistic ceramics (*ceràmica d'artista*). Highlights here include the works of **Antoni Serra i Fiter, Josep Guardiola, Josep Llorens Artigas, Antoni Cumella, Joan Miró** and **Picasso**. Happily, the Palau is prefaced by a lovely park that is regularly enjoyed by local residents who snooze, gossip and read the paper on the park benches. In its gardens you'll find a dragon, a gazebo of parabolic iron arches, and the Hercules fountain—all Gaudí creations brought here from the nearby **Finca Güell**. At the palace entrance stands a statue of **Queen María**

Cristina. ◆ Admission. Tu-Su 9AM-2PM. Av Diagonal, 686 (C Tinet-C Fernando Primo de Rivera) 205.19.67

14 Facultat de Dret (1958, **Guillermo Giráldez Dávila, Pedro López Iñigo** and **Xavier Subias i Fages**) Out of political and logistical expedience (the city's rebellious law students were cramped and cranky in their old quarters), this building housing the Faculty of Law was designed and built in less than a year. Needless to say, this was made possible through the miracle (some might say curse) of prefabrication. One of Barcelona's leading examples of the International Style, the build-

ing is illustrative of that moment in Catalan architectural history when every attempt was made to fill the stylistic void left by the isolationist aftermath of the Civil War. Proponents of such modern architecture may disagree, but we say some voids are best lift unfilled. Above the main door you'll find a sandstone relief by **Subirachs** (fashioned in conjunction with the ceramicist **Antoni Cumella**) that symbolizes *The Law.* ◆ Av Diagonal, 684 (C Fernando Primo de Rivera-Av Pedralbes)

15 Neichel ★★★★$$$$ The carefully orchestrated and intelligently conceived dishes here reflect the genius of chef **Jean-Louis Neichel**, a timid man considered by some a culinary god. His nouvelle cuisine combines his native Alsatian traditions with the sunny flavors of the Mediterranean. The reasonably priced degustation menu is a fine way to worship at his gourmet altar. So is the foie gras with 3 salads covered with fine slices of truffles. Despite its lackluster decor, this is one of the city's leading restaurants thanks to its gastronomic wonders and most interesting wine list. ◆ French ◆ Av Pedralbes, 16 bis (C Beltran i Rozpide-Pg Manuel Girona) Reservations essential. 203.84.08

16 Hotel Princesa Sofía $$$$ (1975, CONSU)
A favorite with businesspeople, this hotel offers the full range of modern, convenient amenities (including parking). One of the city's largest hotels, its 505 rooms generate a good deal of hustle and bustle in the lobby and public areas. A complete renovation is planned, but little had been done at the time of this writing. If redone rooms are available when you stay here, be sure to ask for one, since the vintage 1970s rooms have become pretty dowdy. Among the hotel's out-of-room attractions are an indoor/outdoor pool (a real rarity in Barcelona), a sauna and a gymnasium. You'll find **Gucci** and **Loewe** outlets in the lobby and **Avis** and **Iberia** offices on the premises. **Regine's** disco and piano bar are also on the premises but have a separate entrance. ♦ Pl Pio XII, 4 (Av Diagonal) 330.71.11; fax 330.76.21

17 Masia Torre Rodona (1610) This former country mansion alongside the Hotel Princesa Sofia is now the corporate headquarters of **HUSA** Hotels, of which the Princesa Sofia is a member. If you walk in and politely ask to have a look around, you can get a glimpse of some of the building's lingering 17th-century features. ♦ C Sabino de Arana, 27 (C Doctor Salvador Cardenal)

18 Torres de Oficinas Trade (1969, **José Antonio Coderch de Sentmenat** and **Manuel Valls i Vergés**) These 4 towers of trade and commerce harbor within their undulating, gleaming, smoked-glass curtain wall some major-league international corporate offices. ♦ Gran Via Carles III, 86-94 (C L'Institut Frenopàtic-C D'Europa)

Pedralbes/Sarrià/Sants

19 Nou Camp F.C. Barcelona (1957, **Lorenzo García Barbón, Francesc Mitjans i Miró** and **Josep Soteras i Mauri**; expansion 1982) Beloved home to Barcelona's beloved soccer team, this vast stadium was originally designed to accommodate about 90,000 spectators (43,000 seated). Room for 30,000 more was added for the games of the 1982 World Cup competition. Encompassing an area of nearly 310,000 square feet, it is reputed to be Europe's largest soccer arena. ♦ C D'Arístides-Av Joan XXIII-C Maternitat-Trav Les Corts

20 Parc de L'Espanya Industrial (1985, **Luis Peña Ganchegui**; collaborator, **Francesc Rius i Camps**) Where once stood L'Espanya Industrial, a former textile complex that played an important role in the economic life of the barrio Sants, now stretches a 12-acre park. Flexible of design and varied of function, it represents the collaborative efforts of the neighborhood association, City Hall, and the Basque architect Peña Ganchegui. It is strikingly buffered from the bustling **Estació Central-Sants** train station by a large lake edged with stairs/bleachers culminating in 9 large lookout and lighting towers that emphatically mark the boundary between the *sunken* park and the train station. Running east-west over the lake is an elevated walkway that will access the sports and swimming facilities now being built. The park entrance leading into the heart of the barrio incorporates, via a spacious esplanade dedicated purely to child's play, old buildings that belonged to the textile factory and that, now restored, are used as nurseries and youth centers. The water, a prime park protagonist, scenically embraces some of these antique structures. Scattered throughout the park are various sculptures: some—like **Fuxá**'s *Neptú*, **Casanovas**' *Tors de la Dona* and **Alsina**'s *Braus de l'Abundància*—appropriated from elsewhere; others—like **Anthony Caro**'s *Alto Rhapsody* and **Pablo Palazuelo**'s *Lauda V*—fashioned expressly for the park. So, too, was the huge, playful, black *Drac de Sant Jordi* by **Andrés Nagel** that serves as a kind of artistic link between the park and the **Plaça dels Països Catalans**. Together these 2 new urban spaces make a strong statement about Barcelona's commitment to civic pride of place. ♦ C Premià-C Muntadas-C D'Ermengarda-Rector Triado-Av Roma

21 Plaça dels Països Catalans (1983, **Albert Viaplana i Vea** and **Helio Piñón i Pallarés**) Another salient example of Barcelona's determination to convert yesterday's eyesores into today's visual pleasantries. Formerly known as the **Plaça de l'Estació de Sants**, it was a desolate square (once a parking lot) that merely covered the underground portion of the **Estació Central-Sants** railway station. Chaotic and amorphous, its infrastructure would not even support the weight of the soil required for the tiniest of gardens that might

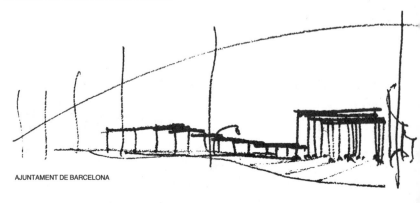

AJUNTAMENT DE BARCELONA

offset some of its vast bleakness. Enter Viaplana, Piñón and their collaborator **Enric Miralles i Moya**. Their mission: to make a pleasing plaza from a sow's ear. Their bold and controversial plan of action: to define the space not through dimension or perimeter, but rather by inserting objects of varying height, weight, mass and proportions that would impart a sorely lacking visual texture. Notable among these are a 49-feet-tall canopied monument with aligned, undulating benches; an undulating pergola whose sinuous covering poetically evokes a steam train's trail of smoke and sports a metallic cat; several podiums sans statues; and a smattering of game tables. The contours of the pink-granite pavement underscoring this highly textured topography subtly create the illusion of a carpet. The end result is one of the most avant-garde public spaces built in Barcelona in recent years. Its aesthetic inspiration derives from abstraction and minimalism, and its compositional criteria are rooted in the antifigurative vanguard of the first quarter of the 20th century. All of which argues for its inclusion among the *machines of symbolic function* deemed art by the Dadaist movement. You may like it, you may hate it, but we doubt you'll be indifferent to it. ♦ Av Roma-C Tarragona-C Viriat-Estació Central-Sants

22 Hotel Numancia $$$ One of the larger NH properties in Barcelona, this one has 140 air-conditioned rooms, a restaurant, cafeteria and parking lot. ♦ C Numancia, 74 (C Caballero-C Marqués de Sentmenat) 322.44.51; fax 410.76.42

23 Edificio de Viviendas (1964, **Taller d'Arquitectura Bofill**) Captained by **Ricardo Bofill**, the Taller de Arquitectura has been a strong, evolutionary force in shaping the new face of Barcelona. Among its earliest municipal projects, this apartment block demonstrates the triumph of originality over obstacles. Presented with an odd-shaped plot of land on a northern corner, Bofill imaginatively exploited it with a vertically cantilevered structure that maximizes sunlight in the individual dwellings. ♦ C Marqués de Sentmenat, 68 (C Nicaragua)

24 Hotel Les Corts $$$ Another businesslike NH property with 81 air-conditioned rooms outfitted with minibars and color TVs. Restaurant, cafeteria and parking offered as well. ♦ Trav Les Corts, 292 (C Nicaragua) 322.08.11; fax 322.08.11

25 Kiku-Chan ★★★$$ A favorite among Barcelona's Japanese population, although there is not a single fish dish, raw or cooked, on the menu. What there is is a selection of salads, noodle and rice dishes, and chicken. Try the spicy soup with noodles, Japanese noodles with onion, or Japanese-style fried chicken with applesauce. Fish and shellfish prepared upon advance request. ♦ Off-beat Japanese ♦ C Numancia, 133 (C Taquígraf Garriga) 410.72.47

26 Hilton $$$$ (1990, **Mir-Coll** and **Piñón-Viaplana y Carmona**) One of the city's newer hotels, it was originally built as a 4-star hotel and then purchased by Hilton and turned into a 5-star experience. Small for a Hilton (both in the number of rooms—290—and, unfortunately, their size), it is otherwise largely up to first-class snuff. Their cramped dimension notwithstanding, the rooms are gracious as

Pedralbes/Sarrià/Sants

well as soundproofed and equipped with radios, minibars, hair dryers, satellite color TVs, and views. The boxy gray structure that contains them is quite unattractive, however. Non-smoking rooms are available, as well as shops, a garage, 24-hour room service, special services for children, an attractive atrium lobby bar, a restaurant and sports facilities. There is also a day-care center for children.

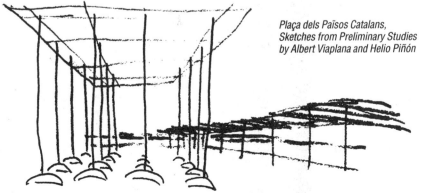

Plaça dels Països Catalans, Sketches from Preliminary Studies by Albert Viaplana and Helio Piñón

Businesswomen take note: on the Executive floors about 15% of the rooms have been devoted expressly to female executives; they feature different color schemes, flowers in the room, bathrobes, special magazines, different lighting, and bathrooms that haven't been *thought out for men*. ◆ Deluxe ◆ Av Diagonal, 589-591 (C Numancia-C Gandesa) 419.22.33; fax 322.52.91

26 Oliver y Hardy ★★★$$$$ Terrace dining here is a romantic dream; indoor dining, a classic, upper-crust experience. The conservatively dressed clientele and club atmosphere of the piano bar tell the socio-economic story. The contemporary cuisine is suitably sophisticated. Try the shellfish salad with raspberry vinegar, fresh pasta with lemon-cream sauce, *salmonetes* with red wine and pears, prawn ragout, and mushrooms *al cafe de París*. Alas, the desserts don't measure up to the rest of the menu. But if you don't pass muster under the doorman's scrutinizing gaze, you won't have to worry about it. ◆ International ◆ Av Diagonal, 593 (C Numancia-C Gandesa) 419.31.81

27 Bulevard Rosa Four floors of shopping with roughly 100 retail outlets in which to indulge your consumer whims. Some familiar names: **Body Shop, Levi Strauss & Co., Sharper Image.** ◆ Av Diagonal, 609-615 (C Gandesa-C Joan Güell) 309.06.50

Within the Bulevard Rosa:

Jardi del Bulevard $$ When viewing the architecture through the enormous picture windows of this establishment, you can almost imagine yourself in Manhattan. The

Pedralbes/Sarrià/Sants

lunchtime crowd of yuppies helps sustain the illusion. The meats (if you remove the sauces), salads and pizzas are good; the pastas, mediocre; and the portions consistently ample. ◆ International ◆ Local 51

28 La Jijonenca ★★$$ This attractive, multilevel eatery serves good, uncomplicated fare like *arroz con salpicón* (rice with seafood salad), smoked salmon, *manchego* cheese, osso buco, and codfish with prawns and mushrooms. At lunch it is abuzz with business types. ◆ International ◆ Av Diagonal, 652-656 (C Marti i Julia-C Numancia) 205.39.14

29 Amalia ★$$$ Comfortable, elegant and refined, this restaurant seems to have been expressly designed for the business lunch. Its only shortcoming—fare that is at best competent (if you stick with the uncomplicated dishes like fresh salmon, steak tartare or the various versions of codfish), at worst, poorly seasoned or overdone. ◆ International ◆ C Nau Santa María, 5-7 (C Numancia-C Caravel-la Niña) 205.64.68

Restaurants/Nightlife: Red   **Hotels:** Blue
Shops/Parks: Green   **Sights/Culture:** Black

30 Pizza Hut $$ No better than it is at home... and sometimes worse. ◆ Pizza/Italian ◆ Av Diagonal, 646 bis. 205.03.15. Also at: C Marina, 225. 348.06.82; C Urgell, 329. 410.62.20; Pg Gràcia, 125-27. 238.30.05; C Sicilia, 382-384. 207.79.11; Rambla Catalunya, 91-93. 487.31.08; C Cartellá, 117-127. 420.01.00

MARI/C DIAGONAL

31 Marisc Diagonal ★★★$$$ One of Barcelona's best and most enchanting seafood restaurants since the owner, a seafood wholesaler, can keep the best for himself. Some suggestions: the *salpicón de pescado y marisco* (a kind of mixed seafood salad), the shrimp, sea snails, *besugo al horno, chipirones* (baby squid) *al la andaluza*, and the sautéed baby octopus. The 3 elegant, spacious dining rooms are also surprisingly intimate. ◆ Seafood ◆ Av Diagonal, 529-531 (C D'Entença-Av Sarrià) 439.79.41

32 La Vaqueria ★★★$$$ The winning combination here is a highly original, tongue-in-cheek decor teamed with consistently good cuisine that straddles the classic and modern kitchens. To be recommended are the fried eggs, carpaccio with parmesan, tortellini, meatballs with cuttlefish, and *merluza* (hake). ◆ International ◆ C Deu i Mata, 139-141 (Ptge Cinc Torres) 419.21.18

33 Edificio Talaia De Barcelona (1970, **Federico Correa i Ruiz, Alfonso Milá i Sagnier** and **José Luis Sanz Magallón**) One of Barcelona's tallest buildings, this *Lego-block* tower has offices on the lower floors and apartments everywhere else except for the top floor, which features a panoramic restaurant. ◆ Av Sarriá, 71 (Av Diagonal)

Meliá Barcelona

34 Hotel Meliá Barcelona Sarrià $$$$ (1975, **Jorge Mir, Rafael Coll, Ignacio Sanchez** and **José María Garcia-Valdecasas**; remodelled 1986, **Oriol Bohigas & Associates**) During remodelling, the facade was altered from the 3rd floor down and the interior was done entirely anew. The lobby now features a noisy cascade of water that inspired the name of the adjoining piano bar, *Drinking in the Rain*, and sometimes drowns out the pianist. The hotel's 311 businesslike rooms feature direct-dial phones, satellite TVs, 24-hour room service, air conditioning and minibars. Two floors are devoted to Royal Service guests who can avail themselves of such added perks as room safes; bathrobes; direct, controlled access to the floor; an independent reception area, with cash desk, for quick check-in and check-out; and telex, fax, messenger and secretarial services. The Royal Service lounge offers Continental breakfast, canapés and all kinds of drinks at no charge. Also on these floors, newspapers are delivered to your door every morning and there is a mini-library stocked with dictionaries, street maps of the city, transportation timetables, and exchange-rate and stock-exchange information. Check-out is flexible and express laundry is charged at normal rates. One of the hotel's culinary and cultural contributions to Barcelona life was the introduction of its famous Sunday brunch. In fact, the Sol group of hotels to which this hotel belongs is duly famous for its fine buffet breakfasts, and the

Meliá Sarrià's Sunday brunch proves a veritable feast. The hotel also offers a gift shop, gym, sauna, solarium and massage service. ♦ Av Sarrià, 50 (C Fra Luis de Granada) 410.60.60; fax 321.51.79

35 Hotel Derby $$$ Just a notch below its *Gran* sibling in terms of amenities, the Derby offers 116 rooms with satellite TVs, air conditioning, videos, music, minibars, and telephones, plus a bar, coffeeshop and garage. ♦ C Loreto, 21 (C Rita Bonnat-Av Sarrià) 322.32.15; fax 410.08.62

36 El Celler de Casa Jordi ★★$$$ While the rusticity of the decor is more subdued here that at **Can Fayos**, the rusticity of its cuisine is more pronouced. The flavorful dishes begin with first-rate ingredients, and a tempting seasonal menu supplements the standard offering. If it's the right time of the year, try the *garbanzos con morro y oreja* (chickpeas with snout and ear—and you thought the brains at Can Fayos were strange), *espinacas* (spinach) *a la catalana*, canelones, *pollo con caracoles y gambas* (chicken with snails and shrimp), *rape* with mushrooms (*setas*) and potatoes, or *pierna de pato con nabos* (duck leg with turnips). Follow regional tradition when it comes to the desserts—*mel i mató*, flan or *crema catalana*. Don't overlook the *anchoas de la*

Escala as a starter or the fine wine offerings. ♦ Catalan ♦ C Rita Bonnat, 3 (Av Josep Tarradellas) 430.10.45

37 Hotel Gran Derby $$$$ The 42 rooms here were clearly designed with the business traveler in mind. Each has a comfortable work area, a small salon where one can receive and entertain guests, a wet bar, minibar, air conditioning, color satellite TV, video and telephone. Twelve rooms are duplexes. Interior rooms are quiet and have a terrace. Corner rooms are slightly more spacious. ♦ C Loreto, 28 (C Rita Bonnat-Av Sarrià) 322.32.15; reservations 322.20.62; fax 419.68.20

37 Can Fayos ★★$$$ For over 20 years Can Fayos has been enjoying continued success. Perhaps it's the rustically Baroque decor of assorted curios and heteroclite objects, but more likely it's the sincere cuisine served in hefty portions. Begin with the *entretenimientos* comprised of olives, anchovies and toasted country bread topped with tomato. Avoid the codfish mousse (you probably would have anyway), *solomillo al whisky*, and *lenguado* (sole) *a la menta*, and stick with the more traditional fare like *sesos a la mantequilla negra* (brains in black butter—it may not sound traditional to you, but trust us, it is), *brandada de bacalao*, *filete de rape* (angler fish) *a la americana*, *fritura de pescados* (fried fish platter), and *la lubina al hinojo* (sea bass with fennel). Also serves a fine *crema catalana*. ♦ Catalan ♦ C Loreto, 22 (C Rita Bonnat-Av Sarrià) 439.30.22

38 Tramonti 1980 ★★$$ This cozy eatery with an eclectic array of art all around is one of our

Pedralbes/Sarrià/Sants

favorite Italian choices in the city. Some of the dishes have a Catalan accent. The **Lombardo** brothers who own and run the place are *molto simpaticos*. ♦ Italian ♦ Av Diagonal, 501 (C Loreto-C Fra Luis de Granada) 410.15.35

39 Foster's Hollywood ★$ Known simply as *Hollywood*, this is the place to come when your taste buds hanker for a burger in the American tradition. The born-in-the-USA menu features a selection of ¼-pound and ½-pound hamburgers (with various toppings) served with cole slaw and french fries and extends to tasty onion rings and spare ribs. Parents will appreciate the special children's menu. ♦ American ♦ Av Diagonal, 495 (C Loreto) 322.10.15

In Barcelona's scientific circles, **Francesc Salvà i Campillo**, a multi-faceted Barcelona doctor of the late 18th and early 19th centuries, is credited with the invention of the telegraph more than 50 years before **Morse**. A member of the Barcelona Acadèmia de Ciències and director of its electrical section, Salvà i Campillo invented the electric telegraph in 1791 and foresaw the imminent development of a wireless telegraph.

Furest

40 Furest An elite outpost of charm and luxury for the fashion-conscious man who likes to browse among such chic brands as Bonneville, Hugo Boss, Ermenegildo Zegna, Henry Cottons, C.P. Company, Cerruti 1881, J. Taverniti, Corneliani, Baumler, Arrow and more. ♦ Av Pau Casals, 3 (Pl Francesc Macià) 201.25.99. Also at: Pg Gràcia, 12. 301.20.00; Av Diagonal, 468. 218.26.65; Bulevard Rosa Pedralbes, Av Diagonal, 609-615, shop Nos. 79 and 95-97

41 Can Jaume ★$ Quick and efficient of service, simple and frank of good food, this place is popular with a heterogeneous crowd of executives, secretaries, homemakers, students and salespeople. You can't go wrong with the *arroz de montaña* (mountain rice), *lentejas estofadas* (lentil stew), *tortilla con gambas* (Spanish omelet with shrimp), squid in its ink, or *fricandó*. ♦ Spanish ♦ Av Pau Casals, 10 (Pl Francesc Macià-C Mestre Nicolau) No credit cards. 200.75.12

Matricula

42 Matricula A fashion *must*. Every season features the most creative and important of the new designers for both men and women. For men: Jean Paul Gaultier, Matsuda, Yohji

Pedralbes/Sarrià/Sants

Yamamoto, Dries van Noten, Comme des Garçons, Armand Basi. For women: Ozbek, Alaïa, Matsuda, Jean Paul Gaultier, Plein Sud, Sybilla, John Richmond. ♦ Av Pau Casals, 24 (C Tenor Viñas) 201.23.08. Also at: Bulevard Rosa Pedralbes, Av Diagonal, 609-615, shop Nos. 82-83. 419.11.00; Galerías Turó, C Tenor Viñas, 12. 201.97.06; La Avenida, Rambla Catalunya, 121. 217.87.02

43 Network ★$$ TV junkies will really feel at home in this vast, multilevel bar/restaurant experience where most tables come complete with a TV screen and you can order everything from tempura to chicken wings, carpaccio to guacamole. ♦ International ♦ Av Diagonal, 616 (C Beethoven) 201.72.38

44 Giorgio Armani For women. ♦ Av Diagonal, 624 (C Ganduxer) 200.99.01

45 Via Veneto ★★$$$$ Behind the Modernist facade of this swank restaurant frequented by bankers and businesspeople lurks an elegant decor that outclasses the largely country-style Catalan fare. Some traditional dishes are the salad of thinly sliced, marinated squid with tomatoes and olive oil and the salt cod with spinach and grilled red pepper. To start, try the salt-cod fritters, hearty country sausage, or anchovy-topped puff pastry. The *salmonetes al carbón* (charcoal-grilled red mullet) is a memorable dish; so is the *foie con vinagre de frambueses* (with raspberry vinegar). ♦ C Ganduxer, 10-12 (Av Diagonal-C Bori i Fontestà) Reservations recommended. 200.72.44

46 Cintia A high-class boutique in a correspondingly high-class neighborhood. The name brands include Jil Sander, Thierry Mugler, Jacqueline de Ribes and Bogner. ♦ C Ganduxer, 32 (C Bori i Fontestà-Pl Sant Gregori Taumaturg) 201.62.83

47 Semon Since 1962, purveyors of Barcelona's finest cold cuts, salads, cheeses, canned goods, pastries, wines, cavas, candies and more. In the back 7 tables comprise **l'indret**, a small, choice restaurant (not unknown to Spain's royal family) that offers a select, imaginative menu at reasonable prices. The house specialty are the blinis with caviar or salmon. Definitely an *insider's* place. ♦ C Ganduxer, 31 (Pl Sant Gregori Taumaturg) 210.65.08. Also at: (store only) C Capità Arenas, 11. 203.74.44

47 D'Alma Christian Lacroix, Valentino—to name-drop just a few of the designing lights found here. ♦ C Sante Fe de Nou Mèxic, 5, 7 (Pl Sant Gregori Taumaturg-C Escoles Pies) 200.37.88

48 Trecce Mostly Italian chic for women. Alberta Ferretti, Mimmina, Moschino, Kenzo, Dolce Gabbana, Graziella Rochi, Les Copains and Erreuno. ♦ C Escoles Pies, 2 (C Santa Fe de Nou Mèxic) 209.07.34

49 Via One of the best shoe boutiques in Barcelona, Via carries the Italian creations of Lorenzo Bolni, Alexandre Nicolete, Pollini...and more. ♦ C Escoles Pies, 3-5 (C Jacinto Benavente) 200.47.83

In the last decade Barcelona has installed over 35 public sculptures, and there are more to come. Offering little pay but great artistic freedom, it has commissioned leading sculptors, primarily from the US and Spain, to erect what they like in the city's more than 150 new or rehabilitated municipal plazas and parks. The roster of sculptors includes **Richard Serra, Ellsworth Kelly, Eduardo Chillida, Joan Miró, Bryan Hunt, Anthony Caro, Antoni Tàpies, Xavier Corberó, Roy Lichtenstein, Claes Oldenburg** and **Beverly Pepper**.

Colegio de les Teresianes

50 Colegio de les Teresianes (1894, **Antoni Gaudí i Cornet**) Early in his career Gaudí focussed on the Gothic style and its structural problems. At the height of his pre-occupation with that architectural genre and its challenges, he designed this building as a school and Mother House for the Teresian order of nuns. Actually begun by someone else, the building's rigid, rectangular shape was an immutable *fait accompli* by the time Gaudí stepped in to take over. Limited funds resulted in the use of simple materials and a notable lack of ornamentation. As a result, some have come to characterize this work as an example of Gaudí in a more functional, less fanciful mode. Still, the building has some memorable features; among them, its windows with false arches, large balcony with brick latticework, the parabolic brick arches that on the first floor form an interesting gallery, its roof battlements, and the ceramic crosses at the corners. The property of the Reverend Mothers of Saint Theresa, the building still houses the **Colegio de Santa Teresa** (a Catholic girl's school), and its main floor and upstairs cloister can be visited most Saturdays 11AM-1PM. Much of the rest of the complex is not the work of Gaudí but corresponds to subsequent additions. ◆ C Ganduxer, 95-105 (C Sant Casimir-C D'Alacant)

51 Hotel Tres Torres $$ Though rather off the beaten track, this 3-star hotel offers 56 rooms at a good price. All have full baths, telephones, TVs, and minibars. The hotel also offers a bar, snack bar and room service. ◆ C Calatrava, 32-34 (C Vergos-C Doctor Carulla) 417.73.00; fax 205.65.06. Reservations can also be made through Marketing Ahead, 433 5th Ave, New York NY 10016; 212/686.9213; fax 212/686.0271

Tibidabo/Gràcia

To the north Barcelona is bounded by the **Serra de Collserola** (which keeps the cold winds at bay), whose tallest peak is **Tibidabo Mountain**. The name *Tibidabo*, so the legend goes, comes from the time when Satan took Jesus to this city's mightiest (all things are relative) mountain to tempt him with the surrounding wonder. *Tibi dabo* (This I give to you), he said to Jesus (i.e., the beauties of Barcelona, an earthly ideal), *if you will prostrate yourself before me and adore me.* Needless to say, Jesus refused, but if nothing else, this tale tells you that Barcelona has always had a pretty high opinion of itself.

Since the time of Satan's futile overture, the mountains' natural endowments have been little tampered with. But while there is still a lot of unspoiled nature in *dem dere hills*, few Barcelonans are inclined to seek recreation in its forests primeval, even though the slopes of **Mount Tibidabo** were made a municipal park in 1908. Barcelona, it seems, not only has long lived with its back to the sea, but also with its back to the mountains. Of course, Barcelona's moneyed

Map Continues on Pg. 96

elite exploited the hills for their magnificent mansions (often called *torres*) blessed with breathtaking views, but to go hiking in the mountains? No, thank you, say the Barcelonans.

In 1900 an enterprising pharmacist and famous manufacturer of cough drops, **Dr. Salvador Andreu i Grau**, envisioned these mountains as a place of leisure that would, in turn, stimulate the sale of his plots of land for the construction of the *torres*. As a result, the Tibidabo area now offers visitors an amusement park, the fascinating **Museu de Autómatas**, a number of fine restaurants, the **Museu de la Ciència**, and, along the avenues leading up to the top, a series of exquisite Modernist mansions, many of which now house offices and luxury flats. To facilitate access to the city's new northern playground, Dr. Andreu's company constructed the **tramvía blau** (blue tram)—the only tram still functioning on the Spanish peninsula today—and the **funicular** to the top of the mountain.

Ascending Tibidabo Mountain by car proves rather circuitous. It's really much better and more fascinating to take the **FF.CC. de la Generalitat** to the tramvía blau—which passes the stately mansions of the **Avinguda Tibidabo**—and then take the funicular to the top where the view is spectacular and there is an amusement park for the children. Also here, at Tibidabo's highest point (about 1679 feet above sea level), stands the much-revered **Templo del Sagrado Corazón** church (a response to the legend of the mountain's Satanic naming, perhaps?).

Between the **Avinguda de la Diagonal** and the top of Tibidabo, Barcelona registers an eclectic mix of the mainstream middle class, the upscale Modernist (highlighted by some famous **Gaudí** endeavors), and the odd and offbeat. Here nestle the former villages

Tibidabo/Gràcia

of **Gràcia** (officially grafted on to the municipal tree in 1898) and **Sant Gervasi.** More lively and less tony than either **Sarrià** (which loosely embraces **Pedralbes**, parts of Sant Gervasi, and a bit more) or Tibidabo, middle-class Gràcia was already a separate village when Barcelona was still surrounded by city walls. Now it is simply another Barcelona barrio, but with a difference. Its plazas are among the city's most enchanting, and among the city's middle class Gràcia is a preferred address. One local guidebook appropriately characterizes it as a *working class area with a sense of community and brotherhood.* It is also the province of artisans' workshops, artists' studios, small galleries, affordable trendiness of all kinds, lively bars and moderate-priced restaurants. Singles seem especially fond of its easy-going friendliness and, of course, its lower rents. It is the kind of place where the residents sit out on the stoops and balconies on summer nights and shoot the breeze.

The name *Gràcia* derives from the **Monasterio de Santa Maria de Jesús de Gràcia** founded by **Alfonso IV** in 1427 at the intersection of **Carrers Aragó** and **Pau Claris**. Destroyed and rebuilt several times, the monastery eventually found a home in what is now Gràcia, which began to take an urban shape in the 1860s and 1870s. Beginning in 1872, it was linked to the city of Barcelona via horse-drawn tram; in 1899, by electric tram. Ever a progressive barrio, it was perched on the ideological edge of revolution for much of the second half of the 19th century. In the final years of that century it published a feminist magazine, and not without reason is one of its plazas called **Revolució Setembre de 1868**.

Map Continued from Pg. 95

Further indication of its independent spirit is the fact that the Catalan theater has made great avant-garde strides in such neighborhood theaters as the famed **Lliure**.

In its own way, Gràcia was (and still is) the California of Barcelona—a place that spawns sects; nurtures radical thinking; cultivates theosophists, vegetarians and anarchists; and harbors a fringe element of gypsies, spiritualists and self-proclaimed witches who find their eccentricities blithely accepted here. Judging from the burgeoning number of ethnic restaurants (particularly South American and North African) springing up here, the barrio has also of late become a favorite among the city's newer immigrants. Above all, this is a barrio for those young in years and/or spirit.

When Gràcia was founded in the 15th century it was, of course, way, way out of town. Now it is not only an integral part of the city, but one of its most *marchoso* (spirited) barrios. Its *fiesta mayor*, celebrated at the end of August, is a highlight of the Barcelona summer for both barrio residents and *outsiders*.

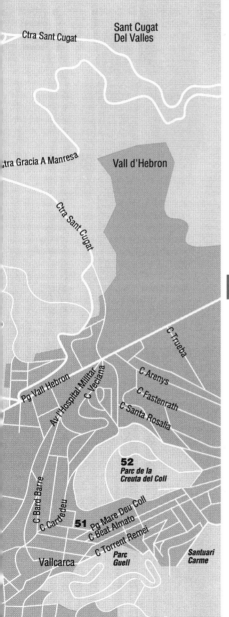

1 Bilbao ★★★$$$ The simple, fresh food here is offered at prices that are not all that painful. No wonder it's a local favorite. The *anchoas* (anchovies) *de Cantabria, cogollitos de Tudela con atún* (lettuce hearts with tuna), *jamón de Jabujo*, grilled shrimp, and squid with garlic and parsley are all dependable choices. The cover (for bread and appetite-whetters) is unconscionably high, however. ◆ Spanish ◆ C Perill, 33 (C Venus) 258.96.24

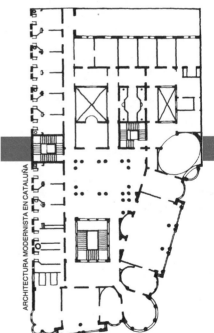

ARCHITECTURA MODERNISTA EN CATALUÑA

2 Casa Fuster (1911, **Lluís Domènech i Montaner**) Marking the point of transition from the broad Pg Gràcia to the narrower C Gran (or Mayor) de Gràcia is one of Domènech's last creative efforts, a synthesis of the influences that distinguished his career. There is a certain Nordic character to the

97

building's crown, a Gothic echo in the moldings framing the windows, a Classicism to the lower floors, and a hint of Venetian color in the use of pink and white marble. Within you'll find the offices of an electric company. Although you can ask to have a look around, the interior retains little of Domènech's original design. ◆ Pg Gràcia, 132 (C Gràcia)

2 Martin's At the moment the most *in* place on the gay scene with a clientele ranging from 17 to 70. There is a dance floor and an upstairs *black room*. ◆ Pg Gràcia, 130 (C Gràcia-C Bonavista) 228.19.73

3 Iglesia y Convento de Pompeia (1910, **Enric Sagnier Villavecchia**) At the core of this church and convent is a triangular cloister patio. The facade facing Av Diagonal marks the church; the other 2 facades correspond to the convent. The church, conceived along traditional Catalan Gothic lines, has 3 naves connected via ogival arches, a polygonal apse crowned with ribbed vaulting, and large windows with pointed arches. The bell tower signals the junction of church and convent. ◆ Av Diagonal, 450 (C Riera Sant Miquel, 1)

4 Roig Robi ★★★$$$ Summer dining on this restaurant's interior terrace is pure enchantment. Elsewhere the rather Minimalist decor is in keeping with the spirit of a menu stressing light, refined cuisine suited to the season. Chef-owner **Mercé Navarro** is a precise stylist and imaginative cook. Try her fresh pasta with cheese and broccoli, scallop salad, angler fish (*rape*) *al pil pil,* roast leg of lamb stuffed with apples and *foie gras,* and, for starters, *fideos con almejas* (thin, crispy noodles cooked in savory fish broth and served with clams). The homemade desserts are worth saving room for. ◆ Nouvelle Catalan ◆ C Séneca, 20 (C Minerva) 218.92.22

Tibidabo/Gràcia

Many historians claim **Columbus** was actually Catalan, born in Barcelona. But since Columbus himself deliberately obfuscated his origins (some say to hide his Jewish roots, come say because he was the son of a tavern owner who was hanged), referring in his documents and testament only to an uncle who had emigrated to Genoa, no one knows for sure where he was born. But those who maintain that he was born in Barcelona say it was in Carrer dels Boters. Still others say he was a descendant of the founders of Barcelona's old Hospital d'En Colom. Those who believe Columbus was a native of Barcelona claim that the treasurer of the Catholic monarchs **Isabella** and **Ferdinand, Luis Santángel,** a childhood friend of Columbus in Barcelona, convinced the queen to sponsor his voyage of discovery.

Barcelona, repository of courtesy, shelter of strangers, hospice of the poor, homeland of the brave, vengeance of the affronted, and gracious confluence of firm friendships; in setting and beauty, unique.

Cervantes

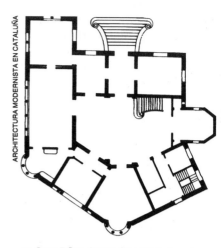

ARCHITECTURA MODERNISTA EN CATALUÑA

5 Casa Pérez Samanillo (1910, **Joan J. Hervás Arizmendi**; modified 1948, **Raimon Duran Renals**) Built as a single-family dwelling for **Luis Pérez Samanillo,** this chateau-like structure constituted then, as now, an elaborate display of Modernism in a highly visible location—a combination that rendered it an architectural milestone in this then up-and-coming part of the city. In fact, the building won the municipal prize for the best work built in 1910. Its original entrance was through a garden on the Av Diagonal side, which was sacrificed, along with a tower, for the construction of the adjoining apartment house. The entrance was then moved to C Balmes and, in 1948, the ground floor was modified by Raimon Duran Renals for the installation of the **Círculo Ecuestre** (Equestrian Circle), which still occupies the structure today. Notable within are the vestibule and staircase. The original interior decoration, which adhered strictly to the stylistic tenets of its time, was by the furniture maker **Joan Esteva**. It is possible, upon polite request, to have a look within. ◆ C Balmes 169-169 bis (Av Diagonal, 502-504)

6 Cervesería José Luis A few rounds of snacks at this sophisticated *tapas* bar could set you back the price of a full meal elsewhere if you're not careful. Beware the helpful suggestions of the staff—they will boost your bill quickly. Quality is commensurate with the prices, however. ◆ Av Diagonal, 520 (C Tuset) 200.83.12

6 Caixa D'Estalvis i Pensions de Barcelona (1973, **Xavier Busquets i Sindreu**) Beginning in the 1970s, big business sought a new image for its buildings: costly materials (better still if they had to be imported), unusual installations, astonishing facades reflected the dawning era of conspicuous consumerism at the architectural level. Here Busquets impresses us with an elegant curtain wall fronted by a sunshade of movable smoked glass that provides insulation from the elements and from sound without obscuring the glass wall beneath. ◆ Av Diagonal, 522-532 (C Tuset)

7 Sutton One of Barcelona's chicest dance halls frequented by a glittering, largely *40something-50something* crowd partial to the samba, salsa, tango, lambada and cha cha cha. Live bands are common in clubs of this caliber, and Sutton usually has one of the best. ◆ Cover. C Tuset, 13 (C Moia-Trav Gràcia) 209.05.37

8 Flash-Flash ★$$$ For over 20 years the fashion, finance and media people have been coming here to see and be seen. The culinary mainstay is a selection of more than 100 different kinds of *tortillas* (Spanish omelets), but you can also have a meat-and-potatoes meal here. While Flash-Flash's trendiness is persistent, the quality of its food harks back to the name—now you see it, now you don't. The atmosphere is friendly and informal. ◆ Tortillas ◆ C Granada del Penedés, 25 (C Balmes-C Tuset) 237.09.90

9 Henry J. Bean's Bar and Grill ★$ Imagine a cross between an English pub and an American Denny's where there's a Bud waiting for you at the bar to help wash down those nachos and potato skins. Chili, hamburgers, ribs and a salad bar (unfortunately rather measly) are some more taste echoes from back home. Come for the happy hour (7-9PM) when the place is really hoppin'. ◆ American ◆ C Granada del Penedés, 14-16 (C Julián Romea-C Balmes) 218.29.98

9 Giardinetto Notte ★★★$$$ Appropriately named *Night Garden*, this was the first restaurant in the city to stay upon until the wee, wee hours (currently 2:30AM). Despite the formidable competition now posed by other late-night entries like **Oliver y Hardy** and **La Vaqueria**, it retains a loyal night-owl following that is partial to its menu mix of the trendy and the traditional Italian. Some recent selections: fettuccini al pesto, *flan de rape con gambas* (angler fish flan with shrimp), *fritura de chipirones* (fried baby squid), risotto with crab and shrimp, magret of duck with port wine and onions, and the ubiquitous carpaccio. ◆ Italian ◆ C Granada del Penedés, 22 (C Balmes) 218.75.36

During the Spanish Civil War, **Franco** commandeered the castle on the Cordorníu-owned **Raimat Estate** north of Barcelona. He tested every bed until he found one that suited him. A female ghost is rumored to appear in that room every night, just before dawn.

Restaurants/Nightlife: Red   Hotels: Blue
Shops/Parks: Green   Sights/Culture: Black

10 La Cova del Drac Typically one of Barcelona's best spots for jazz, La Cova del Drac was conceived in the spirit of the 1950s *hot clubs* of Saint Germain de Prés. Below the cafeteria of the same name, this cafe-style joint exudes a nostalgic intimacy that sets just the right tone for the live performances offered from September through June. At one time or another most of the greats of the jazz world have stepped up onto the Cova's tiny stage and kibitzed with the patrons sitting just a few feet away. ◆ Admission ◆ C Tuset, 30 (C Granada del Penedés) 217.56.42

11 Restaurante Reno ★★★★$$$$ Since 1954, Reno has been catering to Barcelona's more discriminating palates. In the process it has earned mention in the French *Traditions & Qualité* guide. The food, which chef-owner **José Juliá Bertrán** characterizes as Catalan with French overtones, is unerringly delicious, and there is a special menu for every season. The wine list is an oenophile's dream. ◆ Catalan/French ◆ C Tuset, 27 (Trav Gràcia) Reservations essential. 200.91.29

12 Hotel Condado $$$ The 90 recently renovated rooms all have complete baths, air conditioning, direct-dial telephones, and TVs. The rooms with terraces are slightly larger, and those facing the inner courtyard are especially bright and quiet. A restaurant and bar are offered on the premises, and parking is offered next door. ◆ C D'Aribau, 201 (Trav

Tibidabo/Gràcia

Gràcia) 200.23.11; fax 200.25.86. Reservations can also be made through Marketing Ahead, 433 5th Ave, New York NY 10016; 212/686.9213; fax 212/686.0271

12 La Dorada ★★★$$$$ One of several Doradas in Spain (and one in Paris), this restaurant features the seafood served with Andalusian flavor and flair for which owner **Félix Cabeza** is renowned. But you can't go wrong with the rice dishes, either, or the *fideos con almejas* (noodles with clams). Still, the culinary mainstays are the platters of fried fish and, of course, the house specialty— *dorada* (a Mediterranean fish) baked in salt. ◆ Seafood ◆ Trav Gràcia, 44-46 (C Aribau-C Muntaner) 200.63.22

13 Hotel Wilson $$$ The 55 comfortably functional rooms have private baths, phones, music, air conditioning and color TVs. The first-floor cafeteria-bar serves breakfast. Room service and parking available. ◆ Av Diagonal, 568 (C Bon Pastor) 209.25.11; fax 200.83.70

14 Belle Epoque A well-known, uh, face on the nightlife scene, **Dolly van Doll**'s bare-breast-studded spectacle bills itself as the only genuine music hall in town. All in all, this campy cabaret is plain good fun. ♦ Cover. C Muntaner, 246 (Av Diagonal-Trav Gràcia)

15 Kiyokata Restaurant ★★$$ (1912, **Bonaventura Bassegoda Amigó**) As the majority of Japanese visitors to Barcelona are zealous admirers of Modernist architecture, it is quite fitting that this restaurant be installed in the Modernist **Casa Parets de Plet**, whose balconies are characteristically curvaceous and whose windowed galleries are delicately embroidered with wrought iron. Within, where you'll find visiting Japanese businesspeople and increasing numbers of *barceloneses* savoring the traditional, high-quality fare (sushis, sashimis, noodles, marinated raw fish), the decor is more soberly Japanese. ♦ Japanese ♦ C Muntaner, 231 (Av Diagonal-Trav Gràcia) 200.51.26

16 Hotel Presidente $$$ (1966, **José María Ayxelá**) The architect is still the owner of this 5-star hotel whose rooms are generally smaller than those of its first-class peers and whose prices are, therefore, just a tad lower. Recently renovated from stem to stern, its 160 rooms are air-conditioned and have satellite color TVs and minibars. The pleasant mezzanine lounge, bar and restaurant offer a fish-bowl view of bustling *uptown* Barcelona. The hotel also offers a vest-pocket outdoor pool on the 9th floor and parking facilities. ♦ Av Diagonal, 570 (C Muntaner) 200.21.11; fax 209.51.06

17 Xine-la Shop-owner **Silvia** was the first to import Italian shoes to Barcelona and she continues to feature the best names—Moreschi, Sergio Rossi, Pollini, El Vaquero, Moschino—and offer one of the city's largest and most

Tibidabo/Gràcia

exclusive selections. The choice for men is more limited. The accessories are enchanting as well. ♦ Trav Gràcia, 10 (Pl Francesc Macià-C Casanova) 200.11.61

18 Can Tripes $ If you would like nothing better than a home-cooked meal, this is the place to come. Granted, the dishes are Catalan, but there is lots of good ole *t.l.c.* in every low-cost bite. ♦ Catalan ♦ C Sagues, 16 (C Avenir-Trav Gràcia) 200.85.40

19 Byblos ★$ If you like things simple and cheap, this is the place for you. The personable Lebanese owners serve hummus and pita-bread sandwiches stuffed with falafel, schawarma, chicken, or liver Lebanese style. ♦ Middle Eastern ♦ C Marià Cubí, 207 (C Sagues-C Calvet)

---

23 April is 3 holidays in one: the feast of **Sant Jordi**, patron saint of Catalonia; the festival of the rose (custom dictates giving friends and family members a rose and a book); and the death of Cervantes.

19 La Teya ★$ A family-style place that offers a bargain *menu del día* with numerous options to choose from for each of the 3 courses. Those with hearty appetites take note: the daily specials come in heaping helpings. ♦ Catalan ♦ C Marià Cubí, 203 (C Sagues-C Calvet) 200.32.54

20 Universal If designer **Claret Serrahema** had been a bit more Minimalist in his decor, he would have had no work to do at all in outfitting this trendy bar. Suffice it to say, the atmosphere is severe. Still, Barcelona's sophisticated elite and fashion victims frequent the place nightly. There is music downstairs, art of sorts upstairs. ♦ C Marià Cubí, 182-184 (C Sagues) 200.74.70

20 Héroes Every season Héroes creates a line of men's styles that are trendy but not extravagant in either design or price. ♦ C Laforja, 103 (C Sagues) 201.32.90. Also at: Bulevard Rosa, Av Diagonal, 474. Bulevard Rosa, Av Diagonal, 609, No. 24

21 Panchito ★★$ Holy frijoles! Finally we come upon one of the few Mexcian restaurants in town. The food is good and cheap and the decor simple yet exotic. ♦ Mexican ♦ C Amigó, 57 (C Madrazo) 202.21.31

22 E4G The young in age and spirit will find many *cool* looks among the fashions of Esprit, Junior Gaultier, Closed, Armani (jeans) and other arbiters of youthful tastes. ♦ C Tenor Viñas, 7 (C Calvet) 209.08.22. Also at: Av Diagonal, 490. 218.35.44; Bulevard Rosa Pedralbes, Av Diagonal, 609, Nos. 69-70. 419.00.22

22 Franel-la The preferred boutique for teenagers. Also offers a collection of clothes for children ages 6 months to 14 years by the Dutch manufacturer Oilily. ♦ C Tenor Viñas, 1 (C Ferran Agulló) 201.84.79

23 Charo Barcelona's elegant and sophisticated ladies frequent this classic boutique to see the latest by Versace, Ungaro, Thierry Mugler, Les Copains and so on. Also offers elegant evening wear of its own creation. ♦ C Ferran Agulló, 18 (C Tenor Viñas-C Josep Bertrand) 209.13.47

24 Bloque Residencial (1961, **José Antonio Coderch de Sentmenat** and **Manuel Valls i Vergés**) An earlier Coderch residential creation, this one is of the smaller variety and most notable for the intriguing facade that teams brick with jalousie shutters. ♦ C Johann Sebastian Bach, 7 (C Valero)

Restaurants/Nightlife: Red   **Hotels:** Blue
Shops/Parks: Green   **Sights/Culture:** Black

25 Bloques Residenciales (1974, **José Antonio Coderch de Sentmenat**) For most of his working life, Coderch's residential projects were of limited size. Only in his later years did he embark on projects like this one that, because of their extension, have a much greater impact on the surrounding urban landscape. Drenched in greenery, this complex of apartment buildings is certainly an attractive enhancement of that landscape. ◆ C Raset, 21-31 (C Freixa, 22-32)

26 Hotel Rekor'd $$$ Just a few years old, this NH hotel offers 15 comfortable suites with large single beds and convertible sofas. Amenities include color satellite TVs, mini-bars, air conditioning and laundry service. The narrow building of friendly red brick that houses it all is very inviting. ◆ C Muntaner, 352 (C Rector Ubach) 200.19.53

27 Edificio de Viviendas en Duplex (1931, **Josep Lluís Sert i López**) Considered Sert's first important work and one of the most successful examples of Spanish Rationalism, this apartment building demonstrates a familiarity with European Functionalism and with the work of **Le Corbusier**, in whose studio Sert worked while completing his architectural studies. The duplex apartments here were a most unusual offering at the time, when the building represented a somewhat controversial break with the historicism prescribed by the prevailing *Noucentista* tradition. Aesthetically speaking, though, the structure is rather plain and boxy and jarringly breaks tradition with the more ornately Classical buildings found along the rest of the block.
◆ C Muntaner, 342-348 (C Rector Ubach)

28 Casa Fernández ★★★$$ You'll probably be hard pressed to find space at Casa Fernández's long bar or at the communal table in the back. It seems that this new style *cervecería*-restaurant has caught on in a big way by combining the following essential ingredients: original and agreeable decor, top-quality products, traditional and trendy dishes prepared to perfection, and very efficient service. Some standards here are the eggs teamed with different accompaniments, *panaché de verduras* (a kind of ratatouille), lentil stew, cold roast beef and an assortment of mini-hamburgers. Also commendable is the selection of wines, beers and desserts. ◆ Spanish/International ◆ C Santaló, 46 (C Marià Cubí-C Laforja) 201.93.08

29 Clínica Barraquer (1940, **Joaquim Lloret i Homs**) A few years before the Civil War, construction began on this building conceived to be the office, ophthamology clinic, and private residence of **Dr. Barraquer**. The ground floor housed the offices and clinic; the 2nd floor, patients' rooms; and the upper floors, the doctor's private quarters, staff rooms, a solarium and terraces. The building's stylistic references include European Expressionism and Art Deco. It still serves today as the **Centro de Oftalmología**. ◆ C Muntaner, 314 (C Laforja)

30 Melquiades $$ The cuisine here tops the lackluster decor, but not by much. Though prepared correctly, the food lacks *feeling*. While locals consider the menu unimaginative, visitors will find much that's new to them. For example, *pimientos del piquillo rellenos de brandada de bacalao* (peppers stuffed with codfish mousse), tallarines with salmon and mint, and a dish teaming baby squid and clams. The *pan con tomate* (bread with tomato) is good. ◆ Catalan ◆ C Laforja, 68 (C Aribau-C Moliner) 200.13.41

30 L'Entrecote del Marqués ★★★$$ A newcomer, this restaurant offers a menu of popular dishes at popularly low prices. The *salchichón de Vic* (a kind of salami) and ham are excellent. More indicative of the chef's own talents are the salmon carpaccio, the magret of duck with plums and Armagnac, the *suquet de rape al estilo de Cadaqués* (angler fish stew Costa Brava style), and, of course, the *entrecôtes* prepared with various fine sauces. A selection of cheeses and homemade cakes and pastries finishes off the meal. ◆ International ◆ C Oliana, 14 (C Moliner) 201.63.69

31 El Cus-Cus ★$$ At last tally this was still the only place in town to get genuine North African cuisine. Unfortunately, the couscous is not all it should be, but the rest of the dishes are well prepared and authentically seasoned. Try the *chek-kuka*, pepper salad, lamb *tajine*, and the *cabrito* (goat) stuffed with cream of zucchini. ◆ North African ◆ Pl Cardona, 4 (C Laforja-C Marià Cubí) 201.98.67

32 Duràn-Duràn ★★★$$$ Sr. Càndid Duràn offers his clients good value for their money. Here are some solid choices: the lentil salad with vinaigrette and basil, the fish soup, the terrine of foie gras, the *confit de pato con frijoles verdes*, the salmon with pink-pepper sauce, and the filet of bull marinated in sherry. The sauces are light, and everything is done to a turn. Connoisseurs of gourmet coffees and teas will thrill to the selection here. Since the bar is a very pleasant place for an aperitif, make your reservation and come early.
◆ Catalan/French ◆ C Alfonso XII, 39-41 (C Oliana) 201.35.13

33 Hotel Belagua $$$ This NH hotel has 72 rooms with bath and all the comfort, cleanliness, efficiency and convenience the business traveler demands—plus parking. ♦ Vía Augusta, 89-91 (C Laforja) 237.39.40; fax 415.30.62

34 Botafumeiro ★★★★$$$$ Psssst. Just between us, the **King of Spain** comes here for the seafood flown in fresh from Spain's northern region of Galicia. When not steamed, grilled, broiled or served raw, it is dressed in exquisitely diaphanous sauces. Before you plunge in and indulge, however, stop to admire the Modernist building. ♦ Seafood ♦ C Gran de Gràcia, 81 (C Santa Eugénia-C Cigne) Reservations essential. 218.42.30

35 Figaro ★★$ A quintessential Gràcia experience, Figaro fills at lunch with a crowd of clerical workers and at night with young artists and intellectuals. The menu is similarly hip, offering everything from fine *charcuterie* to tiramisu. ♦ International ♦ C Ros de Olano, 4 bis (C Pere Seraf-C Gran de Gràcia) 238.19.22

36 Aimara ★★★$$ The exotic, flavorful food here is lovingly prepared by a Peruvian chef. Specialties include *papas rellenas* (stuffed potatoes), *guiso de conejo o pollo* (rabbit or chicken stew), *frijoles dulces* (a dessert) and passion fruit sorbet. ♦ South American ♦ C Ros de Olano, 12 (C Pere Seraf) 238.14.06

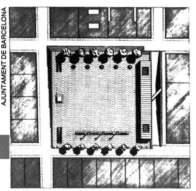

37 Plaça del Sol (1985, **Jaume Bach i Nuñez** and **Gabriel Mora i Gramunt**) As the former village of Gràcia became more and more entwined in the busy urban reality of Barcelona, its small plazas and narrow streets became choked with traffic. A municipal program aimed at recouping some of the barrio's bygone quality of life calls for remodelling no less than 9 Gràcia plazas. Thus far, the transformation of this one, the largest among them, has proved most successful and significant. It involved the construction of an underground parking lot that resulted in a level plaza above that had to be *hooked up* to the surrounding inclined streets via stairs on 2 sides. At the northern end of the plaza is an attractive stand of magnolia trees; at the southern end, rows of plane trees, benches and streetlamps. A glass canopy and sundial (in honor of the plaza's name) complete the very pleasant picture. ♦ C Maspons-C L'Olla-C Planeta-C Valls

38 Casa Vicens (1885, **Antoni Gaudí i Cornet**; expansion 1925, **Joan B. Serra de Martínez**) Conceived in 1878, this house (which looks somewhat like a checkerboard fort) was designed by Gaudí for the ceramicist **Manuel Vicens Montaner** and is considered the master's first truly Modernist work. Of a complex configuration, it is, unlike Gaudí's later works, dominated by straight lines, and its combination stone-and-ceramic construction and adornment represent a very liberal and highly personal interpretation of Spain's medieval *Mudéjar* architectural tradition. Throughout the building we see Gaudí's incipient brilliance and imagination. Note the horizontal, varnished ceramic bands on the lower part of the building; the columns of the upper section with towers at the angles; and the interesting iron gate with dwarf fan palm patterns. Originally, the house had 3 sides facing a garden and shared a common wall with the neighboring convent. The 1925 expansion almost doubled its size. The widening of C Carolines, the expansion of the house itself, and the sale of part of the land it occupied resulted in further serious alterations to Gaudí's original work and the loss of most of the ornamental elements of the original garden, including a gazebo, fountain and waterfall. Still remarkable is the interior decoration of Arabic inspiration (although it is not accessible to the public as this remains a private residence). ♦ C Carolines, 18-24 (Carrero Carolines-Av Princep D'Asturies)

39 Aldea $$ A humble restaurant offering honest fare. The husband is in the kitchen, the wife waits tables. Lunch is restricted to the *menu del día*. Try the *salmón en papillote*, beef fondue, chocolate cake, and apple cake with cream. ♦ International ♦ C Alfonso XII, 76 (C Sant Eusebi) 415.06.23

40 Tuttopasta ★$$$ Not hard to guess what the specialty is here. Try the ravioli with 4 cheeses, the spaghetti al pesto, the carpaccio, or the stuffed *solomillo*. The profiteroles and

CAIXA DE PENSIONS FOUNDATION

AJUNTAMENT DE BARCELONA

chocolate-and-chestnut cake are good too. ♦ Italian ♦ C Sanjoanistes, 28 (C Sant Guillem) 200.55.41

41 Conjunto de Viviendas (1968, **Antoni de Moragas i Gallissà** and **Francesc de Riba i Salas**) Moragas was a member of the **Grup R** that emerged in the 1950s to promote the updating of the national architectural panorama (prostrate since the end of the Civil War) by introducing the new principles of modern architecture and, especially, the organic tendencies typical of the Scandinavian architecture of the time. This apartment block of brick and concrete largely evinces that forward-looking spirit. ♦ C Brusi, 39-43 (Via Augusta-C Sant Elies)

42 Hotel Condor $$$ Another NH hotel, this one is a cut above the **Belagua** mentioned earlier, but otherwise it's business per NH usual in its 78 rooms. ♦ Vía Augusta, 127 (C Aribau) 209.45.11; fax 202.27.13

43 Los Inmortales ★★★$$ The menu here has expanded from pizzas and pastas to include an Italian-Argentine repertoire not to be found in any other Barcelona restaurant that we know of. So sample its selection of good meats, *empanadas de xoclo o carne* (meat pies) and—surprise, surprise—excellent charlotte. You should also be pleased with the house wine. ♦ Italian/Argentinean ♦ C Marc Aureli, 27 (C Copernic) 201.85.14

44 La Carreta ★★★$$ Excellent meats, big portions and low prices are drawing more and more people to this comfortably rustic restaurant. The wine list is outstanding. ♦ South American ♦ C Balmes, 358 (C Putget)

45 Casa-Museu Gaudí (1905, **Francesc Berenguer**) Gaudí lived and worked here from 1906 to 10 June 1926, a few months before his untimely death by streetcar. In December 1926 the house was bought by an Italian couple named **Chiappo-Arietti**. Great admir-

ers of Gaudí, they respected the house's construction, preserved some of the furniture, and made as few changes as possible. They baptized the house **Torre Gaudí**, and in 1960 their heirs offered it to the **Amics de Gaudí** (The Friends of Gaudí), who wished to make a memorial of it. In 1963 it opened as a musuem whose 2 floors, containing furniture and decorative pieces by Gaudí and some of his closer associates, were restored to the way they were in Gaudí's time. An austere, unassuming man in his private life, Gaudí took little interest in his house, its furnishings or his possessions, so you won't find any items of great artistic value or merit. Of interest in the hall is the small chapel with the image of **Saint Anthony**, whom Gaudí adopted as his own personal patron saint. It is said that he used to acknowledge the saint reverently upon entering or leaving the house. The garden outside the house is now a repository for orphaned Gaudiana garnered from a variety of his works. Among them are a grill of palm tree leaves with a stylized palmetto from the **Casa Vicens**; the cross from the main door of the **Finca Miralles**; 3 grills from the **Casa Milà** (aka **La Pedrera**); an iron flower box from the **Casa Battló**; a grill from the **Torre Figueres Bellesguard**; and another grill from the **Finca Güell**. Together these structural souvenirs comprise a small, open-air museum of Gaudí's ironwork. ♦ Admission. M-F 10AM-2PM, 4-7PM, Su, holidays 10AM-2PM, Apr-Sep; daily 10AM-2PM, 4-6PM, Jan-Mar, Oct-Dec

46 Parc Güell (1914, **Antoni Gaudí i Cornet**) In 1922 the municipal government acquired the land and structures of what was originally projected by **Eusebi Güell** and designed by Gaudí to be a self-contained, English-style garden city. Of the planned 61 homes, network of roads, and markets and schools, only

Tibidabo/Gràcia

Parc Güell

2 houses and a few public areas were completed, so the city decided to turn the rolling terrain of **Muntanya Pelada** (492 feet above sea level) and its excellent vistas into a park. The whole area is enclosed by a wall whose main entrance gate in C D'Olot is flanked by

ARCHITECTURA MODERNISTA EN CATALUÑA

2 whimsical pavilions originally destined to be a porter's lodge and administration building. They are both built of stone with brick Catalan vaults topped off with pieces of broken ceramics called *trencadís*. All of Gaudí's work in Parc Güell incorporates sinuous, geometric surfaces, and each of the roofs is crowned by small domes and a tall, spiralling tower terminating in the characteristic Gaudian double cross. Just inside the park entrance a whimsical stairway, adorned with a colorfully conspicuous ceramic lizard, leads to the large hypostyle **Hall of a Hundred** (Doric and seemingly drunk) **Columns** meant to be the market area. In reality you'll find only 84 columns supporting the quarter-sphere domes that in turn support the large, upper plaza (that amounts to a lovely municipal balcony overlooking the city and the sea) rimmed with a twisting, concrete balustrade-bench faced with more *trencadí* decorative work. Both this bench and the beautiful keystones of the hypostyle were a collaborative effort of Gaudí and the architect **Josep M. Jujol**. Some noteworthy structural features found in the park are the large cistern beneath the hypostyle that collects rain water from the plaza by way of the columns themselves and

Tibidabo/Gràcia

the large viaducts supporting the roads whose robust leaning pillars form elegant arches faced with rough-hewn stone. Interestingly, the *sample home* which Gaudí had built for himself was designed by **Francesc Berenguer**, and the second finished house, built for a lawyer named **Trias**, was designed by **Juli Batllevell Arús**. Gaudí, of course, signed off on both of them. The one he lived in from 1906 to 1926 is now the **Casa-Museu Gaudí**. The park also contains 2 natural grottos and one artificial one (where the cistern is). In 1984, UNESCO declared Güell Park a World Heritage site. Recently the entire park has undergone a thorough, and much-needed, overhaul. ♦ C d'Olot, s/n (Coll del Portell-Av Santuari de Sant Josep de la Muntanya)

47 Balmes 413 ★$$ The fare here is fair and so are the prices. A good place to make a meal of *media raciones* (half portions) of shrimp, mussels, squid, and other assorted fish and shellfish. ♦ Seafood/Tapas ♦ C Balmes, 413 (C Castanyer) 211.49.75

48 Restaurante Florian ★★★$$$$ Chef **Rosa Grau**'s gastronomic repertoire is not only ample and varied, but extremely savory and well balanced. You'll find most everything here from a subtle, light tuna carpaccio to a *raging bull* steak fresh from the day's *corrida* or bull-fight (summer only). The place is small and unpretentious. The wines are very fine. ♦ C Bertrand i Serra, 20 (C Mandri-C Torras i Pujalt) Reservations essential. 212.46.27

49 Bonanova ★★★$$$ One of our favorites in the area, Bonanova offers one spacious and one more intimate indoor dining room and, in summer, a pleasant outdoor terrace. The high-quality fare is frank and generous and also a favorite with the area's yuppies. Try the *ensalada de habas a la menta* (bean salad with mint), canelones, or rabbit with snails. And don't overlook the rich selection of wines, champagnes and *cavas*. ♦ Spanish ♦ C Sant Gervasi de Cassoles, 103 (C Reus-Pl Bonanova) 417.10.33

50 La Rotunda (1918, **Adolf Ruiz Casamitjana**) Aka **Torre Andre**, this was designed as a hotel back in 1906. Its location at the beginning of Av Tibidabo (an area that in 1900 was beginning to be settled by Barcelona's upper class) and its striking profile (imparted by the circular tower that begat its name) have made La Rotunda something of an architectural milestone on the Barcelona cityscape. Unfortunately, its original ornamental richness has largely disappeared due to the building's conversion from a hotel to a clinic and the replacement of the building's original attic with a full-fledged additional floor, and inside virtually nothing original remains. All that remains intact and continues to give this building its singular cachet is the temple-like tower's ceramic ornamentation. The work of **Lluís Bru**, its filigree mosaic motifs depict a variety of flora and fauna. La Rotunda is still home to a private clinic. ♦ Av Tibidabo, 2-4 (Pg Sant Gervasi)

51 Mare de Déu de Montserrat Youth Hostel $ (1907) If you don't have a youth hostel card, you can buy one stamp per night to stay in this former Modernist mansion now offering 160 cheap beds. The reception area is done in a colorful Moorish style, and there is a beautiful terrace with a striking view of Barcelona down below. Members of the International Brigade stayed here during the Civil War. Although the hostel technically closes at midnight, it opens its doors at 1AM and 2AM to let in those who have been enjoying the delights of late-night Barcelona. ♦ Pg Mare de Déu del Coll, 41-51 (Ptge Tona-C Castellterçol) 210.51.51

In 1869 **Gaudí** began his university studies in Barcelona's Science Faculty in preparation for later studies at the city's Escola Provincial d'Arquitectura (Provincial School of Architecture). He was an irregular student who preferred spending long hours in the library to going to class.

52 Parc de la Creueta del Coll (Josep Martorell and David Mackay) Built on the site of the old **La Creueta** quarry, this young park occupies one of Barcelona's hills and was conceived as a multipurpose gathering place. Its large piazza and **Eduardo Chillida**'s highly impressive suspended sculpture, *Eulogy to Water*, are its most striking features. You'll also find a lake (used for swimming in the summer despite its most unsavory aspect), an artificial beach, and a pocket of palms. Beyond that there is a large wooded area and walkways punctuated with panoramic vantage points. At the end of the ramp forming an entrance to the park is a tall, flat-faced totem sculpture by **Ellsworth Kelly**. On the crest of the mountain is another sculpture by **Roy Lichtenstein**. ♦ C Cardedeu-C Castellterçol-Pg Mare de Déu del Coll-C Taradell

53 Avenida del Tibidabo To ride along this broad avenue in the **tramvía blau** is to see the happy marriage of money and Modernism. All along the way you'll marvel at the spectacular mansions that speak of Barcelona's turn-of-the-century prosperity.

54 Cafe del Goliard ★$$$ A friendly greeting awaits one and all at this cafe-restaurant offering the latest fad fare. At last visit the menu included eggplant salad, an onion-and-salmon tart over a pepper sauce, a shrimp-and-fish brochette, and ox filet with a marrow sauce. ♦ Eclectic ♦ C Major de Sarrià, 95 bis (Pl Roser) 204.63.10

55 Ca La Tresa ★$$$ The locals really like this neighborhood restaurant and keep coming back for the canelones, anchovies, grilled squid, and veal filet with herbs. ♦ Catalan ♦ C Major de Sarrià, 128 (Pl Sarrià-C Graus) 203.04.29

56 Tram-Tram ★★$$$$ The culinary creations of the young **Guillermo Casañé** are elegant and bursting with personality. The menu covers just about all the bases, from salads and pastas to a hearty lamb with rösti and a subtle steamed hake with vegetables. Offers a very reasonably priced *menu del día* at lunch. It's divine out on the terrace on summer nights. ♦ International ♦ C Major de Sarrià, 121 (C Ramon Miquel i Planas) 204.85.18

57 El Dorado Petit ★★★★$$$$ Attractively ensconced in one of the turn-of-the-century mansions built by the Barcelona elite to escape the summer heat, this fine restaurant is worth the effort required to get here (take a cab). There is somewhat of a colonial feel to the indoor decor laced with mirrors, dark wicker chairs, antique mahogany sideboards and bare wooden floors. The restaurant's highly original menu is market driven (food market, that is) and the pride of owner **Luis Cruañas**, who oversees every aspect of the proceedings with smiling earnestness, is obvious. If San Pedro (a Mediterranean fish) baked with rosemary and topped with a dry white wine sauce is on the menu, try it. Also consider the wild mushrooms grilled with garlic and oil or sautéed with *butifarra* (Catalan pork

sausage) and the dorada (another Mediterranean fish) baked in a salt crust. Or order the *fideus* (tiny strands of pasta fried golden crisp, cooked in fish stock until all the flavor has been absorbed, and then served with a pungent sauce of garlic and olive oil). By no means pass on dessert—many of the choices are homemade and quite unique. Outstanding among them are the *crema catalana* (a lighter version of crème brûlée) and the *recuit*, a molded fromage blanc (like cottage cheese) topped with toasted pine nuts and fragrant wild honey. There is now an El Dorado Petit in New York at 47-49 W 55th St; 212/586.3434. ♦ Mediterranean ♦ C Dolors Monserdá, 51 (C D'Anglí-C Pomaret) Reservations essential. 204.51.53

58 Torre Figueres *Bellesguard* (1902, Antoní Gaudí i Cornet) Vaguely reminiscent of a cathedral, this square *torre*-mansion, built for **Maria Sagués** virtually atop the ruins of the summer palace of the 15th-century **King Martí I l'Humà** (last of the Catalan-Aragon kings), clearly pays homage to the Catalan Gothic style that so fascinated Gaudí throughout his career. The use of materials from the site itself resulted in a chromatic harmony that perfectly integrates the structure with its surroundings. The building's corners correspond to the 4 cardinal points of the compass, and its tower is embellished with stained-glass stripes recalling the Catalan flag, a royal crown, and the 4-armed cross that is the signature mark of Gaudí. Inside, instead of beams, there are thin walls, or ribs, that form arches of varying shapes. In fact, the interior is where Gaudí's brilliance explodes into extraordinary beauty, but the house remains private property and can only be viewed from the outside. ♦ C Bellesguard, 16-20 (C Immaculada-C Valeta D'Arquer)

Tibidabo/Gràcia

Torre Figueres
Bellesguard

CAIXA DE PENSIONS FOUNDATION

59 **Restaurante La Balsa** ★$$$ (1979, **Lluís Clotet** and **Oscar Tusquets**) A sophisticated restaurant with comparably sophisticated prices. Unfortunately, the food is not of the same caliber as the prices or the exotic architectural setting that exudes a strong tropical flavor. Still, many of Barcelona's movers, shakers and celebrities can be spotted here.
♦ Catalan/International ♦ C Infanta Isabel, 4 (C Vista Bella-C Jesús i María) 211.50.48

60 **Museu de la Ciéncia** The hands-on exhibits here, addressing the fields of optics, sound transmission, mechanics, computer science, climate and more, are very popular with children. The *Clik dels Nens* (toddlers' section) for children 3 to 8 was designed by **Xavier Mariscal** and includes bathrooms scaled down to kiddy size. There is also a planetarium whose hours are very variable, so call first.
♦ Admission; children 3-8 free. Tu-Su 10AM-8PM. C Teodor Roviralta, 55 (C Bosch i Alsina) 212.60.50

61 **La Cupula** ★$$$ Installed in a late Modernist mansion dating from 1930, this light, tranquil, out-of-the-way oasis of a restaurant features market cuisine and offers among its various special menus a *light* one for calorie watchers and a children's menu. The dishes (like the habitual yuppie clientele) can border on the pretentious, and they are often unnecessarily elaborate, but you'll do all right if you stick with the fresh, seasonal offerings and leave room for one of the delicious desserts. The

house *gimmick* is a drink menu that tallies 280 different international drinks of varying alcoholic strengths and persuasions. The dining is done on a very pleasant covered terrace.
♦ Catalan/International ♦ C Teodor Roviralta, 37 (C Román Macaya-C Bosch i Alsina) 212.48.88

62 **El Asador de Aranda** ★$$$ (1913, **Joan Rubió i Bellvé**) Housed in one of those Modernist masterpieces, the **Casa Roviralto** (aka **El Frare Blanc**), this restaurant specializes in grilled meats served in copious portions. The various dining rooms are veritable jewels of Modernist decor with a Moorish twist. The house itself was built for the Roviralta family, but its nickname harks back to the property's former occupant, a Dominican convent, parts of which were recycled in the construction of this single-family mansion. For example, the 18th-century chapel was preserved and now houses service facilities for the restaurant. If you climb up to the roof-top terrace you'll see a fabulous view of the sea and the mountains. The restaurant is open every day of the year and you can ask permission to visit within without eating—it is usually granted. ♦ Grill
♦ Av Tibidabo, 31 (C Román Macaya) 417.01.15

63 **Funicular** Spain's oldest funicular, this one offers great views as it carries you to the top of **Tibidabo**. ♦ Pi Doctor Andreu

10 Terrific Things for Kids

1 Barcelona's 2 mountaintop amusement parks (Parc D'Atraccions)—on **Montjuïc** and **Tibidabo**—offer rides for the kids and scenic vistas for the grown-ups.

2 Hands-on learning about optics, sound transmission, mechanics, computer science, and more at the **Museu de la Ciéncia**.

3 Step right up and see the world's only captive albino gorilla at the **Parc de la Ciutadella Zoo**. Then move on to the trained-dolphin show.

4 Wax museums are a perennial favorite with kids, and Barcelona's **Museu de Cera** won't disappoint.

5 Kids love the **Museu Marítim**'s replica of *La Galera Real* and its model of the world's first submarine.

6 And speaking of boats, don't fail to make a family outing on the *golondrinas*.

7 The mimes and clowns that are often among the street performers of **La Rambla** never fail to mesmerize the young ones.

8 Most people don't think *beach* when they think *Barcelona*, but there is one near the Olympic Village and kids love it.

9 The city's cable cars, funiculars and Transbordador Aéreo are just like amusement park rides, so use them whenever possible.

10 If you want to educate a young palate at a reasonable price while indulging in some fine food yourself, take your child to lunch on Saturday at **Orotava**, in the Esquerra de L'Eixample.

64 Parc D'Atraccions Barcelona is likely the only city in the world flanked by 2 mountain-top amusement parks, that of **Montjuïc** and this one. Here you'll find more fine views and a selection of some 30 rides, all renovated in 1990. If you have an aversion to

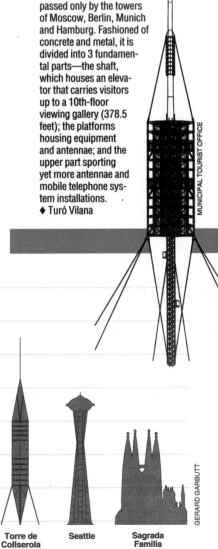

funiculars, you can catch a bus up here from the Pl John Kennedy at the foot of Av Tibidabo. Of interest to both children and adults within the amusement park is the marvelous **Museu de Autómatas** housing a fabulous collection of vintage penny-arcade machines, many of which still function. Among them are soccer games, fortune tellers and puppet orchestras—mostly from the 1920s. Many originally came from the US, and the **Walt Disney** organization once made a bid for the collection with the aim of bringing it back the US. The bid was flatly rejected. The park's hours of operation are highly variable, so contact the tourist office or call before coming. ♦ Admission. Pl Tibidabo. 211.79.42

64 Templo del Sagrado Corazón (1902, **Enric Sagnier**) This falsely Gothic church of artificial stone seems singularly out of place next to an amusement park, but perhaps some Barcelona citizens felt the need to thus exorcise the stigma of Satan's legendary temptation of Christ on **Mount Tibidabo**. Next to the main altar is an elevator that rises to more fine views. ♦ Pl Tibidabo

64 Restaurante La Masia del Tibidabo ★★$$$ Especially popular for Sunday lunches with the family, this large restaurant of nondescript decor has something for everyone on its extensive menu, and it's all quite good. ♦ Catalan/International ♦ Pl Tibidabo. Reservations recommended. 417.63.50

65 Torre de Collserola (1992, **Norman Foster** and **Ove Arup**) This was to be the only telecommunications tower built for the Olympic Games until Spain's telephone company decided to build the controversial **Torre de Calatrava** in the Olympic Ring on Montjuïc. At 854.4 feet, this one is at least taller. In fact, it is the world's 5th tallest, surpassed only by the towers of Moscow, Berlin, Munich and Hamburg. Fashioned of concrete and metal, it is divided into 3 fundamental parts—the shaft, which houses an elevator that carries visitors up to a 10th-floor viewing gallery (378.5 feet); the platforms housing equipment and antennae; and the upper part sporting yet more antennae and mobile telephone system installations. ♦ Turó Vilana

1650'					
1500'					
1350'					
1200'					
1050'					
900'					
750'					
600'					
450'					
300'					
150'					
Moscow	Berlin	Munich	Torre de Collserola	Seattle	Sagrada Familia

GERARD GARBUTT

Esquerra de L'Eixample

Between the maze of narrow **Ciutat Vella** streets to the south and the small streets and plazas to the north that once constituted separate villages in their own right (such as Pedralbes, Sarrià, Sant Gervasi, Gràcia and Tibidabo) topographic order reigns in the **Eixample** grid. When the city walls came tumbling down in 1860, this area of former agricultural activity offered Barcelona's well-heeled citizens and captains of the flourishing textile trade fertile ground for the construction and cultivation of new status symbols. Dovetailing nicely with those ambitions was the contemporaneous flowering of the Modernist movement. As a result

of the happy marriage of the two, Barcelona's Eixample is now one of the world's most interesting architectural enclaves. The symbiotic relationship between prosperity and architectural derring-do endowed the district with magnificent examples of the distinctive Catalan Modernist imagination that took the international Art Nouveau movement to fanciful new heights. A telling sign of the architectural times was the initiation in 1900 of annual municipal architectural prizes.

For Barcelona's bourgeoisie there were suddenly wide open spaces north of La Rambla that beckoned them to abandon the cramped quarters of Ciutat Vella for the spacious possibilities of the Exiample. *Eixample* (*Ensanche* in Spanish) means extension, and it specifically refers here to the expansion of the city carried out in the second half of the 19th century in accordance (to a great extent) with the municipal plan drawn up in 1854 by **Ildefons Cerdà**, commonly referred to as the **Plan Cerdà**. His layout called for streets running parallel and perpendicular to the sea, forming 8-sided blocks with chamferred corners designed to accommodate the wide turns of street cars and give greater visibility to other turning vehicles. These corners later proved favored spots for grocery stores. At the corner of **Carrer Roger de Llúria** and **Carrer Consell de Cent** you'll see the closest approximation of Cerdà's original plan, which also called for interior patio gardens on each block. These rarely materialized, and ultimately most became the province of parked cars. But that is slowly chang-

ing, as Barcelona's general urban overhaul pointedly projects the rehabilitation of the Eixample's interior patios in keeping with Cerdà's original concept.

The first wave of Eixample residents settled in between 1860 and 1890, gravitating toward the center of the new barrio, around the **Passeig de Gràcia**, where they established a zone of high-quality, detached houses with gardens and a sprinkling of commercial establishments. That first Eixample core can now only be experienced through written documents, plans and photographs, because beginning in the 1890s, a second, more commercial Eixample core began to emerge, with businesses occupying the ground floors—much as they do today. Also in the 1890s the first wave of well-heeled Eixample residents was followed

by a middle-class influx of intellectuals, artists and skilled professionals like architects and engineers. As the demand for residences rose, apartment buildings began to vie with single-family dwellings as the structural Eixample norm.

Creatively, the Eixample attains its finest architectural expression within a relatively small area straddling the Passeig de Gràcia between **Carrer D'Aribau** and **Passeig de Sant Joan** and between the **Rondas Universitat** and **Sant Pere** and the **Avinguda de la Diagonal**. The Passeig de Gràcia, which in the city's Barcino days was a path to the mountains and later led from the walled city to the town of Gràcia (now a Barcelona district), is the backbone of the Eixample and the axis that separates the **Esquerra de L'Eixample** (Left Eixample) from the **Dreta de L'Eixample** (Right Eixample). Along it you'll find some of the most outstanding Modernist buildings, including **Gaudí's Pedrera** (see the Dreta de L'Eixample Chapter) and the 3 highly characteristic works by **Domènech i Montaner (Casa Lleó i Morera)**, **Puig i Cadaflach (Casa Amatller)** and Gaudí (**Casa Batlló**) that occupy the **Mançana de la Discòrdia** (Block of Discord) between Carrer Consell de Cent and **Carrer D'Aragó**. Walking up the Passeig de Gràcia from the **Plaça de Catalunya**, you'll see the lamp-benches by **Falqués** with their seats made of *trencadís* (bits and pieces of broken ceramics). Their recent restoration revealed the original maroon-and-gilt ironwork, reinforced the undulating structure, and recovered the original globe-shaped lights. Beneath your feet you'll find the patterned pavement of slate-blue, hexagonal stones that are the work of Gaudí.

More middle class and less status conscious than the Dreta de L'Eixample to the east of the Passeig de Gràcia, this western half of the Eixample has a lower concentration of Modernist works. Among their ranks you'll find vestiges of old institutions of higher learning like the university, the **Seminario Conciliar**, the **Facultad de Medicina** (in the **Hospital Clínico**) and the **Universitat Industrial** with its **Escuela del Trabajo** (School of Work). Also, this half of the Eixample was originally stuck with the bulk of the city services—the Hospital Clínico, fire department, **Plaça de Toros**, **Cárcel Modelo** (a prison) and **Matadero** (slaughterhouse).

Recently, many of Barcelona's Modernist treasures have been rejuvenated, and the Eixample of our day is the commercial heart of Barcelona, headquarters for major-league banks and multinational companies, and an area of upper-middle-class residences. Although half a dozen architects headline the bill of the Eixample's Modernist buildings, some 100 actually participated in fashioning one of Spain's—and perhaps the world's—most singular urban profiles in collaboration with countless painters, decorators, glaziers and artisans. Local authors **Josep Mari** and **José Maria Carandell** affectionately compare the Eixample to an insane asylum, characterizing it as *a place of very rational halls and cells, which are the streets and blocks, inhabited by crazy people, which are the Modernist houses.*

Esquerra de L'Eixample

The best way to discover and delight in its eccentricities is to stroll about, allowing yourself to be continually surprised by the whims of its Modernist conjurers. En route you'll find many modern-day enterprises upholding the spirit of creativity and progress that originally fostered this barrio's uniqueness. Everywhere there are signs of an enduring eagerness to spawn ever-new cultural trends in the arts and design.

Many might still consider today's Eixample, with its penchant for trendiness and cutting-edge cultural displays, *a place of very rational halls...inhabited by crazy people*, but Barcelona has always prided itself on its daring flair for fashion and design, and the Eixample has long been creative headquarters.

1 **Plaça del Catalunya** (1902) Barcelona's center of civic gravity and point of encounter between the old city and the Eixample, this plaza has undergone numerous modifications and face-lifts. Similar in size to St. Peter's Square in the Vatican and the Etoile de Paris, it contains 2 fountains and various sculptures of which *Le Deessa* (The Goddess) by **Josep Clarà** is particularly worth noting. Park benches and gardens provide a serene alternative to the surrounding urban bustle. ♦ Rambla Catalunya-Rda Universitat-Pg Gràcia-C Fontanella

2 **Casa Bosch i Alsina** (1892, **Joaquim Bassegoda i Amigó**) Structures like this one that exhibit formal Neo-Gothic tendencies are typical of the 1890s construction in this transitional area between the waning bourgeoisie barrios of Ciutat Vella and the budding bourgeoisie barrio of the central Eixample. The 2nd-floor gallery originally featured some interesting ironwork. ♦ Pl Catalunya, 8 (Rda Universitat)

3 **Edificio Comercial Hispano-Olivetti** (1964, **Ludovico Belgiojoso, Enrico Peressutti** and **Ernesto N. Rogers**) The Italian BBPR studio that designed this building also authored the famous Torre Velasca in Milan and the restoration of that city's Castle Sforza. Part of **Adriano Olivetti**'s plan for a series of office buildings in the architectural vanguard, this structure represents the introduction of the curtain wall into the historic cityscape of Barcelona, which in this case, thanks to the great sensibility of its design, works well. Note, too, the building's flat roof and chimneys—they are subtle interpretations of Modernism's finials and crowning finishes. ♦ Rda Universtitat, 18 (Pl Catalunya-C Balmes)

LLIBRERIA BOSCH

4 **Llibreria Bosch** Dedicated to bookselling for over 100 years, this is a fine place to look for material in Spanish on almost every subject and for material on Barcelona in assorted languages. ♦ Rda Universitat, 11 (C Balmes-Pl Universitat) 317.53.58. Also at: C Rosellón, 24. 321.33.41

4 **Alt Heidelberg** ★$ An extremely popular place for snacks, sandwiches and full meals at moderate prices. The name unequivocally announces the nationality of most of the food and drink found within, which includes a preponderance of sausages, salads and beers. ♦ German ♦ Rda Universitat, 5 (Pl Universitat) 318.10.32

5 **Universitat Central** (1889, **Elies Rogent**) At the end of the 13th century, Barcelona had a Dominican university called the **Estudi General**, which was basically the medieval equivalent of a liberal arts institution. The Jews at the time also had a center for university studies, but Barcelona's first official university institution was the **Estudi d'Arts i Medicina** (School of Arts and Medicine) founded by **King Martín I** in 1401. In 1450 **Alfonso el Magnánimo** expanded it, adding faculties of theology, law and philosophy. A new building to house these faculties was built in La Rambla beginning in 1536. Distinguished for its Hellenistic and Hebraic studies, this university's activities were vengefully suppressed as punishment shortly after the occupation of Catalunya by **Felipe V**, who moved the university studies to Cervera in 1717 (except for the School of Medicine). The university returned to Barcelona in 1823, was closed again shortly thereafter, and reopened in 1837 (but was without legal sanction until 1842). This Universitat Central building was subsequently built between 1861 and 1889 and until 1958 housed all the faculties except for Medicine. Today, the majority of the University of Barcelona's faculties are strung along the western end of the Av Diagonal. Here in this building, executed in the Neo-Romanesque Catalan style, you'll find the Faculties of Philology and Geology and the **Biblioteca Provincial i Universitària** (Provincial and University Library). The building's facade and vestibule are inspired by the **Monasterio de Poblet**. The beautiful, twin, 2-story patios within are worth a visit. So is the assembly hall with its *Mudéjar* decoration and historical paintings. (Note: *Mudéjar* refers to those Muslims who remained in Castile after the Reconquest and to their art and architecture, which dates from the 12th to the 16th centuries and is characterized by Islamic influence.) The library, which harbors more than 250,000 volumes, contains many important medieval and Renaissance works garnered from the libraries and archives of the monasteries abolished in 1835. ♦ Gran Via C.C., 585 (C Balmes-C D'Aribau)

6 **Casa Jeroni F. Granell** (1904, **Jeroni F. Granell i Manresa**) Not only was Granell the architect on this one, but he was the owner as

well. The ground floor has clearly been mutilated, but it is believed that the remaining windows are the work of Granell's own company. Interesting to visit are the vestibule and the patio. ♦ Gran Via C.C., 582 (C D'Aribau-C Muntaner)

7 **Casa Francisco Farreras** (1902, **Antoni Millàs Figuerola**) This series of 3 contiguous structures (now rental apartments) features a uniform facade fashioned of Montjuïc stone. Although the corner galleries of the chamferred facade are atypically asymmetrical—one being round and extending all the way up and the other triangular and reaching only to the 3rd floor (and forming a balcony on the 4th)—Millàs, whose work is little known, utilized fairly formal Modernist iconography in this building. The ground floor has been greatly altered, and all that is preserved in its original state are the pharmacy in C Villarroel and the vestibules of No. 538 and 540, the former evincing an especially exuberant decorative hand. The top floor constitutes a kind of frieze depicting historical motifs. Also of interest are the bracket decorations on the galleries depicting symbolic feminine figures, the gargoyles, the *sgraffito* and colored-glass ceramic decoration of the vestibules, and the meticulous stonework of the galleries. ◆ Gran Via C.C., 536-542 (C Villarroel)

8 Casa Golferichs (1901, **Joan Rubió Bellver**) One of this architect's first solo endeavours, Casa Golferichs was designed when he was not yet 30 years old and still collaborating with **Antoni Gaudí**. In this highly original structure we can already see emerging some of the essential characteristics that would later distinguish his body of work—the minute design of every element and detail; the use of traditional, indigenous materials, with special emphasis on brickwork; and the interplay of sculpted stone and rubblework. Gaudí's influence is patent here, especially inside, where the passageways were directly inspired by Gaudí's **Episcopal Palace** in Astorga, built between 1887 and 1893. When Rubió built this one-family house, he left part of the plot open for use as a garden. Known popularly as **El Xalet** (the Chalet), local residents once waged a campaign to save it from demolition. It now houses district offices. ◆ Visits Tu-F 5-9PM; Sa 10AM-2PM, 5-9PM. ◆ Gran Via C.C., 491 (C Viladomat)

9 Casa de la Papallona (1912, **Josep Graner i Prat**) First and foremost on this building is the large, well-known, crowning butterfly encrusted with polychrome *trencadís* (broken bits of ceramics). Despite the building's date, Granel resorts to the simple, formal lines of Barcelona's 19th-century architecture—and

Esquerra de L'Eixample

then tops it all off with his fancifully Modernist *mariposa* (*papallona* in Catalán). ◆ C Llançà, 20 (Gran Via C.C.)

10 Plaça de Toros *Las Arenas* (1900, **August Font i Carreras**) In keeping with the stylistic currents common at the turn of the century, this bullring's horseshoe arches and brickwork inlaid with ceramics represent a somewhat romantic interpretation of decidedly Moorish motifs. The smaller of Barcelona's 2 bullrings, this one was recently purchased by the **Fira de Barcelona**, but since its plans for the place were not quite in line with municipal regulations, what will become of this defunct bullring in the future is unclear at the moment. ◆ Gran Via C.C.-C Tarragona-C Diputació-C Llançà

11 El Parc de L'Escorxador (alias Parc Joan Miró) (**Antoni Solanas, Màrius Quintana, Beth Galí** and **Andreu Arriola**) Formerly the site of a slaughterhouse, this park covering an area equivalent to 4 Eixample blocks features abundant trees and recreation areas that make it one of the most popular parks in the city. Emerging from, and reflected in, the pond that graces the large elevated piazza at one end of the park is **Joan Miró**'s tall, polychrome *Woman and Bird* sculpture. In the woods surrounding the pergola on the eastern edge of the park is a path lined with small Miró sculptures. ◆ C Diputació-C Tarragona-C D'Aragó-C Vilamar

12 Quel Fantastico Lunedi ★★★$$$ A wonderful array of traditional Italian cooking—very fresh antipastas, tasty lasagna, escalopines with delicious sauces, great pizzas, sensational tiramisu and classic cappuccino—plus a fine selection of Italian wines. At a remove from the city center, the place had not yet been discovered by the masses when we were last here. ◆ Italian ◆ C València, 26-28 (C Llançà-C Vilamari) 425.39.12

13 Jaume de Provença ★★★★$$$$ Chef **Jaume Bargués** likes to mix the rustic with the modern in his kitchen. Underscoring his various flights of gastronomical fantasy is a solid, earth-bound, professional competence. Here are some choice examples of the happy union: *pastel de esquixada de bacalao* (a codfish concoction in a pastry crust); *lasagna de txangurro con su crema de almejas* (crabmeat lasagna with clam sauce); smoked salmon with 2 caviars; and a roast, suckling lamb filet with fresh pasta and kidneys in an Armagnac cream sauce (yum!). Then, too, there are the Catalan classics: mini-canelones and the *arrosejat* (a savory rice dish, sometimes prepared with cuttlefish). The wine list is commensurate with the cuisine. The decor, alas, is not. The degustation menu is a delicious bargain. ◆ Catalan/International ◆ C Provença, 88 (C Rocafort-C Calabria) Reservations essential. 430.00.29

14 Punto An immense new gathering place for gays with quiet bistro-style tables in the back. Fills up nightly with an elite clientele from the fashion, arts and show business worlds. ◆ C Muntaner, 63-65 (C D'Aragó-C Consell de Cent)

15 Escola de Restauració i Hostalatge Barcelona ★★$$ The staff here are all students-in-training at Barcelona's Hotel and Restaurant School, located on the premises. From start to finish, everything is homemade, and the menu changes not only with the season but, to a certain extent, with the curriculum as well. Though the service may at times be tentative and unpolished, the food is generally very good. ◆ International ◆ C Muntaner, 70-72 (C D'Aragó) 253.29.03

16 Seminario Conciliar (1888, **Elies Rogent**) Just behind the university, this building in the form of a cross with a central dome also echoes the **Monasterio de Poblet**. Today it houses the **Institut Catòlic de Estudis Socials** (the Catholic Institute of Social Studies), the **Escuela Universitaria de Treball Social** (the University School of Social Work) and the **Museu Geològic del Seminari**. ◆ C Consell de Cent, 272 (C D'Enric Granados-C Balmes)

17 Casa Josep J. Bertrand (1905, **Enric Sagnier i Villavecchia**) During his career, Sagnier, one of the Eixample's leading turn-of-the-century architects, adopted a series of solutions for the chamferred facades found throughout the district. Here, in this salmon-colored building, the surfaces of the chamferred corner angles are smooth and just slightly curved, in contrast to the more typical resolution of protruding, glass-enclosed corner galleries. ◆ C Balmes, 50 (C Consell de Cent)

18 Casa Rodolf Juncadella (1891, **Enric Sagnier i Villavecchia**) One of the first turn-of-the-century Barcelona structures to be featured in foreign magazines, this palatial building is of ambitious dimensions uncharacteristic of its peak Modernist period. In 1918 the architect himself remodeled the upper portions of the building to add an additional habitable floor. In the process he left the original terracotta reliefs by **Pere Carbonell** untouched, but added the crowning urns. On the first floor (our second) you'll still find the original mosaic and etched-glass decoration. Also interesting are the wrought-iron grillwork of the interior patio and the wrought-iron screen at the entrance. ◆ Rambla Catalunya, 33 (C Diputació-C Consell de Cent)

19 Casa Rupert Garriga Nogués (1901, **Enric Sagnier i Villavecchia**) The most notable of 3 adjoining structures—Nos. 246 (1908, **Bonaventura Bassegoda Amigó**), 248 (1904, **Salvador Soteras Taberner**) and 250 (1901, Sagnier)—that constitute an interesting Modernist enclave. Although by different architects, they share a penchant for monumental facades incorporating large sculptures. In this one Sagnier rather capriciously combined elements of French Classicism (note the corner tower) with others of Rococo inspiration (note the roof balustrade, cornices and pilasters) and some Modernist flourishes. Of interest among them are, on the ground floor, the lyrical sculptures by **Eusebi Arnau** of 4 feminine figures representing the 4 ages of life, that, like bracket-caryatids, hold up the first-floor balcony. The vestibule (which is the building's most spectacular feature and can be visited) is graced with Classic columns and a monumental, curving staircase illuminated by a large, polychromatic skylight. The building houses the offices of **Enciclopèdia Catalana**, a publishing company. ◆ C Diputació, 250 (Rambla Catalunya)

20 Casa Climent Arola (1902, **Francesc de P. del Villar i Carmona**) Built as Villar's own residence, this elegantly graceful building is just one of the monumental Modernist buildings designed between 1892 and 1907 that converted this block into the legendary **Mançana de Oro** (Block of Gold) of the central Eixample area. ◆ Rambla Catalunya, 27 (C Diputació)

20 Casa Heribert Pons (1909, **Alexandre Soler i March**) Awarded first-place honorable mention in the municipal architectural competition of 1910, this building has suffered repeated modifications that have significantly altered its original aspect, which was greatly

influenced by the Viennese Secessionist style. Contributing greatly to its prize-winning splendor of yore was the sculptural work of **Eusebi Arnau**—most notably his figure of Diana the hunter in the vestibule, which retains its original aspect and can be viewed. The last modification of the building, directed by architect **Jordi Bonet Armengol** in 1978, restored the original form of the central tower that was destroyed by a bomb in 1938. Note the outstanding relief on the facade, an allegorical representation of the arts. Originally built to house apartments on the upper floors and the owner's residence and commercial enterprises on the lower ones, it now houses the **Department d'Economia i Finances** of the **Generalitat de Catalunya**. ♦ Rambla Catalunya, 19-21 (C Diputació-Gran Via C.C.)

21 Casa Pia Battló (1896, **Josep Vilaseca i Casanovas**) Although principally eclectic of style, this building's ornamental details in stone and wrought iron are iconographic reminders of Gothic fantasy. The chamferred facade with protruding, turret-topped galleries at the corners would subsequently prove a much-utilized motif in Eixample architecture. Also notable are the small lanterns at the top of the facade and the interesting use of iron girders, especially in the ground floor openings. As it is now home to offices and apartments, its facade is lamentably blighted with commercial signs and only the vestibule can be readily visited. ♦ Rambla Catalunya, 17 (Gran Via C.C.)

22 Casa Josep Portabella (1896, **Domènec Balet i Nadal**) Another prime example of the Neo-Gothic elements common to the construction of the 1890s in this part of the Eixample close to the old city. The building's renovated aspect (except for the alteration of one set of balconies) remains faithful to the original. ♦ Gran Via C.C., 616 (Rambla Catalunya-C Balmes)

23 Condal Corner A network of more than 50 upscale shops including **Ribé**, one of Barcelona's leading shoe merchants, and **Mils**, a very chic purveyor of porcelains and ceramics whose Lladró offering features some of the more elaborate figurines in the line. The **La Nou** cafe has tables by an interior fountain that are well suited to a brief respite. If you're lucky enough to come at the right time, you'll also be serenaded by a pianist. ♦ Gran Via C.C., 628-632 (Pg Gràcia)

24 Hotel Avenida Palace $$$ This is a rather prestigious address in the business heart of Barcelona offering every comfort and conve-

Esquerra de L'Eixample

nience demanded by businesspeople and tourists alike. The Baroque stairway off the lobby dates from 1952. The 229 air-conditioned rooms and suites all have TVs, minibars, direct-dial telephones and radios. Ancillary services include a beauty parlor, boutique and bookshop. The Rotary Club meets here every Tuesday at 1:45PM. ♦ Gran Via C.C., 605 (Rambla Catalunya) 301.96.00; fax 318.12.34

25 Hotel Calderon $$$ Prime convention territory, the Calderon is distinctive for its modular architecture. Spacious enough to work in, the 263 rooms have satellite TVs, video, air conditioning, direct-dial phones, mini-bars and music. Additional amenities include a sports center with 2 squash courts, sauna, gym, indoor and outdoor swimming pools (a rarity in Barcelona) and parking. ♦ Rambla Catalunya, 26 (C Diputació) 301.00.00; fax 317.31.57

26 Hotel Cristal $$$ Another convention outpost with particularly inviting public areas (especially the lobby). The 150 rooms have the standard complement of air conditioning, direct-dial phones, music and color TVs. Parking available. ♦ C Diputació, 257 (Rambla Catalunya) 301.66.00; fax 317.59.79

27 Hostal Residencia Urbis $$ Installed in a building of the last century, the Urbis offers somewhat seedy but central and economical accommodations. Most of the 59 rooms have complete baths, though some have a shower only. There is a telephone in all and a television in most. No air conditioning, though. Ten triple rooms available. ♦ Pg Gràcia, 23 (C Diputació-C Consell de Cent) 317.27.66; fax 412.28.57

27 Casa Manuel Malagrida (1908, **Joaquim Codina i Matalí**) Though originally built as a multi-family dwelling, Casa Manuel Malagrida has the appearance of a single-family mansion. The French-style cupola, though out of proportion, is the facade's most attractive feature. The decorative work on the spandrels combines vegetable motifs with others alluding to the owner's business activities (he had returned from a stint in South America to become a textile manufacturer)—an eagle (symbolizing Spain) and condor (symbolizing Argentina). In the vestibule you'll still find the original lamps. The premises are now occupied by a bank. ♦ Pg Gràcia, 27 (C Diputació-C Consell de Cent)

28 Hotel Residencia Neutral $ In terms of charm, this lodging lives up to its name, but it is a budget choice in a high-rent district. The bath facilities in its 28 small rooms vary, and colorful floor tiles help rescue the quarters from depressing bleakness. ♦ Rambla Catalunya, 42 (C Consell de Cent, 298) 318.73.70

29 Casa Lleó Morera (1906, **Lluís Domènech i Montaner**; remodelled 1943) Deemed by many experts one of Domènech's most interesting residential structures, the Casa Lleó Morera offers in its vestibule, staircase, elevator and on its first (our second) floor one of the richest and best-conserved displays of Modernist craftsmanship. Note the mosaics, stained glass, marquetry and sculptures. Of course, these were done by the leading artisans of the day, including **Eusebi Arnau** and **Alfons Juyol** (sculptors), **Antoni Serra i Fiter** (ceramics), **Rigalt i Granell** (glass), **Escofet** (floors), **Mario Maragliano** and **Lluís Bru** (mosaics) and **Gaspar Homar** (furnishings and interior decor). In 1906 the building won first prize in the municipal architectural contest. Unfortunately, the ground- and first-floor facades, which once featured magnificent sculptures by Arnau, were severely mutilated in 1943 when remodelling took place for the installation of the luxurious **Loewe** shop. The first floor, originally the residential quarters of the family who owned the building and, therefore, the foremost element of the complex, has since 1987 been the headquarters of the

CHRIS MIDDOUR

Stained glass window, Casa Lleó Morera

Patronat de Turisme, making it possible for you to see some of the Modernist artistry and at the same time pick up some literature about the city. But be discreet. This is not a tourist information office catering to the general public, although it is open to the general public. ♦ Pg Gràcia, 35 (C Consell de Cent) 215.44.77

Within Casa Lleó Morera:

Loewe The Loewe family has been arbiters of classic Spanish good taste for some 150 years. The current proprietors are the 3rd- and 4th-generation heirs of German immigrant **Enrique Loewe Rossberg**, who in 1846 opened a small leather goods store in Spain. Today Loewe, a name-brand symbol of Spanish luxury, has 2 factories, a network of stores around the world, 900 employees, and, judging from our last visit, a long list of Japanese customers in town on business or holiday. ♦ 216.04.00. Also at: Juan Sebastián Bach, 8. 202.36.76; Hotel Princesa Sofía, Pl Pío XII s/n. 330.64.16

29 **Casa Ramon Mulleras** (1868, **Pau Martorell**; remodelled 1911, **Enric Sagnier i Villavecchia**) The **Mançana de la Discòrdia** (Block of Discord), which stretches along the Pg Gràcia between C Consell de Cent and C D'Aragó, was thus dubbed because it accommodates a mixture of Modernist styles by the most outstanding and prolific masters of the day—**Domènech i Montaner** (**Casa Lleó Morera**), **Puig i Cadaflach** (**Casa Amatller**) and **Antoni Gaudí** (**Casa Batlló**). When Sagnier remodelled Casa Ramon Mulleras, the last 2 of these had already been completed. Sagnier—the fourth *master* on the block—completely re-did the facade, adopting, perhaps in counterpoint to his peers, a more Classical and sober stance both without and within that significantly deviates from the stylistic tenor of other works he carried out during the same period. The facade gallery here is remarkable, as are the large hall and main staircase within. The delicate *sgraffito* work depicts dancing ladies. As this is now an apartment house, only the vestibule can be visited. ♦ Pg Gràcia, 37 (C Consell de Cent-C D'Aragó)

Esquerra de L'Eixample

EDITORIAL TEIDE

Casa Lleó Morera   *Casa Amatller*   *Casa Batlló*
(before 1943)

REGIA

30 Museu del Perfume In front this looks like just another *perfumería*—the **Perfumeria Regia** to be exact. But as so often happens in Barcelona, the facade masks buried treasure within. If you ask to see the perfume museum, someone will accompany you to the back of the store and turn on the lights. There you will find over 5000 perfume bottles dating back to the Egyptian days of AD 3000 **Sr. Ramon Planas**, proprietor of the perfumería, began this priceless collection back in 1961. Notable among his collection of commercial bottles, which began to appear at the beginning of the 19th century, is one designed by **Dalí** for **Schiaparelli** in 1942 and fashioned in Baccarat crystal. The wall along the passageway leading to the musuem displays photos of important perfumers of our century. ♦ No admission. Pg Gràcia, 39 (C Consell de Cent-C D'Aragó) 216.01.21

30 Casa Amatller (1875, **Antoni Robert**; remodelled 1900, **Josep Puig i Cadafalch**; vestibule restoration 1989, **Rafael Vila**) The first of the striking structures of the **Mançana de Discòrdia** to emerge from the comprehensive reformation of an already existing structure, Casa Amatller was commissioned by chocolatier **Antoni Amatller**, whose daughter **Teresa** founded the **Institut Amatller d'Art Hispànic**, housed within, in 1942. The sculptures are again the work of **Eusebi Arnau** and **Alfons**

Esquerra de L'Eixample

Juyol. As with almost all of Puig's works, this one mixes elements of the Catalan Gothic (note the style of the arches) with northern European influences (note the crowning finish of the facade) and the naturalist elements typical of Modernism (note the sculptures, ceramics and wrought iron). Certainly the facade here, culminating in a crow-stepped gable, suggests a Dutch or Flemish silhouette of sorts. Also notice the Catalan nationalist theme of Sant Jordi fighting the dragon on the facade. On the first floor (where the Institut is) you'll find some Arnau sculptures and on the top floor some beautiful decorative woodwork by **Gaspar Homar**. You can visit the vestibule and the Institut (M-F 10AM-2PM, 4-8PM). ♦ No admission. Pg Gràcia, 41 (C Consell de Cent-C D'Aragó) 216.01.75

30 Casa Batlló (1906, **Antoni Gaudí i Cornet**) The name Batlló features in many Modernist houses in the Eixample, as this family was one of the leading textile manufacturers of the day. Here Gaudí effectively transformed the building originally erected in 1877 by architect **Emili Sala i Corté**. He added a 5th floor and basements and dramatically altered all the other floors and the facade. With the help of such illustrious collaborators as **Josep M. Jujol** (who authored the abstract composition that covers the Casa Battló and is fashioned of sculptured stone from Montjuïc) and **Joan Rubió i Bellver**, Gaudí created one of the Eixample's most charismatic structures. As he had begun to do in the **Casa Calvet**, he personally took charge here of designing all the elements the project entailed, from the facade to the furnishings, some of which are now on display in the **Casa-Museu Gaudí** in **Parc Güell**. The undulating facade with its distinctive jaw-like, cast-iron balconies is sprinkled with *trencadís* (broken bits of ceramics) and ceramic discs of varying diameter. The garret is finished in fish-scale tiles of various colors and tones. The staircase linking the top floor and the garret terminates in a bulbous shape coated with Mallorcan ceramics and topped off with the characteristic 4-armed cross. Inside, the patio staircase that reaches the roof becomes increasingly smaller as the ceramic decoration fades downward from dark blue to almost white so that the light from the skylight is more evenly distributed. On the roof itself you'll find Gaudí's unique chimneys. Much of Gaudí's original interior decor remains,

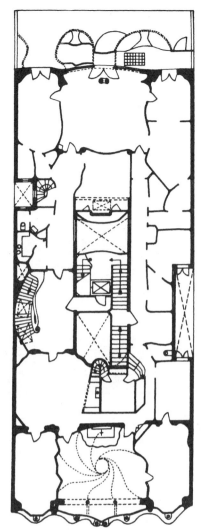

Casa Batlló floor plan

especially on the first floor. You can arrange to see the interior M-F 8AM-10PM by calling the **Cátedra Gaudí** (204.52.50, 8AM-2PM) for an appointment. ♦ Pg Gràcia, 43 (C D'Aragó)

31 Casa Dolors Calm (1902, **Josep Vilaseca i Casanovas**) Elaborate *sgraffito* ornamentation flanks the unitary protruding gallery that was part of Vilaseca's renovation of this 1879 structure by **Josep Déu Busquets**. Vilaseca designed the carpentry work of the gallery, the *sgraffito* decoration, and the sculptural elements found on the ground floor and the cornice, the latter regrettably mutilated by a later modification. The ground floor houses a hardware store and the prestigious **Galería Joan Prats** (daily 10AM-1:30PM, 5-8:30PM), an art gallery established in 1845. Above are apartments. ♦ Rambla Catalunya, 54 (C Consell de Cent-C D'Aragó)

A painter and graphic artist, **Joan Miró** also designed ceramics and stage sets.

31 Forn de Sant Jaume Dating from the 19th century, this purveyor of some of Barcelona's finest chocolates and bonbons started out making bread. After occupying several sites around town, it settled in here where its tempting sweets are made and sold on the premises, as are the homemade *horchata* (a drink made from the *chufa* nut) and ice creams. The adjoining cafeteria, specializing in croissants—plain or stuffed with your choice of chocolate, cheese, foie gras or ham—is an excellent spot for breakfast. ♦ Rambla Catalunya, 50 (C Consell de Cent-C D'Aragó) 216.02.29

32 Orotava ★★★$$$$ Owner **José María Luna** greets everyone here with his own convivial brand of exuberance. Situated in a block lined with art galleries, Orotava exudes a certain artistic flair of its own. More than 60 years old, the restaurant was founded by Luna's father. Some original works by **Miró, Dalí** and **Picasso** mingle with the bohemian-Baroque decor. Seafood and game are the culinary pillars of the menu embellished with varying inventions of Luna's own devising. Tuesday, Friday and Saturday entertainment is part of the evening dining experience. On Saturday at lunch there is a special reduced-price menu for children aimed at grooming them

Esquerra de L'Eixample

to become discriminating gourmets. ♦ Seafood/Game ♦ C Consell de Cent, 335 (Rambla Catalunya) Reservations essential. 302.31.28

33 Casa Antoni Miquel (1888, **Antoni Rovira i Rabassa**; remodelled ca 1900, **Jeroni F. Granell i Manresa**) Around 1900 many facades in the central Eixample area were improved and enriched in an effusive Modernist vein. In remodelling this structure, Granell added the double, protruding galleries with polychromatic glasswork (originally topped by small cupolas), the curved cornice, and the *sgraffito* work—all design elements that regularly featured in the Modernist works of this architect. Today it is an apartment house. ♦ C Balmeš, 54 (C Consell de Cent-C D'Aragó)

Restaurants/Nightlife: Red   **Hotels:** Blue
Shops/Parks: Green   **Sights/Culture:** Black

ALTAÏR

34 **Altaïr Força** This top bookstore for travel books and guidebooks (in a variety of languages) and books on nautical themes believes in practicing what it preaches, so it also rents yachts, sailboats and motorboats, with or without captain. ♦ C Balmes, 69 (C D'Aragó-C València) 254.29.66

35 **Trau** The Trau boutiques are preferred by Barcelona's most elegantly dressed women. Haute fashion confections by Montana, Romeo Gigli and Purificación García are the mainstays of its modish offering. ♦ C València, 260 (Rambla Catalunya) 215.15.77. Also at: C Fernando Agulló, 6. 201.32.68; Bulevard Rosa Pedralbes, Av Diagonal, 609. 419.51.11

35 **Leoni** Next door to **Trau**, similarly timely fashions for men. ♦ C València, 260 (R Catalunya-Pg Gràcia) 215.36.49

35 **Artespaña** A showcase for Spain's artisans in all imaginable genres, Artespaña is a nationwide chain. Ceramics quickly come to mind, of course, but there is much, much more here, and it's all first rate. ♦ Rambla Catalunya, 75 (C València) 215.61.46

36 **Fundació Antoni Tàpies** (1886, Lluís Domènech i Montaner; restoration and modernization 1990, **Roser Amadó** and **Lluís Domènech**) The former publishing headquarters of the **Editorial Montaner i Simón**, this buildings vies with Gaudí's **Casa Vicens** for the honor of being the

Esquerra de L'Eixample

first Catalan Modernist building. Gaudí aside, Domènech i Montaner is one of the 4 or 5 most important European architects of the turn of the century. The supporting structure here is totally metallic—iron columns and steel beams—and the decoration combines *Mudéjar* motifs with symbols such as cogs and 5-pointed stars. The building's recent restoration paved the way for the installation of the Fundació Antoni Tàpies, a foundation created by the Catalan painter **Antoni Tàpies** in 1984 to promote the study and understanding of modern art and culture. It stages exhibitions of art from all over the world and engages in important scholarly research on 20th-century art. It also sponsors lectures and conferences. It physically comprises 3 exhibition rooms and a library. A hideous, tangled sculpture by Tàpies crowns the top. Among its holdings are,

of course, the world's finest and most complete collection of works by Tàpies, with representative masterpieces from every phase of his prolific career. The library gathers together literature and documentation on the art and artists of our century and includes an extensive archive of published and unpublished material on the work of Tàpies. In keeping with the founder's interest in the presentation of non-Western cultures, the library also includes an exhaustive collection of works devoted to the art and culture of the Orient. ♦ Admission. Tu-Su 11AM-8PM. C D'Aragó, 255 (Rambla Catalunya-Pg Gràcia) 487.03.15; fax 487.00.09

37 **El Bulevard Rosa** Comprised of over 100 diverse shops and eateries, this was Barcelona's first shopping mall. ♦ Pg Gràcia, 55 (C València-C D'Arago') 309.06.50. Also at: Av Diagonal, 470. 309.06.50; Av Diagonal, 611-615. 309.06.50

Within El Bulevard Rosa:

El Bulevard dels Antiquaris Over 70 shops devoted primarily to high-quality art and antiques.

37 **Tzazou** Mostly Moschino for women. ♦ Pg Gràcia, 59 (C València) 487.23.26

38 **Casa Domènech Estapà** (1909, **Josep Domènech Estapà**) Built by and for the architect himself, this house combines stone and brick in much the same way he used them in the **Fábrica de Gas** in Barceloneta. Here you'll find a lateral gallery balanced on the other side by a row of geminated windows and iron balconies running in between. The top 2 floors and the crowning gable were added later by **Josep Domènech Mansana**. The vestibule of this apartment house, which can be visited, is notable for the ornamental wood and acid-etched glass handiwork of the interior door. ♦ C València, 241 (Ptge Domingo-Rambla Catalunya)

Hotel Regente

39 **Hotel Regente** $$$ (1915, **Salvador Viñals i Sabaté**) Installed in the former apartment house **Casa Evarist Juncosa**, this building's current crown supporting the hotel sign was added later. What the original crown was like is no longer known, but the current one completely breaks the building's architectural consonance. A pleasant choice for bedding down, the Regente has a small swimming pool and sunbathing area on the roof. The 78 air-conditioned rooms are compact and contemporary and equipped with TVs and telephones. Parking on the premises. ♦ Rambla Catalunya, 76 (C València-C Mallorca) 215.25.70; fax 487.32.27

39 Casa Evarist Juncosa (1909, **Salvador Viñals i Sabaté**) Another Casa Evarist Juncosa, this one containing hints of **Gaudí**'s **Casa Calvet** in the treatment of the facade and hints of the architect **Sagnier** in the conception of the interior spaces and vestibule, which can be visited and is noteworthy for its ceiling, furnishings, wooden soffit, stairway, and the windows opening on to the patio—all rendered with great delicacy and artistic sensibility. ♦ Rambla Catalunya, 78 (C València-C Mallorca)

40 E. Fornet D'En Rossend One of the few places outside the Soviet Union where you'll find a bread line—and with good reason. For a quick, healthy snack, follow your nose to its fresh-baked breads (baked in the back), many of which are high in fiber. Also offers an assortment of snacks, pastries and sandwiches to go. In the business since 1927. ♦ Rambla Catalunya, 82 (C València-C Mallorca) 215.43.94. Also at: C Rossellón, 228. 215.14.47; Provença, 68. 230.55.54

40 Hostal-Residencia Windsor $ A pleasant, 15-room hostel where rooms without a WC and shower come 2 to a full exterior bath with tub. The rooms are clean and carpeted (the singles are very small, though), and the halls and TV room are elegantly appointed for this category of accommodation. ♦ Rambla Catalunya, 84 (C Mallorca) No credit cards. 215.11.98

41 Drugstore No, this is not a pharmacy, but an assortment of a dozen or so shops plus a bar, restaurant and supermarket—all open 24 hours a day every day. ♦ Pg Gràcia, 71 (C Mallorca) 209.65.97

42 Hotel Condes de Barcelona $$$ (1896, **Josep Vilaseca i Casanovas**) Installed in the **Casa Enric Battló** of Neo-Gothic inspiration, this sophisticated hotel opened in 1986. The composition and balance of the facades are impeccable in this structure that marks Vilaseca's earliest flirtation with the Modernist aesthetic, most evident in the lyrical, floral tilework of the top-floor buttresses. Despite extensive remodelling within, the hotel's facade is original (except that there used to be enclosed balconies along the chamferred corner). The real Conde de Barcelona (**King Juan Carlos'** father) checks in from time to time, as do other European aristocrats. Each of the 100 rooms has a balcony and the full set of upscale amenities. Plans are to add 80 more rooms by 1992. Don't miss having a peek at the original Modernist stairway within. ♦ Pg Gràcia, 75 (C Mallorca) 487.37.37; fax 216.08.35

42 Novecento Attention lovers of Art Nouveau and Art Deco! Specializes in antique jewelry. Prices range from reasonable to ridiculous. ♦ Pg Gràcia, 75 (C Mallorca) 215.11.83

43 Beverly Feldman Shoes—glittering, glamorous, gorgeous shoes by American designer Beverly Feldman. ♦ C Mallorca, 259 (Pg Gràcia) 487.03.83

43 Casa Angel Batlló (1896, **Josep Vilaseca i Casanovas**) The 6 crowning arches correspond to 3 identical buildings successfully camouflaged by a completely homogeneous facade. The largest project this architect undertook for the Battló family, these structures now house the **George G. Byron Cockteleria** along with numerous apartments. ♦ C Mallorca, 253-257 (Pg Gràcia-Rambla Catalunya)

43 Hostal-Residencia Ciudad Condal $ Housed within the **Casa Angel Batlló**, this economical hostel offers a mere 11 rooms that are scrubbed sparkling clean. Streetside rooms have balconies; interior rooms overlook a garden. The singles have showers and WCs only; the doubles have complete baths. ♦ C Mallorca, 255 (Pg Gràcia-Rambla Catalunya) No credit cards. 215.10.40

•PER UOMO•
LA MAGLIA

43 Per Uomo Fine men's fashions including such timely trademarks as Brooksfield, Hugo Boss, Moschino, Henry Lloyd, Harry & Moore, and Michelsons. ♦ C Mallorca, 251 (Pg Gràcia-Rambla Catalunya) 487.00.14. Also at: C Calvet, 51. 201.37.69

••••
ALEXANDRA
HOTEL

43 Alexandra Hotel $$$ When this hotel was redone just a few years ago, municipal decree required its vintage facade to be reconstructed

Esquerra de L'Eixample

to its original aspect, although the facade truly pales in comparison to most of this barrio's Modernist wonders. The current interior design is the work of **Gaudí** follower **Joan Pera**. The 75 rooms, all doubles, are equipped with full baths, air-conditioning, satellite TVs, and music. The buffet breakfast is one of the best and most extensive we've come across anywhere. Parking on the premises. ♦ C Mallorca, 251 (Pg Gràcia-Rambla Catalunya) 487.05.05; fax 216.06.06

43 Ocre A great place for gift items ranging from the ultra-sleek to the tongue-in-cheek, from the ultra-practical to practical jokes. ♦ C Mallorca, 251 (Pg Gràcia-Rambla Catalunya) 215.30.09. Also at: C Marià Cubí, 193. 201.14.27

Restaurants/Nightlife: Red   Hotels: Blue
Shops/Parks: Green   Sights/Culture: Black

44 Alfredo Villalba This women's fashion store offers a small, select collection by the designer whose name it bears. He is from Málaga, but lives and works in Madrid. His sumptuous and exclusive designs are executed in the finest materials from Italy. The *look* is one of refinement, elegance, feminity and sensuality. Each design is produced in very limited numbers, so if you don't like dressing like everyone else, this is a good place to shop. ♦ Rambla Catalunya, 88 (C Mallorca) 215.05.42

45 doncarlos A sophisticated fashion outlet for women featuring mostly Italian labels. Byblos gets the majority of the retail votes here, followed by Les Copains and Vis à Vis. The space is spacious and chic, the line of accessories superb. ♦ C Mallorca, 236 (Rambla Catalunya) 216.04.07

46 Casas Joan B. Pons (1909, **Joan B. Pons i Trabal**) This unit is comprised of 2 buildings of different dimensions treated as one. Its affinity with the nearby buildings at Nos. 85-87 bears mentioning since, despite being by different architects, their balconies and ground-floor treatments are quite similar. All the elements of the facade—the stained-glass windows, the sinuous, wrought-iron railings—are ornamented with vegetable motifs. The buildings house apartments and the **Centre Medic Veterinari de Barcelona** (Barcelona Veterinary Center). ♦ C Balmes 81-81 bis (C València)

46 Casas Frederic Vallet Xiró (1910, **Josep Barenys i Gambús**) Together with the **Casa Joan B. Pons** and the neighboring **Casa Jaume Larcegui** (No. 83), these 2 houses form quite an architecturally homogeneous unit, which was more homogeneous before their ground floors were substantially modified. All are now regrettably gloomy with soot. ♦ C Balmes, 85-87 (C València-C Mallorca)

47 El Caballito Blanco ★$$$ Simple, home-style fare in a simple setting. Typical dishes include *macarrones al gratén* (a local version

Esquerra de L'Eixample

of macaroni and cheese), canelones, *garbanzos estofados* (chickpea stew), grilled sea bass and beef stew. ♦ International ♦ C Mallorca, 196 (C D'Aribau) 253.10.33

48 Sí Senyor ★★★$$ The contemporary decor

with elegant booths suggests a sophisticated diner; but the food and wine list are first-class. If you want to treat your palate to a fine Catalan wine, request the Gran Toc de Cavas Hill, a wine produced in limited quantities in a small family vineyard founded last century. It goes especially well with one of the house specialties that you must try—the *arroz negre* (black rice) prepared with squid ink. ♦ Catalan/International ♦ C Mallorca, 199 (C D'Enric Granados-C D'Aribau) 453.21.49

48 El Bodegon ★$$$ Modest decor and simple cooking are featured at this informal neighborhood restaurant. Some of the dishes sport humorous names, like the *minifalda* (miniskirt)—an assortment of salads. We recommend the *cogollos de Tudela con anchoas* (lettuce hearts with anchovies), *ensalada de pulpo* (octopus salad), *estofado de patatas con sepia* (potato-and-cuttlefish stew), clams, *callos* (tripe) and *costillitas de cordero* (tiny lamb chops). ♦ Seafood/Spanish ♦ C Mallorca, 197 (C D'Aribau) 253.10.17

49 La Raspa $$ Since the food is nothing special, you might want to pop in just for a drink to have a look at the downstairs decor—the walls are completely covered with scenes recalling seaside Barcelona at the turn of the century. ♦ Seafood ♦ C Mallorca, 188 (C D'Aribau-C Muntaner) 451.16.31

50 Ideal Cocktail Bar Since 1931 this cozy bar has been quenching the thirst of the city's citizens and visiting businesspeople. The decor is reminiscent of an elegant English pub. The house *cava* is nice and dry and sometimes they serve Moet & Chandon by the glass. Stop by before or after dinner or for an aperitif before lunch. ♦ C D'Aribau, 89 (C Mallorca) 253.10.28

50 Tasca Marcelino ★★$$ An authentic, old-fashioned restaurant where the flavor of days gone by lingers in the food and decor. Savory *tapas* line the downstairs bar, and the display case is full of fresh fish and whole roasted chickens. Come here for breakfast, lunch, dinner or in between. There are tables upstairs for complete repasts and, in summer, a handful of tables outside where you'll likely find a mixed clientele oohing and aahing over the *caracoles de mar o de montaña picantes* (sea snails or spicy mountain snails), grilled sardines, assorted fried fish, *butifarra con judías* (Catalan sausage and beans) and *conejo con all i oli* (rabbit with garlic mayonnaise). ♦ C D'Aribau, 89 (C Mallorca) 253.10.91

51 Da Daviano ★★★$$$ A family greeting awaits all comers to Da Daviano, one of Barcelona's favorite Italian restaurants. The bar and salon below are reserved for sandwiches. The few tables upstairs have a kitchen view. It's best to begin with a plate of Parma ham and other assorted Italian charcuterie. Then choose among the wonderful assortment of pastas, risotti, *saltimboca a la romana* or *escalopinas alla pizzaiola*. A few grilled meat and fish offerings round out the menu. The homemade tiramisu is to die for. ♦ Italian ♦ C D'Aribau, 90 (C Mallorca) 253.98.33

52 Chicoa ★★$$$ The decor is rustic, the clientele loyal. Most begin with the *entremeses de mariscos fríos* (hors d'oeuvres of assorted cold shellfish), *fideos negros con sepia* (black noodles with cuttlefish), or *el refrito de frijoles con anchoas* (refried beans with anchovies) and then go on to the *suquet de langosta* (lobster stew), *calamares y almejas* (squid and clams), or any of the versions of *bacalao* (codfish). ♦ Spanish ♦ C D'Aribau, 71 (C Mallorca-C València) 253.11.23

53 El Rey ★★★$$$$ Here part of the menu greets you live and in person in the form of fish and shellfish that will soon be grilled, fried, sautéed, sauced or eaten raw—as you like. If you're in the mood for something more complex, try the *arroz negro con sepia* (black rice with cuttlefish), canelones with shellfish and fish, *merluza* (hake) with anchovy sauce, or *dorada* (a Mediterranean fish) baked in salt. ♦ Seafood ♦ C València, 204 (C D'Aribau) 253.49.85

54 Muffins ★★$$$ Basically the same menu as **Chicoa** around the corner (the owners are the same), except that some of the orchestrations are more sophisticated here. Likewise the decor. Try the *tallarines con verdura and marisco* (pasta with vegetables and shellfish), *calamarcitos rellenos de gambas* (small squid stuffed with shrimp) and the different versions of *bacalao* (codfish). ♦ Spanish ♦ C València, 210 (C D'Aribau) 254.02.21

55 Yamadori ★★★$$$ The first and still one of the best of Barcelona's Japanese restaurants. You'll find a sushi bar and a menu of typical Japanese fare, some of which is rendered with a slight Spanish accent. ♦ Japanese ♦ C D'Aribau, 68 (C València) 253.92.64

56 Sibarit ★★$$$$ Somewhat pretentious of decor and pompous of menu, this restaurant's regrettable first impression is soon mitigated by the success of its cuisine. You can't go wrong with *ensalada de setas y langostinos* (salad with mushrooms and prawns), marinated salmon, goose foie gras with port wine, *lubina* (sea bass) with fennel, steak tartare—or the wine list. You might want to pass on the lackluster desserts. ♦ International ♦ C D'Aribau, 65 (C València) 253.93.03

57 Hotel Dante $$$ The 81 spotless rooms here each have a bath, air conditioning, color satellite TV, video, minibar, telephone, music and 24-hour bar and room service. The eclectic room furnishings are from an assortment of stylistic eras. Parking available. ♦ C Mallorca, 181 (C D'Aribau-C Muntaner) 323.22.54; fax 323.74.72

58 Hotel Ficus $$ Another spotless hotel that makes a good first impression. Its 85 rooms with tiled floors are outfitted with telephones and televisions. The 6th and 7th floors have 3 choice rooms with terraces facing the street. ♦ C Mallorca, 163 (C Muntaner-C Casanova) 253.35.00; fax 451.18.38

59 Hotel Master $$$ This simple and sophisticated businessperson's hotel offers 84 airconditioned rooms with minibar, telephones (in the bath too), TV, and books for bedtime reading. There is parking too. ♦ C València, 105 (C Villarroel-C Comte D'Urgell) 323.62.15; fax 323.43.89

60 Universitat Industrial (factory Batlló 1875, **Rafael Guastavino i Moreno**; adaptation and new buildings 1931, **Joan Rubió i Bellvér**) The conspicuous 230-foot-high brick chimney here is one of the vestiges of the old embroidery factory of the family Batlló, whose textile installations occupied this site until 1895.

Esquerra de L'Eixample

Though there have been many transformations since, some original features remain— the 5-story structure that housed the looms and the subterranean structure of the current **Escola D'Enginyeria Tècnica** (School of Technical Engineering). At the beginning of our century the city acquired the Batlló complex for the establishment of the **Centro General de Enseñanza Tècnica** (Center for General Technical Instruction), and instead of tearing down the old buildings as originally planned, they were rehabilitated beginning in 1915 and complemented by new constructions later on. You can freely walk inside this university complex, although in some buildings access depends on the good mood or good will of the people in charge. ♦ Bounded by C Comte D'Urgell-C Rosselló-C Villaroel-C París

61 Hotel Nuñez Urgel $$$ This rather unpre-possessing hotel offers 121 surprisingly comfortable rooms with baths, air-conditioning, phones, music and TVs. There are parking facilities and a restaurant and bar on the premises. ♦ C Comte D'Urgell, 232 (C Còrsega-C París) 322.41.53; fax 419.01.06

62 Xix Kebab ★★★$$$ The culinary roots here are Syrian, so this is *the* place to come for *mezzes* (an assortment of cold appetizers that can be a meal in itself), hummus, marinated chicken and lamb, and lamb shish kebab. Only the couscous is of little interest. ♦ Syrian ♦ C Còrsega, 193 (C Villarroel-C Casanova) 321.82.10

63 Il Commendatore ★$$ A restaurant-pizzeria whose decor imitates, down to clothing hanging from a washline, the aspect of an Italian street. The pizzas and pastas are good enough to cause long lines to form outside the door on Friday and Saturday nights. ♦ Italian ♦ C Comte D'Urgell, 247 (C Buenos Aires-C Londres) 322.55.53

64 Dragon Inn ★★★$$$ Reputed to serve the best Chinese food in the city, the Dragon Inn respects tradition but is not afraid of innovation. Among the classics, you'll find won ton soup and Peking duck; among the innovations, various fish and shellfish dishes deliciously seasoned—like the *mariscos fritos con mantequilla* (shellfish fried in butter), the steamed fish, *calamares fritos con jengibre y cebollitas* (squid fried with ginger and little onions), *langostinos con salasa de tomillo* (prawns in a thyme sauce), *cangrejo al horno con jengibre y cebollitas* (oven-baked crab with ginger and little onions), and prawns sautéed with ginger. For dessert try the *buñuelos de plátano y manzana* (banana-and-apple dumplings) or the caramelized apple. The decor is agreeably elegant and exotic. ♦ Chinese ♦ C Buenos Aires, 12-14 (C Comte Borell-C Comte D'Urgell) 419.19.29

Esquerra de L'Eixample

65 Jean Pierre Bua Fashion victims take note. Jean Pierre Bua and his loyal partner **Luis Balagué** have become famous by dressing Barcelona's vanguard. Every season they comb Europe for new designing talents in men's and women's fashions. ♦ Av Diagonal, 469 (C Villarroel) 439.71.00

66 Fancy Men Here men can dress themselves from head to toe in Gianni Versace, Gianfranco Ferrè, Missoni and Les Copains. ♦ Av Diagonal, 463 (C Villarroel-C Casanova) 430.64.20

Barcelona's premier festivals, the **fiestas de la Mercé**, honor one of Barcelona's 2 patron saints, the Virgin of Mercy. Held the week of 24 September, they entail a series of concerts, theatrical performances, parades, and other public displays of glee that crescendo to a grand finale involving music and fireworks.

66 Next Door Very exclusive, sophisticated and elegant designs for men. Also lines of casual wear imported from Italy, France and England and underwritten by such up-to-the-minute names as New York, Paul Smith and Homme faible et merveilleux, one of France's most amusing and creative brand names. ♦ Av Diagonal, 461 (C Villarroel-C Casanova) 439.59.28

67 Casa Company (1911, **Josep Puig i Cadafalch**) This single-family house is clearly unusual among Eixample buildings for its more traditional, house-like profile. It also tests the chronological and conceptual borders of Modernism, since some consider it a clearly *Noucentista* (an architectural blend of Modernism and stylized Classicism) structure. Although it belongs to Puig's so-called *white period*—characterized by modest, simple lines and layouts and decorative restraint—most experts feel this has nothing at all to do with the *Mediterraneanism* of *Noucentisme* but, in this case, rather more with the forms of Viennese Secessionism. There is remarkable ironwork on the windows and figurative *sgraffito* work on the gables that depicts the Assumption of the Virgen and garlands of flowers. In 1940 **Dr. Melcior Colet** installed his gynecological practice here and had the interior redone by **Santiago Marco Urrutia**, a prestigious furniture designer and interior decorator who was in the forefront of the vanguard movement in his field. The building now houses the **Museu de l'Esport Melcior Colet** (a sports museum). ♦ M-Th 10AM-2PM, 4-7PM. C Casanova, 203 (C Buenos Aires)

68 Grand Passage Suites Hotel $$$ Converted in February 1990 from an apartment house to a hotel, all the rooms here (which, as the name indicates, are suites) are outfitted with all the state-of-the-art comforts. And there's a garage. ♦ C Muntaner, 212 (C Londres) 201.03.06; fax 201.00.04. Reservations can also be made through Marketing Ahead, 433 5th Ave, New York NY 10016. 212/686.9213; fax 212/686.0271

Within the Grand Passage Suites Hotel:

Cafe de Londres ★★★$$$ First feast your eyes on the trendy decor and the '70s paintings by **Guinovart** that give the place its unique personality. Then feast on the food, which is better than that found in some of the fancier, higher-priced establishments around town. The cuisine of chef **Antonio Pacheco** is modern but devoid of useless frills. Some recommendations: the *canelones de pescado y marisco* (with fish and seafood), *ensalada de*

lengua de corderito lechal y lentejas (salad of baby lamb's tongue and lentils), *calabacines rellenos de oca al queso* (zucchini stuffed with goose and topped with cheese), salmon carpaccio, *solomillo de buey a la salsa de pimientos rojos* (filet of beef with red-pepper sauce), *pollo al curry* (curry chicken), *troceado de corderito a la menta fresca* (minced lamb with fresh mint) and *albóndigas de pescado con guisantes y almejas* (fish balls with peas and clams). ♦ Eclectic ♦ C Londres, 103 (C Muntaner) 414.15.55

69 El Barkito ★$$ This restaurant's name (*the little boat*), its facade, and its nautical decor are big tip-offs as to what you're likely to eat here. The cooking is simple and sincere. Some things to try: the *pimientos piquitos con anchoas de la Escala* (chopped peppers with anchovies), *pulpo vinagreta* (octopus vinaigrette), *navajas a la plancha con ajo y perejil* (grilled razor clams with garlic and parsley), fried fish, *dátiles de mar* (a Mediterranean shellfish not found on most menus, so you really should try it here) and the sardines. ♦ Seafood ♦ C Còrsega, 225 (C Muntaner) 430.51.60

70 Zsa Zsa No, the Persian carpets at the entrance do not signal a rug merchant, just a tony, trendy cocktail bar with corresponding clientele and rickety tables fashioned of trays. ♦ C Rosselló, 156 (C Muntaner-C D'Aribau) 253.85.66

71 La Mercantil Peixatera ★★$$ Occupying the former premises of a garage for repairing cars, this spacious restaurant is open and lofty. It's also a great place to come for a full meal or for noshing on small plates of anchovies, fried fish or grilled *gambas* (shrimp). ♦ Seafood ♦ C D'Aribau, 117 (C Provença-C Rosselló) 253.35.99

72 La Fira The highly original decor of this bar incorporates much of the old paraphernalia from the former **Apolo** amusement park that once existed in Av Paral.lel. At the bar you can sit on chain swings or old seats from rides.

In the back there is a *churrería* offering candy, popcorn and other assorted snacks. There is also a fascinating collection of automated penny-arcade machines, some of which work. All this plus Phil Collins, George Michael and their top-10 contemporaries providing the musical backdrop. The crowd is young, but the imaginative decor is worth a look no matter how old you are. ♦ C Provença, 171 (C Muntaner-C D'Aribau) 323.72.71

73 La Xampanyería A romantic spot to sample more than 40 different *cavas* and champagnes and perhaps nibble some pâté or chocolate. ♦ C Provença, 236 (C D'Enric Granados) 253.74.55

74 Els Balcons ★★$$ This restaurant is located one flight up behind what appears to be the door to an ordinary apartment. Formerly this was the photographic studio of **Blay Saura Cirere**, the owner, whose wife is in charge of culinary matters. Saura's children are involved in art, architecture and design, and many of the city's leading architects frequent this simple restaurant with clean, modern lines. The artwork on the walls is by one of Saura's daughters. Notable among the many fine dishes on the menu are the *macarrones al pescado* (with small pieces of shrimp and angler fish) and the *calamares con chocolate* (squid in a delicate chocolate sauce)—an interesting contrast of flavors. ♦ Pasta/Seafood ♦ C Provença, 203 (C Balmes-C D'Enric Granados) 254.60.83

75 Casa Esteve Recolons (1905, **Pere Bassegoda i Mateu**) The lower floors of this apartment house are attractively adorned with graceful balconies entwined with wrought-iron

Esquerra de L'Eixample

flowers that are, however, not noticeably Modernist. The top floor and gable flourishes are, though. Worthy of a passing glimpse are the vestibule, finely crafted doors, ceilings and elevator—a veritable symphony of wood, iron and glass. ♦ C Rosselló, 192 (C D'Enric Granados)

76 La Avenida Another mall tucked away like pirate treasure behind a portal giving no clue as to what lies within. Although a mall is a mall is a mall, check out the curiosities at **Zabriskie**. ♦ C Rosselló, 233 (C Balmes-Rambla Catalunya)

77 Spaghetti Express $ McDonald's goes Italian at this self-service restaurant featuring fresh pastas. ♦ C Rosselló, 239 (Rambla Catalunya) 238.22.16

Restaurants/Nightlife: Red   **Hotels:** Blue
Shops/Parks: Green   **Sights/Culture:** Black

78 Nick Havanna Though the high-tech decor by **Eduard Samsó** and **Alfredo Arribas** is strictly '80s, this remains a *must* on the '90s nightlife scene. Everyone from the upscale walks of life drops in at some point during the weekend when you can barely squeeze in one more yuppie at the bar. Has the dubious distinction of starting the trend for ever trendier bathrooms. ◆ C Rosselló, 208 (C Balmes-Rambla Catalunya) 215.65.91

79 Aramis Installed within the **Casa Manuel Verdú** (1903, **Maurici Augé i Robert**), this shopping stop is urged if your tastes are classic and your money coffers overfloweth. ◆ Rambla Catalunya, 103 (C Provença) 215.16.69

80 Casas Pilar y Josefa Albiñana de Regàs (ca 1898, **Francesc Berenguer i Mestres**) These 2 identical houses once owned by 2 sisters have undergone a radical face-lift. At street level you'll find one of Barcelona's leading outlets for intimate apparel, **Santacana** (215.04.84). La Perla is the high-priced trademark of choice here. ◆ Rambla Catalunya 92-94 (C Mallorca-C Provença)

80 Casa Ferran Cortés (1902, **Enric Sagnier i Villavecchia**) The only survivor of a group of 3 identical houses that first employed elements of Barcelona's budding Modernist movement. The original undulating crown was lost during a renovation. ◆ Rambla Catalunya, 96 (C Mallorca-C Provença)

81 La Bodegueta A lingering antique outpost in the increasingly trendy, state-of-the-art Eixample. A limited selection of sandwiches and tapas are served at 3 or 4 small tables, and above the 4-stool bar are old liquor barrels which now serve decorative purposes only. Great for a pit stop. ◆ Rambla Catalunya, 100 (C Provença) 215.48.94

81 Groc For over 20 years the designs of **Toni Miró** have been a popular favorite with the men and women of Catalunya's upper class

Esquerra de L'Eixample

and artistocracy. He favors natural fibers and offers pret-a-porter as well as custom tailoring. ◆ Rambla Catalunya, 100 bis (C Provença) 215.74.74

82 Sargadelos The imaginative, colorful, hand-painted porcelain sold here is straight from the factory in the Galician village of Sargadelos. As this is the factory's own store, the selection here is the most extensive and the prices are the lowest. ◆ C Provença, 274 (Rambla Catalunya) 215.01.79

83 Llibreria Francesa A good selection of books on myriad subjects in various languages and a good place to find polyglot material on Barcelona. Why *Francesa*? The owners are French, it seems, nothing more. ◆ Pg Gràcia, 91 (C Provença). 215.14.17

83 Adolfo Domínguez One of Spain's leading designers in recent years, Domínguez came to attention in the US when he designed **Don Johnson**'s *Miami Vice* TV wardrobe for a season. In essence, he is Spain's Armani, a designer who revolutionized male attire with his distinctive angular design statements. He offers similarly unattractive designs for women. ◆ Pg Gràcia, 89 (C Provença) 215.13.39

84 Mauri Established in 1939, this 4-in-one emporium in a 100-year-old building is part pastisserie, *bomboneria* (candy store), *saló de te* (tea room) and *xarcuteria* (delicatessen). Its pastries, other sweets and ice creams are homemade. At the small cafe tucked between the pastry shop and the delicatessen you can sample the wares or have lunch (no dinner served). ◆ Rambla Catalunya, 102 (C Provença) 215.10.20

84 Casa Dolors Vidal de Sagnier (1894, **Enric Sagnier i Villavecchia**) For a time this was the architect's own house, and almost assuredly the windowed, Neo-Gothic upper gallery crowned by medallions was his studio. The lower gallery was a 1906 addition by the architect himself. Most striking is the burgundy-and-yellow facade graced with a figure carrying the Greek letter *omega*. ◆ Rambla Catalunya, 104 (C Provença-Ptge Concepció)

85 Casa Antónia Costa (1904, **Josep Domènech i Estapà**) Within the Modernist movement, Domènech i Estapà projected a highly personal vision. Rooted in eclecticism and incorporating elements from the vanguard, his works exhibit an individualistic style. Within the central Eixample, this is probably his most representative residential work. One highly characteristic element that often distinguishes his designs can be found here—the circular forms used to finish off the building. But even more interesting is the introduction of 2 covered galleries extending upward from the 2nd floor and creating a kind of *double facade*. More so than some of his other works, this building is formally Modernist, an attempt to distill the functional and the grandiloquent modes that characterized his contribution to the **Palacio de Justicia** and his design of the **Catalana de Gas y Electricidad**. The vestibule of this apartment house is all you can visit. ◆ Rambla Catalunya, 122 (C Còrsega)

86 Casa Serra (1908, **Josep Puig i Cadafalch**) Winner in 1908 of the prize for the best building built in 1907 (it couldn't win the prize in 1907 since it wasn't finished yet). Radically transformed and mutilated by numerous modern interventions, all that remains of the original Casa Serra are the 2 wings that form an angle facing the Rambla Catalunya. In its day this was one of the best examples of a single-family Modernist *palacete* (mansion) with a significant garden along the Av Diagonal, which then was becoming a preferred address for the city's upper class. Nevertheless, the structure was never used as a single-family residence and ended up being adapted to house a religious secondary school. Between 1940 and 1950 the religious community that owned the building executed several expansions and, in 1966, wanted to tear the original structure down. After 15 years of tug of war among the owners, various citizens' and cultural groups, the city and state administrations, and the press, it was finally decided to tear down part of it (1981-82) and build another structure behind it. It was subsequently taken over by the city and adapted for municipal offices. Tidbits of the original work remain within, but are not accessible to public view. The sculpture work of the medallions and coats of arms on the door are by **Eusebi Arnau**. ♦ Rambla Catalunya, 126 (C Còrsega)

87 Bel Air ★★★$$$ A sophisticated restaurant specializing in market cuisine, rice dishes and stews—all rendered with a nouvelle touch when it comes to quantity and presentation. Installed in a turn-of-the-century mansion, this is a most pleasant dining experience all around. ♦ Catalan ♦ C Còrsega, 286 (Rambla Catalunya-C Balmes) 237.75.88

88 Casa Francesc Fargas (1911, **Francesc Fargas i Margenat**) Former owner and architect Fargas clearly evinced Secessionist tendencies here, especially in the sculptural treatment of the ground floor and the cornice, as well as in the design of the ornamental ironwork. ♦ C Balmes, 156 (C Còrsega-C París)

89 Velvet One of Barcelona's recent crop of trendy, *designer* bars, Velvet's decor is from the hand of **Alfredo Arribas**. There are 2 entrances, both unmarked and both highly imaginative. Don't miss the bathrooms or the bar stools shaped like buttocks. The DJ really mixes it up, playing everything from '60s to the latest rap. ♦ C Balmes, 161 (C Còrsega-C París) 227.67.14

90 Casa Paul Martí (1909, **Domènec Boada i Piera**) This very attractive structure in pastel green with charcoal grey shutters has nothing else particularly noteworthy about it. It is neither grandiose nor exuberant like the structures of the more central Eixample area—it is just plain pretty and, therefore, worthy of attention. ♦ C Còrsega, 271 (C D'Enric Granados-C Balmes)

91 Casa Francesc Cairó (1907, **Domènec Boada i Piera**) Though there is little unique about this Modernist building, except perhaps the vestibule, it is really too pretty to be missed, so keep an eye out for it. ♦ C D'Enric Granados, 106 (C Còrsega-C París)

92 Petit Paris ★★$$$ Don't let the name fool you. It's more reflective of the ambience and decor than the food. The featured cuisine is market-fresh Catalan and a good bet is the *solomillo* (sirloin steak). ♦ Catalan ♦ C París, 196 (C D'Enric Granados) 218.26.78

In 1520 Spain's first cookbook, the *Libre del Coc*, was published in Catalan.

93 Cristal Park Restaurant ★$$$ Chef **Enrique Fernández** specializes in steak tartare and terrine of shrimp and codfish. ♦ International ♦ C París, 192 (C D'Enric Granados-C D'Aribau) 217.06.27

94 Hotel Astoria $$$ Lodged in a classic-style building built in 1953, this hotel impresses with its 4 solid columns in the lobby. It was completely renovated in 1987, and all of the uncarpeted rooms are air-conditioned and have direct-dial phones and TVs with a video channel. Most of the rooms have separate sitting rooms with a sofa, and some have a windowed terrace. There are also 4 duplex rooms with separate sitting rooms upstairs. ♦ C París, 203 (C D'Enric Granados) 209.83.11; fax 202.30.08

95 Casa Miquel Sayrach (1918, **Manuel Sayrach i Carreras**) The architect of this singular structure was the son of the owner. One of the later Modernist structures in this area, it is clearly influenced by the work of Gaudí, particularly in the upper reaches. The hallway features interesting organic shapes, and on the first floor you'll find one of Barcelona's most select and pricey restaurants, **La Dama** (★★★$$$$), where the fine French-Catalan cuisine of **Josep Bullich** is served amidst an elegant Modernist decor. ♦ Av Diagonal, 423-425 (C D'Enric Granados)

96 Edifici Astòria (1934, **Germán Rodríguez Arias**) This building's composition is an interpretation of the work of one of the masters of

Esquerra de L'Eixample

the modern movement, **Walter Gropius**. It is also one of the most complex structures built in Spain at the time since besides being residential it incorporated a cinema and a bar. ♦ C París, 197-199 (C D'Aribau)

97 Casas A. Pascual y Cia (1913, **Antoni Millàs i Figuerola**) Of interest in these 2 structures are the Modernist decorative elements within. In the vestibule of No. 175 note the mosaic floor, the carved-wood banister, and the grillwork of the elevator. In No. 177 also note the elevator grillwork. ♦ C D'Aribau, 175-177 (C Londres)

Gaudí's Modernist residential masterpiece, **Casa Batlló**, was put on the block on 25 April 1991 for a mere $100 million. Not so extravagant considering that the owners have paid $3.5 million in upkeep over the past 3 decades.

98 Casas Sociedad Torres Hermanos (1906, **Jaume Torres i Grau**) These 3 contiguous structures are one of the best sets of Modernist buildings remaining in the city, although they are little known because their architect was not one of the movement's leading lights. The facade on the chamferred corner, built between 1905 and 1907, displays 5 planes with *sgraffiti* decoration separated by pilasters. The facade on C D'Aribau is crowned with a beautifully sinuous cornice. The facade on C Paris is reminiscent of **Gaudí**'s **Casa Calvet** built a few years earlier. Of interest are the vestibules (which can be visited), the patios within, and the pharmacy on the ground floor of the center building. ◆ C París 180-182 (C D'Aribau)

99 Casa Conrad Roure (1902, **Ferran Romeu i Ribot**) Conrad Roure—lawyer, comedian and journalist—commissioned Romeu—an architect of limited, but high-quality production—to create this uncharacteristically squat, 2-story building that seems out of place in the Eixample, especially given its subdued facade—very simple above and slightly more gregarious below. The entrance is embellished with a large arch containing 2 columns with floral capitals and decorative reliefs in a Gothic vein and an insignia bearing an oak—*roure* in Catalan—alluding to the building's proprietor. It is worth visiting the vestibule whose tilework incorporates a Renaissance design, revived by the architect **Antoni M. Gallissà** at the end of the 19th century, that became one of the most popular decorative motifs of Modernism. Until 1961 this building housed a Montessori school; now it houses the municipal **Escuela de Música** (School of Music). ◆ C D'Aribau, 155 (C París-C Còrsega)

99 Gregory's This bar's luxurious confines are popular among yuppies, executives and other assorted businesspeople. To facilitate the fun, the house organizes special parties—Monday is Lady's Night, Tuesday is Andalusian Night with *sevillanas* (a kind of flamenco folk dance) danced all around, and Thursday it's the

Esquerra de L'Eixample

rumba catalana (which is to say, a swinging time). ◆ C D'Aribau, 153 (C Còrsega-C París) 410.82.70

99 Maritim This spacious, cozy bar with rooms eponymously reminiscent of a boat is luxurious and comfortable...and romantic.
◆ C D'Aribau, 153 (C Còrsega-C París)

100 Quilombo There is live music every night at this wonderfully informal little club on one of Barcelona's most popular nightlife streets. The mostly ethnic music runs the gamut from flamenco to Andean and more. Feel free to sing along if you happen to know any of the tunes—or request one that you do. ◆ No cover. C Aribau, 149 (C Còrsega) 439.54.06

Restaurants/Nightlife: Red   **Hotels:** Blue
Shops/Parks: Green   **Sights/Culture:** Black

101 Koyuki ★★$$ Both visiting and resident Japanese with a yen for home-style dishes like mama used to make come here at lunch and dinner. The cuisine follows tradition: soups, sashimis, boiled fish, and noodle and rice dishes. ◆ Japanese ◆ C Còrsega, 242 (C D'Enric Granados) 237.84.90

102 Barcelona Divina ★$$$ More lively at dinner than at lunch, this restaurant's culinary aspirations exceed its technical grasp, but if you stick with more traditional, less complex fare you should do all right. For example, the *ensalada tibia de foie gras de pato y alcachofas* (warm salad of duck foie gras and artichokes), *suquet de pescado y marisco* (fish and shellfish stew), or *solomillo* (sirloin) with a grain mustard sauce. The c*oup de grace* desserts, however, are worthy of the restaurant's rather immodest name. Try the *bavarois de mango*, assortment of flavored flans, and *milhojas de fresitas con crema y coulis de frambuesa* (flaky pastry with strawberries and cream topped with a raspberry sauce). The wine cellar is good too. ◆ International ◆ C D'Aribau, 137 (C Còrsega-C Rosselló)

Barcelona Design

Barcelona first developed a taste for cutting-edge design in the heyday of Modernism at the turn of the century. Though it has never since relinquished its hold on the daring and the bold, the political vicissitudes of 20th-century Spain periodically put a damper on the city's artistic bent, although Barcelona did get away with a lot of things no other Spanish city could—avant-garde art exhibitions and the sale of condoms and banned books during the Franco era.

In the 1960s Barcelona once again began to make bold strides into the vanguard of industrial, graphic and interior design. All you have to do is take a look around to see that aesthetics matter in this city and that design pervades public and private life. On a municipal level this is evident in the roster of architects and sculptors re-shaping the urban profile—among them **Richard Meier, Ricardo Bofill, Arata Isozaki, Gae Aulenti, Victorio Gregotti, Beverly Pepper, Eduardo Chillida, Roy Lichtenstein** and **Ellsworth Kelly**—the numerous new and refurbished public parks, plazas, promenades and roadways; and the decoration and decor of countless shops, restaurants and clubs around town.

It is a most telling fact that almost all the winners of Spain's Ministry of Industry's National Design Prize in both the individual and corporate categories have been from Barcelona. In the world of furniture, some names to look for are **Josep Lluscá, Jorge Pensi, Gabriel Ordeig, Carlos Riart, Pete Sans, Alberto**

*Enric Satué,
logo for Up
& Down
nightclub*

Lievore and **Gabriel Teixidó**. In graphic design, **Enric Satué, América Sánchez, Yves Zimmermann, Carlos Rolando, Mario Esquenazi, Josep Maria Mir,**

Carlos Rolando, menu covers

Joaquim Nolla, Claret Serrahima, Francis Closas, Mercedes Azúa, Ricard Badía, Alfonso Sostres, Pati Núñez and **Josep Bagá**; in interior design, **Correa-Milá, Sòria-Garcés, Pau-IDP, Pep Cortés, Oriol Bohigas, Miguel Milá, Jordi Galí, Freixas-Argentí-Mirando, Piñón i Viaplana, Eduard Samsó, Alfredo Arribas** and **Oscar Tusquets**.

*América Sánchez,
logo for KGB
nightclub*

The man of the designing moment, however, is indisputably **Xavier Mariscal**. Born in Valencia in 1950, Mariscal began his career in Barcelona drawing and publishing comics that were considered *underground*. Later he branched out into illustration and the design of textile prints and furniture. He burst onto the international scene together with the mythical Memphis group in Milan and later through his participation in *Les avant-gardes de la fin du XXème siècle* at the **Centre Georges Pompidou** in Paris and the **Documenta** of Kassel. He then tried his hand at painting and sculpture and began designing lamps, rugs, ceramics and shoes. With the selection of his dog figure, **Cobi**, as the Olympic mascot, Mariscal ARRIVED. His fancies can now be found all over town—the giant *gamba* (prawn) atop the Moll de la Fusta's **Gambrinus** restaurant, the bar stools in Passeig de Gràcia's **Maná Maná** restaurant, and the interior decor of the **Poble Espanyol's Las Torres de Avila** (done in collaboration with **Alfredo Arribas**), to name a mere few. Part *enfant terrible* and part Renaissance man, Mariscal has the Midas touch when it comes to design.

*Xavier Mariscal,
designer,
Olympic mascot*

Dreta de L'Eixample

The eastern half of the Eixample is prime architectural turf, and aficionados of the art will find much to marvel at here. Primarily developed during the first half of the 20th century, the **Dreta de L'Eixample** (Right Eixample) exudes, for the most part, an understated elegance and an architectural assuredness that comes from being truly classy. While largely devoid of museums, monuments, flocks of restaurants, and the feverish trendiness of its sibling **Esquerra de L'Eixample** (Left Eixample), it contains some very significant Modernist milestones—to wit, **Domènech i**

Montaner's **Hospital de Sant Pau** and **Gaudí**'s **Casa Milà** (aka **La Pedrera**) and **Sagrada Familia** cathedral, one of Barcelona's best-known landmarks. Between them runs the **Avinguda de Gaudí** dotted with street lamps by **Falqués**.

At the end of the 19th century, this was the more upscale of the 2 Eixample quarters, and in **Carrer de Mallorca** you'll find the **Casas Simon**, **Montaner** and **Thomas** that typify the stately mansions that sprouted up in this barrio between 1870 and 1890. In fact, the Dreta de L'Eixample—especially the triangular area between the **Passeig de Gràcia**, **Carrer D'Aragó** and the **Avinguda de la Diagonal**—is home to a greater number of structures of greater artistic interest than the Esquerra de L'Eixample. Here you can barely walk down the street without being bowled over by some graciously wonderful architectural notion. Whenever possible, you should have a look inside as well, as the ornamental work tends to be truly exceptional.

Further walks along **Carrers València**, **Consell de Cent**, **Diputació** and **Gran Via C.C.** between the Passeig de Gràcia and **Passeig de Sant Joan** will yield an additional cache of extraordinary Modernist buildings. In addition to their characteristic iconography and rich decoration, these buildings are notable for their distinctive layouts. The typical construction on this side of the Passeig de Gràcia consists of a ground floor, usually having 3 to 5 openings, given over to shops or stores (formerly often selling draperies, since textiles were a specialty of the Catalan industrial revolution). Unlike in the US, where the top floor is most often the penthouse province of the owner or the more monied tenants, in the Dreta de L'Eixample the floor above the ground floor (known as the principal or main floor) was occupied by the proprietor and overlooked the garden located in the interior of the block. This floor usually features a large, ornate gallery on the front facade and is accessed by a wide staircase from the hall or vestibule, often separate from the staircase leading to the upper floors where the tenants live.

Coincidentally, in the increasingly polarized political atmosphere preceding the Spanish Civil War, this would have been the Eixample of the *right* ideologically as well as geographically. Today it still continues to be more sedate, staid and conservative than the *left* Eixample.

Map labels:
C Mas Casanoves
C Llorens I Barba
C Santa Carolina
C Rosalia Castro
Trav Gracia
52 Hospital de St Pau
C Torre Velez
Ptge Flaugier
Av Gaudi
51
C Sant Quinti
C Freser
C Castillejos
Ptge Villaret
C Cartagena
C Dos Maig
C Independencia
C Xifre
C Rogent
C Bassols
C Enamorats
namorats
C Corunya
C Clot
Av Meridiana
29
n Via C. C.
lbes
Plaça de les Glories Catalanes
28
C Bolivia
C Pamplona
C Alaba
C Tanger
C Avila
C Sancho Avila
C Badajoz
C Ciutat Granada

1 El Corte Inglés
The Macy's of Barcelona—indeed of Spain—this is the country's most suc-

cessful department-store chain. One of its nicest features is the 9th-floor cafeteria (★★$$) which offers an impressive luncheon buffet that, with luck, you can accompany with a marvelous city view. In summer, you can dine al fresco on the terrace. ♦ Pl Catalunya, 14 (Rda Sant Pere) 302.12.12. Also at: Av Diagonal 617-619. 322.40.11

2 Locutorio de Telefónica The place to make international calls and avoid the highway robbery of hotel surcharges. They take credit cards here, and there is one Direct USA phone with an AT&T operator waiting at the other end, but, as you can imagine, it's in great demand. ♦ M-Sa 8:30AM-9PM. C Fontanella, 4 (Pl Catalunya)

3 Casa Victorià de la Riva (1899, **Enric Sagnier i Villavecchia**) Noteworthy for the circular tower at one of the chamfered corners that subsequently became a common architectural feature on buildings throughout the Eixample. In this case, the more elaborate tower stands in contradiction to the greater simplicity of the facade, which has been renovated. ♦ C Alí Bei, 1 (C Girona)

4 Casa Modest Andreu (1906, **Telm Fernàndez i Janot**) One of the few known works by this architect, this building is worthy of mention for its beautiful wrought-iron balconies alone, but the vestibule also offers a lovely glass door with stunning reliefs and a remarkable staircase and elevator. ♦ C Alí Bei, 3 (C Girona)

5 Casas Joaquim y Antoni Marfà (1902, **Manuel Comas i Thos**) Here we're talking about 2 houses (owned by 2 brothers) whose architectural resolution is identical and whose conspicuous, enclosed gallery is centered on the adjoining facades. The stylistic inclinations predate Modernism and are similar in key areas to the **Casa Moysi** (Rambla Catalunya, 23) designed by the same architect and built in 1893. Comas signed the building on the facade. ♦ C Alí Bei, 27-29 (C Bailén-Pg Sant Joan)

Dreta de L'Eixample

6 Estació del Nord (1915, **Demetri Ribes Marco**) Actually Ribes is responsible here for the central structure linking 2 buildings built in 1861 and the 2 sections of the main facade that flank it. The attention to detail evinced in the carpentry work, the bathrooms, and the rails of the ticket windows reveals his profound concern with quality and design. In this former train station, the architect intelligently combined the Modernist vernacular with traditional artistry, the forms of the Viennese Secessionist movement, and the rational functionality of the ironwork architecture typical of the markets, trade pavilions, train stations and industrial buildings constructed during the

last quarter of the 19th century. This is now the central bus terminal for all national and international buses, so there is free access to its architectural highlights. Nearby you'll find the new home of the **Arxiu de la Corona d'Aragó** (Archives of the Kingdom of Aragon), moved here from the Barri Gòtic. ♦ Av Vilanova, s/n (C Nàpols)

7 Casas Tomàs Roger (1894, **Enric Sagnier i Villavecchia**) These 2 buildings and the **Casas Antoni Roger** occupy most of this block and make a monumental impact. Built several years later than the Casas Antoni Roger, these were actually built in 2 stages: first the one at No. 37 and then the one at No. 39. Of particular note is the former's vestibule with its monumental profusion of decorative fancies and its grill separating the staircase to the main floor (the domain of the building's owner) and the staircase to the upper floors (domain of the tenants). Like the Casas Antoni Roger, the buildings incorporate Classical elements, which run here to Corinthian and Tuscan columns, plateresque reliefs and sculptured brackets. Originally, both sets of Roger edifices also featured very similar crowns. ♦ C Ausiàs Marc, 37-39 (C Bailén-C Girona)

8 Casas Antoni Roger (1890, **Enric Sagnier i Villavecchia**) This is the first work Sagnier did for an upper-class Catalan family and clearly reflects his client's economic muscle. Conceived in a medieval vein, the execution of the buildings also incorporates some Classical tendencies. Although this is really 2 houses with 2 separate entrances, the facade masquerades as a homogeneous whole. The houses are a good example of the architectural period just preceding the explosion of Modernism, and it is interesting to note that Sagnier's 1888 resolution of the chamferred facade in the style of a Catalan Gothic mansion foreshadows a stylistic motif that would characterize some of the most important Modernist works. The vestibule is also worth a look. ♦ C Ausiàs Marc, 33-35 (C Girona)

9 Casa Antònia Burés (1906, **Juli Batllevel i Arús**) In terms of traditional structural and decorative elements, this is perhaps the most representative structure in this area of the Modernist spirit prevailing during the first decade of the 20th century. Most eye-catching are the ground-floor mullions that, in the form of pines, extend to the base of the main-floor galleries. Rumor has it that these naturalist flourishes were the work of **Enrich Pi** (*pi* means pine in Catalán), the master builder who executed the project. ♦ C Ausiàs Marc, 42-46 (C Bailén-C Girona)

10 Casas Francesc Burés (1905, **Francesc Berenguer i Mestres**) Even though the building's plans are signed by the architect **Miquel Pascual i Tintorer**, it seems that the real author of this structure is Berenguer. This is because Berenguer never received the official title of *architect* and was thus unable to sign the construction plans. Never mind. The building still represents a high point in Modernism, its vestibule and main floor representing the epitome of the period's decorative arts artistry. ♦ C Ausiàs Marc, 30-32 (C Girona)

11 Casa Antònia Puget (1907, **Roc Cot i Cot**) Another instance where the architectural responsibility is not quite clear. The plans are signed by Cot, but sources from the period attribute the supervision of the work to **Ramon Viñolas** and say that Cot only participated in the finishing touches and decoration of the building. In any case, this attractive brick building was thought worthy of consideration for the first-class City Hall architectural prize of 1907. ♦ C Ausiàs Marc, 22 (C Girona-C Bruc)

12 Casa Manuel Felip (1913, **Telm Fernàndez i Janot**) The building plans date from 1905, but work did not begin until 1911. The building next door (No. 20), built years before, was commissioned by the same man and designed by the same architect. Though the kinship of the 2 edifices is evident, there are some telling differences: the stone rails of the first edifice are rendered in iron on the second, and the lateral galleries of the first have been eliminated in the second to put a smoother, more homogeneous face on things, more in keeping with the tastes of advanced Modernism. ♦ C Ausiàs Marc, 16-18 (C Girona-C Bruc)

13 Casas Joaquim Cabot (1904, **Josep Vilaseca i Casanovas**) Vilaseca's first purely Modernist works, these 2 buildings occupy a triangular plot of land. Nos. 12-14 sport large—almost disproportionately so—galleries and decorative *sgraffiti* depicting white flowers on a red background. The primary attraction of Nos. 8-10 is the beautiful sculptural work by **Vives** and **Albareda** on the facade. Sprouting from the floral brackets is a complete gable of leaves and stems gathered together with a ribbon. The vestibule merits a visit for the design of its walls and ceilings and its lamps. ♦ C Roger Llúria, 8-14 (C Ausiàs Marc-C Casp)

14 Casa Calvet (1900, **Antoni Gaudí i Cornet**) Built for the company **Hijos de Pedro Mártir Calvet**, this is Gaudí's first apartment house in the Eixample proper. The social significance of this fact is that this building marked the start of an emphasis on *quality* multi-family dwellings, and here Gaudí personally took charge of the design of every element (a good example is the entrance hall). In 1900 Barcelona began awarding municipal architectural prizes, and Casa Calvet won the first one for the highest quality building constructed during the previous year. Of the 3 buildings Gaudí built within the Cerdà Eixample, this one is more typical of the traditional bourgeois residence of the district. Its more conventional facade (made of Montjuïc stone like that of the **Casa Batlló**) terminating in double Baroque-like gables does not reflect the imagination Gaudí would shortly demonstrate in the Casas Batlló and **Milà**. Adorning the upper part of the edifice

Casa Calvet

are the heads of **Sant Genís** (the actor), **Sant Genís** (the notary)—both patron saints of the owner's native village, Sant Genís de Vilasar—and **Sant Pere Màrtir**, the personal patron saint of **Sr. Calvet**, a textile producer, whose ground-floor offices were also designed by the architect. Perhaps the most beautiful and significant design elements of the Casa Calvet are the complementary details—the peepholes, door handles and the furnishings of the first 3 floors (many of which are now in the **Casa-Museu Gaudí** in Parc Güell), which were the domain of the building's owner. The vestibule too, is interesting for its wall tiles, brass lamps, benches, murals, and the elevator

Dreta de L'Eixample

fashioned of glass, wood and iron. You may be able to sneak a peek at it, but generally the public must be content to view this building from the outside only. ♦ C Casp, 48 (C Roger Llúria-C Bruc)

14 Casa Antoni Salvadó (1904, **Juli Batllevell i Arús**) In juxtaposition to the adjoining Modernist Casa Calvet, Batllevell here opted for an architectural repertoire rooted in strict historicism, although the meticulous care taken with the materials and workmanship is a typical Modernist trait. The vestibule is a prime example. The current, clashing crown is the result of a misguided renovation. ♦ C Casp, 46 (C Roger Llúria-C Bruc)

15 Casas Pascual i Pons (1891, **Enric Sagnier i Villavecchia**) These 2 independent buildings (originally the properties of **Alexandre Pons** and **Sebastià Pascual**) constructed as a single unit represent one of Sagnier's first, and most literal, Neo-Gothic constructions. Surviving a profound remodelling in 1984 are the staircase, iron lamps and glasswork of the vestibule. Most of the building is now occupied by the offices of the insurance company **La Catalan de Seguros**. ♦ Pg Gràcia, 2-4 (Rda Sant Pere-C Casp)

16 Casas Antoni Rocamora (1917, **Joaquim Bassegoda i Amigó**) On the face of things this series of houses, one of the largest structural undertakings to be found in the Eixample, appears to be a single unit. It also appears that Joaquim, who signed the plans, executed the construction in conjunction with his brother **Bonaventura**. The 3 buildings, which have a decidedly French Gothic accent, have separate entrances and a uniform stone facade. The interplay of the facade's structural and ornamental elements gives rise to lintels, arches, cornices, brackets and railings that recall plateresque bas-reliefs. Together with the nearby **Casas Pascual i Pons**, they constitute one of the Eixample's most attractive architectural displays. ♦ Pg Gràcia, 6-14 (C Casp)

17 Hotel Barcelona $$$ A modern hotel mere meters from the Pl Catalunya with 63 air-conditioned rooms equipped with TVs, minibars and the usual set of straightforward, modern creature comforts. Parking too. ♦ C Casp, 1-13 (Pg Gràcia) 302.58.58; fax 301.86.74

18 Casa Llorenç Camprubí (ca 1900, **Adolf Ruiz i Casamitjana**) A very attractive example of Ruiz's work at the turn of the century, this represents a very personal interpretation of the prevailing trend toward the Neo-Gothic. Note the beautiful bi-level gallery. ♦ C Casp, 22 (C Pau Claris-Pg Gràcia)

19 Laie ★$$ Providing food for both stomach and thought, this combination cafe-restaurant and bookstore takes its name from the pre-Iberian settlement that allegedly

Dreta de L'Eixample

existed on Montjuïc. Stop in for coffee and a pastry or for lunch, and pick up a book or stick-mounted newspapers of the day to read as you munch. The atmosphere is refined and intellectual. The brief menu changes frequently. Similarly brief is the wine list. In the morning various breakfasts are served, and in the afternoon Laie takes on the guise of a tea room and offers many varieties of tea. ♦ Catalan ♦ C Pau Claris, 85 (C Casp) Cafe, 302.73.10; bookstore, 318.17.39

20 Hotel Granvia $$ For over half a century this hotel, now a **Best Western** affiliate, has occupied this small Victorian-style mansion dating from the end of the 19th century. The 48 rooms have telephones and minibars and feature such old-fashioned flourishes as brocaded upholstery. The splendid 2nd-floor salon is gilded and chandeliered and leads onto a spacious outdoor terrace. ♦ Gran Via C.C., 642 (Pg Gràcia-C Pau Claris) 318.19.00; reservations 302.50.46; fax 318.99.97

21 Casa Ramon Oller (1871, **Eduard Fontseré**; remodelled 1901, **Pau Salvat i Espasa**) Most notable about this building is the completely new structure that emerged from Salvat's 1901 remodelling. The 1871 structure was strictly Classical, and Salvat's modification consisted of remodelling the facade and the vestibule, redistributing the apartments, adding a glass-encased gallery on the interior patio, and adding another floor. Most interesting, however, is the ornamental work—the wrought iron of the galleries, the grillwork of the balconies, the *sgraffiti*, and the laborious elaboration of the front door's capitals, adorned with figures of animals laced with oak leaves and laurel. Step into the vestibule and have a look at the sculptural work on the marble staircase leading to the main floor. ♦ Gran Via C.C., 658 (C Pau Claris-C Roger Llúria)

22 Hotel Ritz $$$$ (1919, **Eduardo Ferrés Puig**) The stately graciousness of years gone by lives on in the Ritz's great salons, its elegant rugs on marble floors, and its sparkling chandeliers. For many years this was the center of Barcelona's social life. With the inauguration of the **Palau de Pedralbes** in 1924, the hotel became a focal point for visiting nobility, and their parties at the Ritz are legendary. During the Spanish Civil War the hotel served as lodging for the members of the Non-Intervention Committee of the League of Nations. During WWII many ambassadors made their homes here. And all along presidents, kings, statesmen, captains of business and industry, and well-heeled regular folk have regularly called it a night here. The **Duke of Windsor** checked in when he left Great Britain with **Mrs. Simpson**. In fact, upon asking for the bill, the Duke suggested, half in jest, that they not charge him much because now he was just like so many other English people suffering from the war. When playing at the nearby **Palau de la Música**, **Arthur Rubinstein** stayed here. Other notable guests have included **W. Somerset Maugham**, **Cantinflas** and **Sophia Loren**. Over lunch here **Prince Faisal** learned of his brother's assassination and left the table a king. A recent renovation has put a fresh polish on everything, but the 149 rooms maintain their exquisite turn-of-the-century ambience and traditional furnishings while offering all the latest technological amenities. The hotel's 12 suites all feature *Roman baths*. The hotel's **Diana Restaurant** (★★★$$$$) offers an international menu sprinkled with daily Catalan specials. Its custom-made rug of hand-knotted wool

---

Restaurants/Nightlife: Red   Hotels: Blue
Shops/Parks: Green   Sights/Culture: Black

recalls the shades and designs of the era of the hotel's birth. Venetian-style curtains adorn the windows. Piano music accompanies the meals. The hotel also has a bar, garden, gift shop, parking service and quick check-out (though why anyone would want to rush off is not clear to us). ♦ Deluxe ♦ Gran Via C.C. 668 (C Roger de Llúria) 318.52.00; fax 381.01.48. Reservations can also be made through the Leading Hotels of the World, 800/223.6800

23 Ticktacktoe ★★★$$$ Now somewhat worn at the edges, this once haute trendy, *over-designed* restaurant (with bar and billiard hall) can happily coast on the reputation of its food alone. Though its menu moves with the times, it does strike some popular traditional notes. We can recommend the *ensalada de cigalitas* (prawn salad), *perfumado arroz con almejas* (perfumed rice with clams) and the carpaccio. ♦ C Roger Llúria, 40 (Gran Via C.C.-C Diputació) 318.99.47

24 Hotel Havana Palace $$$$ (1887; 1991, remodelled, **Josep Juanpere Miret** and **Antoni Puig Guasch**) At the heart of this brand new hotel is a 6-story patio crowned with a glass cupola, surrounded by a piano bar, restaurant, gift shop and lounge area. You'll also find a health club, private garage and business center. The 150 soundproofed rooms and suites feature exclusive furniture designs, lavish, Carrara-marble baths and the full complement of amenities, including bathrobes. Previously this was the Havana Hotel, but the original Neo-classical facade of 1887 and its lovely 19th-century clock are all that remain the same. Within all has been conjured anew. The official rating of this hotel is *5-Star-Monumental*—a new category that distinguishes properties that in addition to being sybaritically luxurious are also of historic or architectural significance. ♦ Deluxe ♦ Gran Via C.C., 647 (C Bruc) 487.24.74; fax 216.08.35

25 Casa Ramon Vilà (1916, **Joan Maymó i Cabanellas**) In this late Modernist work the waning of the movement's ornamental effusiveness can be seen, both in the facade and the vestibule, which is decidedly more Classical in tone. The stylistic *swan song* of Modernism here is the gallery. ♦ C Girona, 46 (Gran Vía C.C.-C Diputació)

26 Monumento al Doctor Robert (1910, **Josep Llimona**; reconstruction 1985) Perhaps the city's most characteristically Modernist monument, this municipal tribute to beloved Barcelona mayor **Bartomeu Robert** features a grouping of figures atop a stone fountain. At the very top is a bust of Dr. Robert being kissed by an allegorical figure representing *Glory*. The latter 2 figures are in stone, the other 7 are bronze. Although the architect **Domènech i Montaner** was initially associated with the project, he apparently abandoned it before the final configuration was fixed in stone, so to speak. In fact, the affinity of the stone base with the facade of **Casa Milà** (finished afterward) has incited much speculation that perhaps **Gaudí** had a hand in the monument's design. At first, this monument was erected in the Pl Universitat. During the Civil War it was dismantled, and in 1979 re-erected on its present site. ♦ Pl Tetuán

27 Plaza de Toros Monumental (1916, **Ignasi Mas i Morell, Domènec Sugrañes i Gras** and **Joaquim Raspall i Mayol**) Actually, Mas and Sugrañes remodelled and expanded Raspall's previous bullring on this site known as **El Sport**—inaugurated only 2 years earlier—to give Barcelona its largest bullring. At that time the city had 3 bullrings—this one, one in Barceloneta, and Las Arenas. As in the case of Las Arenas, the ornamentation here is a romantic interpretation of Moorish and, in this case, some *Mozarabic* motifs. (Note: *Mozarabic* refers to the Spanish Christians living in Muslim Spain and to their art and literature, which flourished especially in the Kingdom of León in the 10th and early 11th centuries). The decorative tilework is attributed to the Italian **Mario Maragliano**. ♦ Gran Vía C.C., 749 (Pg Carles I-C Lepant)

28 Plaça de les Glòries Catalanes It is in this plaza that Barcelona's main arteries—Av Diagonal, Gran Via C.C. and Av Meridiana—meet. The original **Plan Cerdà** and the former plan of **León Jaussely** of 1905 both called for this to be the heart of the city. After the removal of the train tracks once serving the nearby Estació del Nord, those intentions have

Plaça de les Glòries Catalanes, Teatre Nacional

TALLER D'ARQUITECTURA

133

finally come closer to fruition with the construction of 2 circular plazas, one above the other—the lower one joined to Av Diagonal and Av Meridiana and the upper one to Gran Via C.C.—at whose core is an expansive plaza of greenery the size of 2 Eixample blocks. This new complex also includes a park designed in collaboration with the sculptor **Beverly Pepper** and the new **Teatre Nacional** (National Theater) by **Ricardo Bofill**. Elliptical in shape, covered by a metal-and-glass roof, and occupying 22,300 square feet, this theater contains 2 auditoriums (one seating 1000 and another 500), a vestibule designed as a winter garden, a bar and restaurant, a library, and an exhibition hall. The steps leading up to it may also be used as seating for outdoor events. Opposite the National Theater, between C Lepant and C Padilla, is the Pl Arts where you'll find the new **El Auditori** (Auditorium) by **Rafael Moneo** built around a central patio and crowned by a semi-open cupola. It features 3 performance halls accommodating audiences of 2600, 700 and 150; a cafeteria; a restaurant; and a library spread across 3 floors offering a reading room, and record, sheet music and video libraries. On the 2nd and 3rd floors is a museum of music; on the 3rd, the **Conservatori Municipal** (Center of Advanced Music Studies). This is the permanent home of the **Orquesta Ciutat de Barcelona** (Barcelona City Orchestra), the **Banda Municipal** (Municipal Band) and the **Cobla Municipal** (Municipal Brass Band).

29 Mercat Els Encants Every Monday, Wednesday, Friday and Saturday from 7AM to sunset the streets around the Pl de les Glòries Catalanes transform themselves into Barcelona's version of London's Portobello Rd. At this diverse flea market you'll find virtually everything, including the occasional antique treasure at a bargain price. ♦ C Dos Maig-C Independència

30 La Manduca ★$$ Small of tables and somewhat contorted of interior architecture, this slightly offbeat eatery serves wonderful home-style food. If it's the season for wild mushrooms, start with them as an appetizer. Other-

Dreta de L'Eixample

wise, try the anchovies or the *chipirones* (baby squid). Those who like cod will find 4 versions to choose from; those who like tripe might consider Manduca's rendition with garbanzos. Also to be recommended are the *albóndigas* (meatballs) with potatoes—simple but savory. ♦ Catalan ♦ C Girona, 59 (C Diputació) 302.31.37

31 Casa Marcel-lí Costa (1862, **Felip Ubach**; remodelled ca 1902) Ubach was one of Barcelona's most prolific architects of the mid-1800s. Originally the building was commissioned by **Teresa Quadreny** on behalf of the **El Ensanche y Mejora de Barcelona** (the Eixample and Barcelona Improvement), an organization formed to develop the Eixample. As happened with many other early Eixample structures, this one was modified at the turn of the century. As a result, it sprouted a gallery and updated balconies, and the lower floors were converted into commercial space. ♦ C Diputació, 299 (C Roger Llúria)

32 Passatge de Permanyer (1864, **Jeroni Granell i Barrera**) As close as Barcelona gets to English-style mews, this street of low-profile, Post-Romantic houses is a block-long oasis of quiet admist urban bustle. Some of the buildings remain residences, some have been abandoned. The handful of such passatges to be found in the Eixample were deviations from the Plan Cerdà and were, at first, not meant to accommodate buildings. They soon did, however, and this passatge is the most interesting of them all for its architectural coherence. The houses are short and relatively small with gardens in front. ♦ C Pau Claris-C Roger Llúria

33 Hotel Diplomatic $$$ The last resort among the city's crop of 5-star hotels simply because the room decor is really not up to top-of-the-line snuff. Rather, it is suggestive of the more garish aspects of Hollywood in the 1950s—patterned carpets in bold, bright patterns often clashing with other decorative elements—despite the fact that the hotel was completely renovated as recently as 1988. Its 217 rooms and suites are all facing the street and soundproofed and have air-conditioning, TVs, VCRs, direct-dial phones, background music and room safes. The hotel's public areas are in better taste than the rooms and include 4 bars, a restaurant, coffeeshop, outdoor swimming pool and private garage. The main office of **Europcar** is in the hotel, making it very convenient to arrange a rental. ♦ C Pau Claris, 122 (C Consell de Cent) 317.31.00; fax 318.65.31

34 Horno Sarret (1866, **Felip Ubach Corbella**; remodelled ca 1906) The **Forn de Pa Patisseria** on the ground floor is most noteworthy for the ornamental work encasing the 2 doors: the molded wood dynamically undulates around the entryways and contrasts with the more Classical coat of arms in the center depicting a woman sowing wheat. Inside you'll find one door that is a simplified reproduction of the original one and sports vegetable motifs both in the woodwork and the acid-etched glass. ♦ C Girona, 73 (C Consell de Cent)

35 Betlem A classic example of the Eixample's traditional corner grocery store and a good place to pick up upscale picnic supplies, including all manner of tempting cheeses, cold cuts, tinned goods, wines and more. ♦ C Girona, 70 (C Consell Cent) 232.41.55

Restaurants/Nightlife: Red	Hotels: Blue
Shops/Parks: Green	Sights/Culture: Black

36 Conducta Ejemplar ★★$ To *wet* your appetite, start off with a *caipirinha* (a potent Brazilian cocktail). Then try one of the excellent salads. Next, fill up on 10 varieties of meat successively cut and served to you on your plate. All this and a nice decor too. ♦ Brazilian ♦ C Consell de Cent, 403 (C Girona-C Bailén) 231.51.12

37 Scala A dinner/cabaret that amounts to a vaudeville show expensively re-packaged and high-teched for the '90s. You'll see everything here from animal acts to jugglers, magicians and topless dancing girls. The stage management of these mega-productions featuring over 60 performers is absolutely mind-boggling. The stages move up and down, and some of the special effects are right out of Spielberg. For dinner you can choose among different set menus or order à la carte. There is a dance floor for patrons as well. ♦ Admission; cover for the second show. Pg Sant Joan, 47-49 (C Consell de Cent) 232.63.63

38 Mesón Los Pacos ★$$$ To eat well here you must know your way around the endless menu. Here are some suggestions: the *cogollos de Tudela con anchoas* (hearts of lettuce with anchovies), *empanada gallega* (savory, stuffed pastry), *parrillada de pescados y mariscos* (platter of fish and shellfish), and *costillitas de cabrito a la parrilla* (grilled goat—yes *goat*—chops). ♦ C Bailén, 83-85 (C D'Aragó-C Consell de Cent) 231.49.06

39 Hotel Europark $$ Sixty-six newly renovated rooms occupy this narrow building. All have baths, air-conditioning, telephones, TVs and music. No frills, no pretensions, just middle-of-the-road comfort. ♦ C D'Aragó, 325 (C Girona-C Bailén) 257.92.05; fax 258.99.61

40 Casa Isabel Pomar (1906, **Joan Rubió i Bellver**) This skinny, cathedralesque building is one of the few multi-family dwellings Rubió designed. He took great care with the finishing touches of the facade—the ceramics, the wrought-iron work—and his compositional solution to the building's constrained horizontal dimensions earned it a 2nd-category nomination in the municipal architectural contest of 1907. ♦ C Girona, 86 (C D'Aragó)

41 Mercat Concepció A scaled-down version of **La Boquería**, this produce market inhabits a lovely structure. The adjoining 13th-century Gothic church was originally built by the order of St. James of the Cross where Via Laietana now meets C Jonqueres. Both the church and its marvelous 14th-century cloister were carefully dismantled and, under the supervision of architect **Meroni Granell**, moved and reassembled here between 1871 and 1888. ♦ C D'Aragó, 311 (C Girona-C Bruc)

42 L'Aram ★$$$ A welcome surprise on this street largely devoid of good gastronomic options. The rustic decor befits the owner's warm, friendly greeting. Her innovative dishes include *lentejas francesas estofadas con crestas de gallo* (French lentil-bean stew with rooster combs). ♦ Eclectic ♦ C D'Aragó, 305 (C Bruc-C Roger de Llúria) 207.01.88

43 Conservatori Superior de Música (1916, **Antoni de Falguera Sivilla**) This block of the Dreta de L'Eixample is unusual for the municipal outposts—market, district offices, etc.— that are generally more typical of the more pedestrian Esquerra de L'Eixample. This music conservatory's towers recall **Puig i Cadafalch**'s **Casa Serra** and **Casa de les Punxes** and are akin to the neighboring towers of the municipal building of C D'Aragó designed by **Pere Falqués**, who apparently originally designed this building, which was subsequently modified by Falguera in 1916. The main entrance is framed by a beautiful sculptural grouping by **Eusebi Arnau**. Don't miss the grand salon within that extends all the way up to a wondrous skylight. ♦ Free access during class hours. C Bruc, 104-112 (Ptge Pla-C València)

44 Casa Manuel Llopis Bofill (1903, **Antoni Maria Gallissà i Soqué**) Gallissà was one of the most outstanding collaborators of **Elies Rogent** and **Domènech i Montaner**, with whom he worked on the Universal Exhibition of 1888. In fact, Domènech put him in charge of one of the workshops installed in Domènech's intended cafe-restaurant in the Parc de la Ciutadella where he supervised the work of architects, sculptors, ceramicists, glaziers and blacksmiths in the manner of England's Arts & Crafts workshops. Still, Gallissà's own architectural production is scarce, and this well-known building is his most important. A careful attention to detail is patent throughout but most notably so in the galleries, balconies and the extraordinary treatment of the ground floor, whose arches link it with the rest of the facade. Gallissà's familiarity with the revived crafts' artistry of the day is particularly evident in his use of glass ceramics in the roof, vaults and soffits; his use of *sgraffiti* in geometric and floral patterns on the facade; his use of iron as a structural element in the galleries and projecting cornices; and his use of sculptured stone in the pilasters, columns and capitals. The vesti-

bule repeats in corresponding detail the themes of the facade. The building's crown and central gallery have been slightly modified. ♦ C València, 339 (C Bailén)

45 Iglesia de Les Saleses (1885, **Joan Martorell i Montells**) This multi-peaked and spired church of Gothic inspiration falls within the Neo-Medievalism that preceded the full flowering of the Modernist movement. The pictorial decorative work of the presbytery is by **Enric Moncerdà**. ♦ Pg Sant Joan, 88-92 (C València)

The Sagrada Familia is . . . the reflection of the sound of the people. Woe the day that it is halted!
Joan Maragall

46 Barnils ★★$$$ The competent, contemporary cooking here is reflected in such popular dishes as *pimientos del piquillo rellenos de gambas y pescado* (peppers stuffed with shrimp and fish) and *habas con langostinos* (broad beans with prawns). The toasted country bread with tomato is delicious, as are the homemade desserts and the assortment of sorbets. ♦ Catalan ♦ C Roger de Flor, 204 (C D'Aragó-C València) 207.77.57

47 Casa Planells (1924, **Josep M. Jujol i Gibert**) A frequent collaborator of Gaudí's (e.g., the **Casas Battló** and **Milà** and numerous elements of **Parc Güell**), Jujol is an architect of great imagination and a stickler for details. Here, in this structure utilizing limited resources, he achieves a strong sense of Constructivism. In eschewing ornamental concessions, his dynamic resolution of this difficult corner edifice also demonstrates an affinity with central European Expressionism. ♦ Av Diagonal, 332 (C Sicilia)

48 Templo Expiatorio de la Sagrada Familia (completion uncertain, **Antoni Gaudí i Cornet**, et al) To finish or not to finish, that is the controversial question. Even unfinished, this is indisputably Barcelona's best-known landmark—despite the scaffolding and constant clack-clack-clack of chiseling that have become fixed features of this monumental work-in-progress. It all began in 1869 when bookseller **Josep Maria Bocabella Verdaguer**, founder of an association devoted to Sant Josep, decided to copy in Barcelona the house of Nazareth and build, to

house it, a church dedicated to the Sagrada Familia (Sacred Family). The original plans by **Francesc de Paula del Villar Lozano** called for a Neo-Gothic church, and work began in 1882. But when only the crypt

had been started, dissension between the architect and the Works Council interrupted the project. In 1883 Gaudí took over and, restricted somewhat by Villar's original plans, finished the crypt, which now contains Gaudí's sepulchre. He then let his architectural imagination run wild and devised an ambitious symbolic scheme for the construction of the remainder of this modern cathedral of outlandish proportions—a height of 557.6 feet; a nave and apse measuring 311.6 feet; a transept measuring 196.8 feet; the width of the nave measuring 49.2 feet and that of the lateral aisles measuring 24.6 feet, for a total width of 147.6 feet; and the width of the transept measuring 98.4 feet. If it is ever finished, this will be Europe's largest cathedral. Gaudí's preliminary drawings for it were in the Neo-Gothic style. The apse, completed in 1893, and the overall verticality of the structure are characteristic of this style, but as work proceeded, Gaudí's intentions became increasingly naturalistic. As always, it was his way to improvise as he went along. His guiding plan, never spelled out in definitive architectural detail, was highly symbolic. It called for 3 monumental facades corresponding to the Nativity, the Passion and Death, and the Glory of Christ. The central dome, which rises high above the others and culminates in a cross at whose center we see a lamb, was to symbolize Christ and be surrounded by 4 slightly lower domes bearing the symbols of the 4 Evangelists: the eagle, the ox, the lion and the angel. The 4 towers of each of the 3 facades would together represent the 12 Apostles, and the tower crowning the apse, the Virgin Mary. Only the **Fachada del Nacimiento** (Nativity Facade) was completed (1893-1904), though. It reaches a height of 351 feet and is ardently mystic in its expressionism. When Gaudí died in 1926, only one tower of its 4 had been finished. The architect **Domènec Sugrañes** finished the other 3 copying off the first one. Work stopped in 1936 when Gaudí's crypt and study burned. Beginning in 1952, it started again, financed by private donations

CAIXA DE PENSIONS FOUNDATION

Gaudí

If architecture were a religion, Antoni Gaudí y Cornet would be hailed as a prophet of extraordinary vision. In a Barcelona studded with Modernist jewels, his structures stand boldly apart. Often acting as both architect and designer, he was absorbed in his work down to the smallest detail. Plans were mere guideposts; he improvised as he went along. Imaginative to the point of eccentricity, he never repeated himself—no 2 of his buildings are alike. Yet they are all recognizably Gaudí.

It's not surprising, then, that Gaudí himself was a bit of an oddball. Moody and austere in his personal life, he seems to have channeled all his exuberance and extravagance into his creations. For the last 43 years of his life he worked on the Sagrada Familia cathedral. For the last fifteen years he turned down all other commissions and ultimately ended up moving into the workshop on the construction premises.

A frugal vegetarian who took long walks, he led the life of a celibate bachelor in his later years. In fact, he had become such a recluse by the time he was run over by a tram in 1926 and died in the hospital 2 days later that initially his passing went unrecognized.

Born in 1852 into a family of artisans, Gaudí learned early on the crafts that he would later bring to bear full force in his oeuvre. A metalworker by training, he received his architectural degree in 1878, taking 9, rather than the customary 5, years to complete his training.

For him architecture was not a profession, but a calling. A deeply religious man, especially later in life, he thought of himself as the humble instrument of a divine power. He conceived not buildings but *visions*. He never lectured or wrote about his profession, creations, philosophy or theories. His mission was Modernism, and Barcelona was his pulpit.

At once functional and fantastical, his works, like a good sermon, endure and continue to provoke reaction. On the 100th anniversary of his birth in 1952, Barcelona declared all of his buildings historical monuments, thus preventing them from being demolished and procuring government funds for their continued wellbeing. They are also listed among the World Trust Properties protected by UNESCO.

Schools of La Sagrada Familia

and based on what few drawings and sketches had survived the fire. Many argue that the subsequent work only detracts from the uniqueness of the Gaudí original. Clearly, the special genius evident in his Nativity Facade at the eastern end of the structure contrasts sharply with the coarseness of the recent construction of the **Passion and Death Facade** on the western side. Beneath the Passion Facade is a museum displaying the original Villar designs and tracing in photos, fragments and plans the evolution of the Sagrada Familia. It also addresses other Gaudí works in photographic detail. To date, the following parts of the cathedral have been built: the apsidal crypt; the crypt in the western lateral aisle; the crypt in the eastern lateral aisle; the crypt in the transept; the Nativity Facade; the apse (outer wall); 4 of the 50 sections which will comprise the cloister; the Passion Facade; the walls and great windows of the nave (to a height of 98.4 feet); the foundations of all the interior columns, with an average depth of 82 feet; and half of the columns of the nave, to a height of 65.6 feet. It has been said that Gaudí knew he could never finish such an ambitious project and that he planned for future generations to take over in their own architectural vernaculars. Instead, the continuing construction is based on sketches made by Gaudí's collaborators and admirers that never received Gaudí's explicit approval. At the time of his death Gaudí had also finished the parish schools, the priests' residence, the drawing workshop, the photographic studio and the archives. The school (twice rebuilt) and priests' house remain. The other structures burned down in 1936. ♦ Admission. Daily 9AM-7PM. Pl Sagrada Familia (C Provença-C Sardenya-C Mallorca-C Marina) 255.02.47

Dreta de L'Eixample

49 La Llesca ★$$ A typically quaint *tapas* bar and restaurant that prides itself on its *escalivada* (made from peppers, eggplant and onions), *terrasco al horno* (oven-roasted back—not rack—of lamb), homemade canelones, and *pollo* (chicken) in a champagne sauce. ♦ Catalan/Spanish ♦ Av Gaudí, 12 (C Marina-C Lepant) 255.31.30

It would be a betrayal to even think of finishing the Sagrada Familia . . . without genius. Let it remain there, like a huge rotting tooth.

Salvador Dali

50 Dino's ★$$$ A favorite for businesspeople at lunch, Dino's offers a largely traditional menu regrettably sprinkled with a few dishes that trip all over themselves trying to be fancy. No problems, though, with the *rossejat de fideos* (noodles cooked in fish broth and served with a garlic mayonnaise), *arroz negro con sepia* (black rice with cuttlefish), and the *crema catalana* (very good). ♦ C Còrsega, 562 (C Lepant-C Padilla) 236.51.38

Gaudí

51 Cafeteria Pizzeria Gaudí ★$ More than just fresh pasta and pizza. Also Catalan specialties and hearty meat dishes. Sleek, contemporary decor. ♦ Italian/Catalan ♦ Av Gaudí, 44-46 (C Padilla-C Castillejos) 255.67.56

52 Hospital de Sant Pau (1912, **Lluis Domènech i Montaner**) Judging from the entrance, one would guess this was a church rather than a hospital complex. The last will and testament of Catalan banker **Pau Gil**, which called for the construction of a large medical center in Barcelona, underwrote part of its construction. Many consider it the finest Modernist complex ever built. Its layout, featuring independent pavilions, reflects the prevailing sanitary and hygienic theories of the day. A central avenue cuts obliquely through the rectangular complex covering more than a million square feet (equivalent to about 9 Eixample blocks). The problems of linking the various pavilions and providing the common services they require were taken care of via a vast network of underground connections. The execution of the project falls into 2 phases. The first, and definitive, phase (1902-11) clearly reflects Domènech's direct involvement in the prominent use, both structurally and decoratively, of the traditional techniques that are an important characteristic of Modernism. Note the systematic use of brick vaulting and the high-quality ornamentation featuring floral designs, ceramic appliqués, sculptures,

Dreta de L'Eixample

mosaics, tiles and stained glass. Among the numerous artisans and artists who participated in the project were **Francesc Labarta** (who designed the mosaics and the tiles subsequently made by **Mario Maragliano**), **Eusebi Arnau** (who did the statue of Pau Gil), **Francesc Modolell** (who did the architectural sculpture work), and **Pau Gargallo** (whose work here is a clear example of Catalan Expressionism, a vanguard movement following on the heels of a declining Modernism). You'll find his work on the northern and southern facades and in the vestibule of the administrative pavilion. The angels of the surgery pavilion and the cross at its entrance are also

his creations. During the first phase, $\frac{1}{4}$ of the projected work was completed before the bequeathed funds ran out. It was then decided that the **Hospital de la Santa Creu**, created in 1401, would abandon its site near La Rambla and occupy the remaining terrain here. In 1912 the second phase of construction began, in which the architect's son, **Pere Domènech**, played an important role, especially after his father's death in 1923. In 1930 **King Alfonso XIII** officially inaugurated the medical center. You can readily walk in and survey the turrets, tiles and brickwork of the various buildings that comprise the complex. Certainly as far as hospitals go, this is the most pleasant one we've ever seen. ♦ C Sant Antoni Maria Claret, 167-171 (C Cartagena-C Mas Casanovas-C Sant Quintí)

53 Casa Macaya (1901, **Josep Puig i Cadafalch**) Garnering a mention in the municipal competition of 1902, this striking building, built shortly after the **Casa Amatller**, now houses the **Centre Cultural de la Fundació Caixa de Pensions** (Cultural Center of a Catalan bank), which comprises 2 downstairs rooms regularly offering art exhibitions (admission charged) and, upstairs, a magazine room, library, *fonoteca* and *videoteca*. The *fonoteca* offers the possibility of listening, free of charge, to a collection of classical, jazz and other assorted music from around the world made available by UNESCO. The downstairs bookstore is devoted to art and design. The original patio of the house was covered in the 1980s to create a bar and an area for concerts. The only original interior decorative elements that remain are the tiles and *sgraffiti* of the vestibule. On the outside, the large, smooth areas of white stucco reveal a Mediterranean influence that in years to come would typify the smaller mansions designed by this architect—such as the **Casa Company** in the Esquerra de L'Eixample. Among the ornamental work on the 2 doors, note the capital sculpture by **Eusebi Arnau** depicting commonplace scenes—a man on a donkey, another on a bicycle. ♦ Tu-Sa 11AM-2PM, 4-8PM; Su 10AM-3PM. Pg Sant Joan, 108 (C Provença-C Mallorca) 258.89.07

54 Casa Jeroni F. Granell (1903, **Jeroni F. Granell i Manresa**) Built strictly as an apartment house, this structure is more egalitarian of aspect than most in the Dreta de L'Eixample, lacking as it does a gallery signalling the proprietor's *main* floor. A typical example of Granell's highly personal style, this building, like many others by him, is readily identifiable by the sinuous, serpentine *writing* framing and weaving among the windows, doors and *sgraffiti*. In this case the graceful, green flower relief motif on a pale rose background makes for an especially eye-catching facade. Also of note is the vestibule, which can be visited. ♦ C Girona, 122 (C Mallorca-C València)

Restaurants/Nightlife: Red **Hotels:** Blue **Shops/Parks:** Green **Sights/Culture:** Black

55 Casa Eduardo S. de Lamadrid (1902, **Lluís Domènech i Montaner**) Followers of the work of Domènech will be interested to know that some critics consider this his first true Modernist work. Whether that is the case or not, it is the only one of its typology—i.e., an attached, multi-family dwelling—that he did in the Eixample. ♦ C Girona, 113 (C Mallorca-C València)

56 Casa Sofía García (1914, **Juli Maria Fossas Martínez**) Fossas' body of Modernist work is rather limited and dates basically from 1900-15. In this particular structure he wavers between the Modernist aesthetic and the tenets of Classicism common to the earliest Eixample works. The 2 polygonal, main-floor galleries and the rhythmic order of the rectilinear balconies underscore the Classical compositional elements. The Tudor arches of the ground floor and the curved pediments of the crown, whose decorative relief work is barely perceptible, are a passing stylistic nod to Modernism. The decorative work of the vestibule is equally parsimonious. Modernism reasserts itself with a vengeance in the ground-floor **Farmacia Puigoriol**, however. Elaborate carpentry and glasswork cover practically the entire exterior surface area. The design is by **Mariano Pau**; the carpentry by **Francesc Torres**; the lamps by **Pere Anglés**; and the marblework by **Nogués Hnos**.
♦ C Mallorca, 312 (C Girona)

57 On de Rocs This shop offers a large selection of architectural orphans salvaged from demolition sights. Though most of the items here would be hard to pack into your suitcase, it's still fun to sift through the fireplaces, statues, staircases, street lamps and much more dating from the 18th century to the 1930s.
♦ C Bruc, 120 (C Mallorca-C València)

58 Casa Francesc Farreras (1900, **Antoni Millàs i Figuerola**) One curious bit of architectural trivia: although the building plans were signed by the illustrious **Lluís Domènech i Montaner**, bibliographic entries of the period attribute the structure to Millàs. The vestibule, which can and *should* be visited, is richly decorated. Note the *sgraffiti* of the walls, the stained glass, the carpentry work, and the plaster of Paris ceiling simulating a coffered, wooden one. But above all, take a look at the ironwork of the staircase and the elevator, both the work of **Josep M. Jujol**. Designed in 1913, the elevator is one of the most distinctive works to be found in the Eixample.
♦ C Mallorca, 284 (C Bruc-C Roger Llúria)

59 b.d. Ediciones de Diseño (1898, **Lluís Domènech i Montaner**) In its original, 2-story state, this building, **Casa Thomas**, served as the residence and studio of its owner, **J. Thomas**. In 1912 his heirs enlarged it. The expansion plans were signed by **Francesc Guàrdia i Vial** (Domènech's son-in-law), but with the authorization of Domènech i Montaner, which leads many to believe that he had an important hand in adding the 3 new floors to his former structure, especially since the lower floors were not altered (except for the addition of 2 galleries) and the original, crowning towers were reconstructed anew atop the new top floor. The tilework—featuring eagles—of the original structure was extended throughout the new facade, resulting in a seamless, stylistic harmony. Fittingly, Casa Thomas is now home to b.d. Ediciones de Diseño, a store offering both vintage and up-to-the-minute designs in all manner of home furnishings by leading national and international designers. Particularly appealing are its Gaudí, Domènech i Montaner and MacKintosh reproductions. ♦ C Mallorca, 291-293 (C Bruc-C Roger Llúria) 258.69.09

60 Palau Ramon de Montaner (1893, **Lluís Domènech i Montaner**) Originally, this plot of land was to accommodate 2 mansions designed by architect **Josep Domènech i Estapà** for the owners of the publishing house **Montaner i Simon**. Only **Francesc Simon**'s house was built as originally conceived, and it has since disappeared. This, the house of Ramon de Montaner, was begun based on Domènech i Estapà's design, but for some unknown reason the project passed to the hands of Domènech i Montaner, a cousin of the owner, although, the records indicate architect **Antoni M. Gallissà** as the project supervisor. In any event, the structure clearly reflects a change in designing hands. Domènech i Estapà's elegant eclecticism dominates the lower portion of the facade, while the upper portion reveals Domènech i Montaner's trademark expressivity—most pointedly the Modernist floral decoration of the buttresses and the lovely, multicolored ceramic friezes of the facade. He is also the author of the wonderful interior staircase that ascends through the magical illumination of a polychrome, stained-glass skylight. The sculptural elements of the entrance are by **Eusebi Arnau**. This is now the headquarters of the **Delegació Govern a Catalunya** (the seat of the representative of the Spanish national government) and is open to the public Saturday 10AM-1PM. ♦ C Mallorca, 278 (C Roger de Llúria)

Dreta de L'Eixample

61 Stress A gay hang out open day and night. During the day things are calm and women are admitted. At night things can get a bit wild.
♦ Av Diagonal, 353 (C Bruc) 207.55.15

61 Casa Pilar Bassols (1916, **Gabriel Borrell i Cardona**) A good architectural example depicting the stylistic tone of the end of the Modernist era, this building is a bit unusual in having 2 streetside facades, each treated quite differently. The main facade on Av Diagonal is completely of stone; the one on the lesser C Provença is much simpler of adornment and instead of stone features stucco imitations of ashlars. ♦ Av Diagonal, 355 (C Bruc)

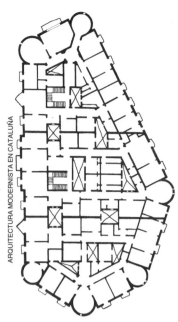

62 Casa Terrades (1905, **Josep Puig i Cadafalch**) Aka **Casa de les Punxes**, this Modernist apartment building with medieval castle overtones and a pronounced Nordic Neo-Gothic tone is Puig's best-known. One of the largest and most singular works of the period, it received an honorable mention in the 1905 municipal architectural competition for being one of the best buildings erected during 1904. Its nickname (meaning *House of the Spikes*) derives from the pointed spires crowning the 6 circular towers scattered across this hexagonal block and from the gable ends of the facades, some of which sport soffits of tilework devoted to symbolic or legendary themes. One of them on C Rosselló reads *Sant Jordi, patró de Catalunya, torneunos la llibertat*— a message soliciting liberty that during the Franco years amounted to a most daring statement of protest. The building's rich use of brickwork is strikingly complemented by the refined delicacy of the jambs, lintels and the

Dreta de L'Eixample

flowered balconies so exquisitely wrought by **Manuel Ballarín**. Also of interest are the triangular galleries. Some of the vestibules of the building are accessible. ♦ Av Diagonal, 416-420 (C Rosselló-C Bruc)

Maybe the Sagrada Familia is fated to remain unfinished. Its creator, Gaudí, was killed in 1926 by a tram while contemplating his work from the street . Ever since, Barcelona has not been able to decide what to do with it.

Restaurants/Nightlife: Red   **Hotels:** Blue
Shops/Parks: Green   **Sights/Culture:** Black

63 Can Pere ★$$ This rustic restaurant has built up a faithful following with its generous portions at moderate prices. Though there are some trendy listings on the menu, you're better off sticking with the more traditional dishes like *paella mixta, entremeses Can Pere* (assorted hors d'oeuvres), *zarzuela* (a local variant of bouillabaisse), *parrillada de pescado* (a platter of grilled fish) and *gambas al ajillo* (shrimp in a garlic and olive oil sauce). ♦ Spanish ♦ C Rosselló, 264-266 (C Bruc) 257.40.20

64 Bienservida ★$$ The name of this restaurant (*Well Served*) is unfortunately in complete contradiction to its sad decor. But the regulars come for the good, home-style cooking in the form of canelones, *tortilla a la paisana* (a Spanish omelet), *macarrones, judías verdes con jamón* (green beans with ham), *zarzuela* (a local bouillabaisse), *calamares* (squid), *pollo asado* (roast chicken) and *butifarra asada con judías* (Catalan sausage roasted with beans). ♦ Catalan ♦ C Rosselló, 305-307 (C Girona) 257.85.87

65 D Barcelona On entering you'll find a large quantity of useful and useless gadgets ranging from 1940s and '50s reproductions to up-to-the-minute designs. In the back is an art gallery that stages high-quality monthly exhibitions of contemporary art. ♦ Av Diagonal, 367 (C Rosselló) 216.03.46

66 El Tinell A large antique outlet specializing in Victorian furnishings ranging from pianos to lamps, bronze figures and armchairs. ♦ C Pau Claris, 190 (C Rosselló) 215.52.48

67 Palau Quadras (1904, **Josep Puig i Cadafalch**) Here Puig was responsible for remodelling and enlarging a former rental property to convert it into a residence for the Barón de Quadras. His intervention was so profound, though (even the main entrance was moved from C Rosselló to Av Diagonal), that practically all that remains of the original building are some structural elements. The layout derives from the typical Gothic mansions of Barcelona—a central patio at the building's core from which the main staircase leads to the upper floors. But it's the virtuosity of the building's Gothic ornamentation that stands out most. The sculptural work was conceived by **Eusebi Arnau** and executed by **Alfons Juyol**. At one corner of the gallery you'll see yet another scene of Sant Jordi squaring off with the dragon. The facade in the back on C Rosselló contrasts greatly with the Av Diagonal facade in conserving to a large extent the rational simplicity of the original facade that typified the Eixample's pre-Modernist days. Inside you'll find the **Museu de la Música**, but after the fine first impression made by the main facade, Puig's decorative work on the first floor within is a disappointment. ♦ Admission. Tu-Su 9AM-2PM. Av Diagonal, 373 (C Pau Claris)

68 Casa Comalat (1911, **Salvador Valeri i Pupurull**) This Modernist building goes to decorative extremes, especially in the vestibules. Its 2 facades (one on Av Diagonal and the other on C Còrsega) differ greatly. The former is more symmetrical and elegant; the latter, with its undulations and ceramic decorations in a decidedly Gaudí vein, is more spontaneous and, in our opinion, the more intriguing. The Av Diagonal facade was somewhat affected by the renovation of one of the neighboring buildings. Also, during restoration work in 1987, some of its sculptural elements were lost, including 2 feminine figures that had flanked the cupola. Unfortunately, the remarkable hallway featuring mosaics and stained glass in organic shapes and vivid ochre and violet hues is impossible to visit. ◆ Av Diagonal, 442 (Pl Rei Joan Carles)

Within the Casa Comalat:

SiSiSi This fashionable bar was designed by **Gabi Ordeig** and is one of the benchmarks of today's trendy Barcelona nightlife. ◆ 217.57.73

69 Mordisco ★$ At lunch you'll find this place buzzing with PR types, decorators, designers, photographers and other artsy professionals. The decor features some works by **Xavier Mariscal**. Hamburgers and stuffed rolls are the culinary trademarks. The salad selection is ample and good. Beyond that, the menu toes the national line. ◆ Spanish ◆ C Rosselló, 265 (Pg Gràcia) 218.33.14

70 Yanko One of Spain's premier leather merchants. The quality of its shoes, handbags and luggage is first-class, and the styling is chic. ◆ Pg Gràcia, 100 (C Rosselló) 215.33.61

VINÇON

71 Vinçon Once upon a time there was a Jew, a German and a Catalan. In 1929 they established a company importing and wholesaling fine porcelain from Germany. During the Spanish Civil War the Jew, **Enrique Levi**, emigrated to New York. **Hugo Vinçon** (a German and a Jew) and **Jacinto Amat** (a Catalan) opened a small retail store at this location. Starting in 1967, the store began to import top-quality German furniture in the latest designs, and the rest is home-furnishings history. As profits soared, the company kept gobbling up more and more surrounding space, including the former studio of painter **Ramón Casas**, which is now fittingly the area devoted to the artistic exhibitions and design displays Vinçon stages every 4 weeks. The store itself now extends the entire block from Pg Gràcia through to C Pau Claris and offers anything you could want in the way of high-tech, state-of-the-art housewares, from light bulbs to barbecues, safes and luggage. In all, they carry nearly 10,000 products for the home in cutting-edge designs by contemporary masters the world over. Arrangements can be made to ship purchases. ◆ Pg Gràcia, 96 (C Rosselló-C Provença) 215.60.50; fax 215.50.37

71 Casa Milà (aka La Pedrera) (1910, **Antoni Gaudí i Cornet**) Now deemed one of Modernism's most imaginative wonders, the Casa

Cartoon lampooning Casa Milà

Milà was something of a laughing stock in its youth. Curved walls in the apartments? Come on, get real! The last completed work by Gaudí, built between 1905 and 1910, it was begun right after he finished the Casa Batlló. At one point Señora Milà brought a lawsuit against the architect alledging that the finished product was not what the original, more ambitious plans called for. She was right, of course—such was Gaudí's improvisational modus operandi—but Gaudí was still vindicated in court, perhaps in part because even before it was finished Casa Milà's architectural significance had been officially acknowledged. In 1909, it was classified as a *monument* and thus exempted from the municipal ordinances of its day. In 1911 it was selected as one of the best works of 1910, but was disqualified because many of its finishing touches had not yet been finished. The plan of the apartment house breaks totally with the type of houses typically found in the Eixample. Within, one

Dreta de L'Eixample

Casa Milà plan

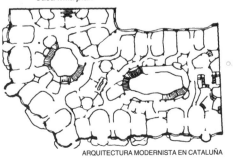

ARQUITECTURA MODERNISTA EN CATALUÑA

of the most notable departures from the Eixample norm was the elimination of a grand stairway in deference to an elevator as the main mode of access to the upper floors (supplemented by a service staircase). The large dwellings are arranged along the undulating facade and around 2 large interior patios, one circular and the other elliptical in shape. From these arises a spiral staircase leading to the first floor and a ramp leading to the undergound parking area.

Casa Milà

The building employs an audacious structure based on columns of stone and brick and a metallic web that eliminate the need for load-bearing walls. Both inside and out Gaudí maximizes the use of the curve. It is probably fair to say that there is not one straight wall to be found here. The building's endlessly undulating facade presents an eroded appearance and is fashioned of rough stone that puts one in mind of a quarry (*pedrera* in Catalán). The wrought-iron balconies are by **Josep Maria Jujol**, as are some of the ceilings and some of the carpentry work. The roof (which you must visit) features a phantasmagoric set of chimneys and surrealistic ventilation towers. The building's current owner, the **Caixa de Catalunya** (a bank), plans to restore it and open much of it up as a museum. In 1984 Casa Milà was declared a World Heritage site by UNESCO. Free guided visits are offered Monday-Friday 10AM-1PM and 5-7PM and Saturday 10AM-1PM, although this schedule may well vary until the museum is officially opened, so call first. On your own you won't be able to peek beyond the interior courtyard. ♦ Pg Gràcia, 92 (C Provença) 215.33.98

Dreta de L'Eixample

72 The Chicago Pizza Pie Factory $ A taste of the USA brought to you by the My Kinda Town Group of Restaurants based in London, which also brings you **Henry J. Bean's Bar and Grill**. The funky decor of ceiling fans and street fans is somehow archetypal. Pizzas, chili con carne and fried chicken are the staples here and can be accompanied by ample helpings of salad. ♦ American ♦ C Provença, 300 (C Pau Claris-Pg Gràcia) 215.94.15

73 Banca Catalana (1968, **Josep Maria Fargas i Falp** and **Enric Tous i Carbó**) Since installing a modern bank headquarters along one of the city's most important architectural avenues was a very delicate matter indeed, the company solicited proposals from among Catalunya's architectural elite. The result is this structure with a modular facade of prefabricated pieces outlined along its perimeter in gold metal to distinguish it from its neighbors. We can't quite decide whether we like it or not. Do you? ♦ Pg Gràcia, 84 (C Mallorca)

74 Maná Maná ★$$ A sophisticated snack bar and restaurant specializing in sandwiches of all kinds, pizza, pasta, ice cream, sorbets, milk shakes and fresh fruit juices. The coffee here is some of the best in town and is offered with a variety of exotic embellishments. The whimsical bar stools were designed by Olympic-mascot creator **Xavier Mariscal**. ♦ Pg Gràcia, 78 (C Mallorca) 215.63.87

74 Robert Clergerie Elegant women the world over regularly set foot in this store that carries on a century of tradition by still making all its shoes by hand. Considering the comfort, quality and timely designs, the prices aren't all that unreasonable. ♦ Pg Gràcia, 76 (C Mallorca-C València)

75 Casa Joan Coma (1907, **Enric Sagnier i Villavecchia**) Beginning in 1904, Sagnier carried out an extensive transformation to put a Modernist face on this building constructed in 1882. He added a main-floor gallery, new balcony railings and a stone front throughout. His efforts won a special mention in the municipal architectural awards of 1908. ♦ Pg Gràcia, 74 (C Mallorca-C València)

75 Hotel Majestic $$$ Behind this Neoclassical facade resides a businesslike hotel whose 336 comfortable rooms (done up in the beige-and-brown businesslike manner of the '60s) have air conditioning, safes, satellite televisions, radios and minibars. ♦ Pg Gràcia, 70-72 (C Mallorca-C València) 215.45.12; fax 215.77.73

PATA NEGRA

76 Cafeteria Restaurant Pata Negra ★$$ A contemporary eatery with a selection of newspapers at the disposal of diners. Very popular at lunch. Tasty *tapas* (try the vegetarian *tortilla*) and sandwiches at the bar. The L-shaped dining area is bigger than it looks at first sight and offers a full menu of traditional Spanish dishes. ◆ Spanish ◆ C Pau Claris, 155 (C Mallorca-C València) 215.44.05

77 Les Ostres ★★$$$ A solid, sophisticated choice with dining on 3 levels and at the bar. The top level is best, for here you'll find 3 romantic tables for 2 in the gallery windows. In honor of the restaurant's name, try the oysters. Follow up with any of the fine fish dishes. ◆ Seafood ◆ C València, 267 (C Pau Claris) 215.30.35

78 Casa Pau Ubarri (1904, **Miquel Madroell i Rius**) This building bears mention primarily for the crowning glories of its tower-like galleries. The coat of arms on the facade is that of the owner, the **Conde (Count) de San José de Santurce**. ◆ C València, 293 (C Roger de Llúria-C Bruc)

79 Casa Josefa Villaneuva (1909, **Juli Maria Fossas i Martínez**) The Modernist aesthetic adopted by Fossas here is most closely aligned with the spirits of **Gaudí** and **Rubió i Bellver** (consider the **Casa Batlló** and **Casa Pomar**, respectively). The columns supporting the balconies of the chamferred gallery (topped with a spire) look like human skeleton bones. Although Fossas throws in some Rococo decoration on the lintels and roof parapet, this is undoubtedly his best Modernist work. Beginning in the 1920s, he increasingly moved away from this movement to embrace the new *noucentista* aesthetic whose tendencies are more Classical and monumental. Though not readily apparent, this structure was conceived as 2 buildings. Their symmetrical composition was disfigured when one of the chamferred corner galleries was eliminated. ◆ C Roger de Llúria, 80 (C València)

80 La Barcelonina de Vins i Esperits A small, upscale place to snack on select pâtés, homemade cheeses, all manner of smoked things and other assorted *tapas*. The prime attraction is the 500 different wines, many of them displayed along one wall. Quiet and classy. ◆ Tapas ◆ C València, 304, bajos (C Pau Claris-C Roger Llúria) 215.70.83

Restaurants/Nightlife: Red   Hotels: Blue
Shops/Parks: Green   Sights/Culture: Black

81 The Daily Telegraph An English-style pub with an ample cocktail menu and a very limited selection of sandwiches. Good spot to break for a brew and a game of darts. Some 20 foreign beers offered, including Guinness. ◆ C Pau Claris, 139 (C València-C D'Aragó) 215.17.79

82 Casa Marfà (1905, **Manuel Comas i Thos**) Within the Eixample this is one of the best-preserved examples of the use of a Neo-Medieval vernacular that is here marked by a blend of the Neo-Romanesque and the Neo-Gothic. Oddly enough, the building dates from the time when Modernism was in full flower. Even within the architect's own body of work, it stands out as unique. Of special interest is the entrance, featuring 3 large arches resting on short columns with floral capitals and wooden doors carved with Gothic motifs. The vestibule too, merits a visit, most especially for the monumental stairway that leads to the main floor and is topped with a magnificent, polychrome, triangular skylight. The facade bears the architect's signature. ◆ Pg Gràcia, 66 (C València)

83 Galeries Halley Another maze-like mall with some 40 commercial establishments. At its core is a cafe where you can rest up between spending sprees. ◆ Pg Gràcia, 62 (C València-C D'Aragó)

84 Madrid-Barcelona ★$$ Generations of Barcelonans have come here for the *sesos a la romana* (brains), *fideos a la cazuela* (noodle casserole), *callos a la madrileña* (tripe) and the baked apple with ice cream. Judging from the permanent crowd at the bar and the lunch and dinner crush at the tables, they're on to a good thing. ◆ Spanish ◆ C D'Aragó, 282 (C Pau Claris) 215.70.26

85 El Gran Colmado ★★$$ Although the quality of the food tends to fluctuate, you should come here to experience this curious cross

Dreta de L'Eixample

between a grocery store and a restaurant. The variable menu weds tradition with trendiness. The steak tartare, one of the best we've had, is consistently good. Also typically good are the *ensalada de foie gras a la vinagreta*, *calabacines rellenos de frutos de mar* (zucchini stuffed with seafood), *arroz a la cazuela* (rice casserole), carpaccio, *conejo con caracoles* (rabbit with snails), veal filet with foie gras sauce, and salmon with *angulas* (baby eels). The desserts are iffy. A communal table accommodates lone diners desiring some company. ◆ Catalan ◆ C Consell de Cent, 318 (C Pau Claris-Pg Gràcia) 302.26.26

Day Trips

Monasterio de Nuestra Señora de Montserrat

For almost 1000 years Montserrat (meaning serrated mountain) has been a sacred spot for Catalans. Situated some 45 miles from Barcelona, it is easily accessible via the N-II. You can also take the daily half-day bus tour offered by Julià Tours, Plaça Universitat (318.38.95) or the FF.CC. de la Generalitat (205.15.15) from Plaça d'Espanya to the cable car running to the top of the mountain.

Catalunya's leading pilgrimage center, Montserrat is where the faithful come to pay their respects to the **Black Virgin**, known popularly as **La Moreneta**, a polychrome image dating from the 12th century that was miraculously found on this mountain. Since the 9th century the mountain has harbored hermitages. Since 1205 it has been endowed with a monastery. The original one was destroyed by **Napoleon**'s forces in 1812; the 2 large buildings you see today are from the 19th century.

Although you cannot actually visit the monastery inhabited by some 80 Benedictine monks, the vast complex itself includes a 16th-century basilica where the venerated Black Virgin resides; and a museum comprised of an old section containing religious paintings, a Biblical collection of archaeological artifacts, and a collection of Jewish liturgical items, and a new section housing a contingent of 19th- and 20th-century secular paintings. Museum hours are daily 10:30AM-2PM and 3-7PM, 1 July-31 October and Holy Week; daily 10:30AM-2PM (old museum) and 3-6PM (new museum), 1 November-30 June

There are also several hotels, restaurants and a string of food stalls and souvenir shops.

Montserrat's **Escolanía** (Boys' Choir), founded in the 13th century, is one of the oldest in the world. Daily visitors are moved by its singing of the *Salve* at 1PM and 7:10PM and, on Sunday and religious holidays, by its singing of the Mass.

The surrealistic topography of Montserrat is high drama—so high, in fact, that it inspired **Wagner**'s scenography for the opera *Parsifal*. Paths and funiculars crisscross the mountain leading to its various hermitages. Outstanding among them are **Sant Jeroni** where, on a clear day, you can see from the Pyrenees to the Balearic Islands; **Santa Cecilia** with an 11th-century Romanesque church; **Santa Cova**, where, legend has it, the image of the Black Virgin was miraculously found; **Sant Miguel**, from which you have a fine view of the monastery; and **Sant Joan**, which also offers a series of splendid vistas. Along the path leading to the Santa Cova are 15 monuments devoted to the Mysteries of the Rosary; some of them are by such leading Modernist figures as **Gaudí** (First Glorious Mystery, 1916), **Puig i Cadafalch** and **Josep Llimona**.

If you go to Montserrat by car, stop along the way in **Santa Coloma de Cervelló** to see Gaudí's crypt of the **Church of the Sacred Heart**, which today is the village church. A much-admired work, it in many ways foreshadowed his Sagrada Familia. Of aesthetic interest within are Gaudí's wood-and wrought-iron benches. The church is officially open to the public M-Sa 10:15AM-1:30PM and 4-8PM, and Su and holidays 10AM-2PM, but these hours may vary due to church functions. Still, the exterior alone is worth the slight detour.

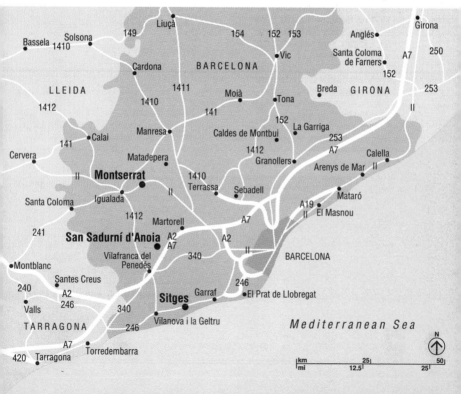

San Sadurní d'Anoia

The Catalan region of the Penedés, which runs from the Montserrat Massif to the Mediterranean Sea, is home to about 90% of Spain's *bodegas* (wineries) producing *cava* (sparkling wines). The acknowledged capital of this region is San Sadurní d'Anoia—just 25 miles from Barcelona, via the A-2 (Exit 27)—where you'll find several *bodegas* offering informative tours and tastings. Most well-known among them are

Codorníu (891.01.25) and **Freixenet** (891.07.00). Codorníu, in the business since 1872, is Spain's oldest *cava* winery with some 16 miles of underground caves. An added bonus on its guided tour is the Modernist structure by **Josep Puig i Cadafalch** (1898) that now houses the **Codorníu Museum** and was designated a national monument in 1987 (the only industrial structure to be so honored). In recent years Codorníu has expanded its production into California's Napa Valley. Founded in 1889, the house of Freixenet also offers a tour and tasting. Recently it has expanded its operations into California's Sonoma Valley and into France.

A Taste of Cava

Cava is Spain's answer to champagne. Since European practice restricts the use of the name *champagne* to the sparkling wines that come from that particular French region, other countries must call their sparkling wines something else. Spain calls them *cavas* (originally a Catalan word meaning wine cellars). *Cava* was first made in Catalunya in the 1870s from the fine, local, white grape varieties *parellada*, *xarel-lo* and *macabeo*. In the 1890s and 1900s it became the elegant drink of choice in the sophisticated Modernist cafes of Barcelona. In the 1920s the industry took off and the nation at large developed a taste for *cava*. Now much of the world has happily done likewise.

Cava connoisseurs swear by Catalunya's *brut natures*. Elaborated with a *licor de expedición* (dosage) composed of cava from the same lot, these are among the driest, crispest, freshest, most natural of all *cavas* (personally, we love them). Rarely produced in commercial quantities, they are hard to come by outside of Catalunya. Not so with many of the other *cavas* whose international availability is quite a recent phenomenon.

Sitges

Just 45 minutes by car (along the C-246) or train from Barcelona, Sitges is a seaside town cosmopolitan well beyond its size. A tourist enclave as early as the 19th century, it was a favored refuge among the intellectuals of the Modernist movement. In fact, the well-known painter **Santiago Rusiñol** set up residence here, as did many of Barcelona's well-heeled families, whose mansions (some of them Modernist of mien) line the **Passeig Marítim**.

Besides its beaches, boutiques and its summer party atmosphere, Sitges offers 2 choice museums in its quaint old quarter that make the trip worthwhile year-round. **Cau Ferrat** (C Fonollars, s/n 894.03.64), the former residence of Rusiñol, is a 19th-century retreat fashioned of two 16th-century fishermen's houses. Its displays include a collection of Rusiñol's own works as well as some by **Picasso** and **El Greco**, and an interesting assortment of wrought-iron objects, archaeological curios and decorative tiles. Adjacent you'll find the **Museu Maricel de Mar** (894.03.64), the former home of **Dr. Perez Rosales**, an avid collector of medieval, Renaissance and Baroque furnishings, tapestries and porcelain. He also acquired a 14th-century chapel in its entirety! Both museums are open Tu-Sa 9:30AM-2PM and 4-6PM; Su 9:30AM-2PM.

If you go to Sitges by car, try your luck at the **Gran Casino de Barcelona, Sant Pere de Ribes** (893.36.66), just 3 miles out of town along the C-246. This elegant casino occupies a 19th-century Romantic structure and offers not only the full complement of games of chance but a fine restaurant (★★$$$$) as well. If you just want to dance, there's a disco. The casino is open daily 6PM-5AM, 1 June-30 August; M-Th, Su 5PM-4AM, F-Sa 5PM-5AM, 1 September-31 May; closed Christmas Eve. Your passport is required for admission, and there is a fee for entry. Open-air shows are offered from mid-July through August; call 893.15.04 for information.

Catalonia, the region that Barcelona capitals, accounts for a quarter of Spain's industrial production, one-fifth of its gross national product, one-fifth of its exports, and one-third of the foreign investment (and nearly all the Japanese investment) in the country. It also attracts more than one-third of the tourists. It is considered to have the best schools, hospitals, roads and general infrastructure in Spain.

Day Trips

The Catalonia and Andalusia regions of Spain are both known for their brandies. But while a distinctive Spanish brandy has been produced in Andalusia since at least the 16th century, the history of Catalan brandy-making is much shorter, beginning only in the last century. Most Catalan brandies are produced in the Penedés area from Parellada, Xarello and Macabeo grapes, resulting in a brandy similar in style to French Cognac. Some of the major Catalan producers are **Torres, Mascaró** and **Manuel Giró**.

Architectural Highlights

Gothic Barcelona

The predominant architectural motif of Barcelona's **Ciutat Vella** (Old City) is Gothic (12th-16th centuries), although in numerous cases the style has been retroactively reproduced, reconstructed or simply imitated. Even the main facade of the Barri Gòtic's headlining **Cathedral** dates from our own century, and the Gothic facades of the **Palau de la Generalitat** and the **Casa de la Ciutat** have been somewhat eclipsed by later construction. Surprisingly, some of the best examples of Barcelona's Gothic construction are found not in the Barri Gòtic but along La Ribera's **Carrer Montcada**. In 1974 the architectural import of its Gothic mansions was duly acknowledged with the declaration of the street as a national *Conjunto Monumental Histórico Artístico* (a national historic and artistic treasure).

Plaza del Pi with the Iglesia del Pi on the left

Catalunya's own local brand of Gothic is most evident in such religious structures as the **Iglesia del Pi**, the **Iglesia de Betlem**, the **Monasterio de Pedralbes**, and, most of all, the **Iglesia de Santa María del Mar**.

Modernism

Around 1892, the Modernist movement, Barcelona's (and Catalunya's) distinctively unique rendition of Art Nouveau, began to gel in the worlds of art, music, literature and architecture. Giving the passing nod to Art Nouveau's architectural traditions, Modernism took off in daring directions unmatched anywhere else in the world. Its defiant stance against the encroaching mechanization of life and work revived the decorative crafts of yore with a creative vengeance.

From 1900 on, architecture became the movement's fundamental manifestation, and the role of the architect reached deeply into the realm of design. Directly involved with even the smallest of decorative details,

Antoni Gaudí carried Modernism to its boldest horizons, endowing Barcelona with some of the world's most remarkable edifices. His **Casa Milà, Casa Batlló, Casa Vicens** and **Palau Güell**, though brilliant, were a mere prelude to the visionary **Sagrada Familia**, the epitomic expression of his genius.

Lluís Domènech i Montaner, another brilliant Modernist master, enriched the city with his incomparable concert hall, the **Palau de la Música Catalan**, and the **Hospital de Sant Pau**.

The Eixample's **Mançana de la Discòrdia** (along the western side of Passeig de Gràcia between Carrer Consell de Cent and Carrer D'Aragó) constitutes a précis of Modernism with its buildings by Gaudí (Casa Batlló), Domènech i Montaner (**Casa Lleó i Morera**) and Josep Puig i Cadafalch (**Casa Amatller**)— an enlightening mix of Modernist styling.

Many lesser, but still incredibly striking, Modernist structures populate the ordered expanse of the Eixample's streets, offering admirers of the genre many hours of strolling pleasure. Among them you'll find a number of commercial establishments that, although situated in older buildings, were newly outfitted at the turn of the century in the Modernist mode. Pharmacies were especially receptive to the new trend, and many have survived to our day with their decoration intact. Note the **Farmàcia Sastre i Marqués** (1905, Puig i Cadafalch) at Carrer Hospital, 109; the **Farmàcia J. de Bolòs** at Carrer València, 256; the **Farmàcia Puig-Oriol** (1913) at Carrer Mallorca, 312; and the **Farmàcia Genové** (1911, **Enric Sagnier**) at La Rambla, 77.

Casa Milà front gate grillwork by Antoni Gaudí

Architectural Highlights

many Modernist architects supervised a contingent of collaborating artisans in an effort to integrate the applied arts with the core architectural structure. The wrought iron, artificial stone, *sgraffiti*, mosaics, stained-glass and other decorative expressions were not mere adornment, but rather integral parts of a structurally organic whole.

What I can say for certain is that the task of the urbanists of the Barcelona City Council has been a very important element in the effort that all of us have made to launch the name of Barcelona internationally, recover the lost dignity of our urban landscape, and create an atmosphere of controversy and discussion in a Catalan society threatened by conformism, ideological uniformity, and the fear of confrontation.

Pasqual Maragall, Mayor of Barcelona

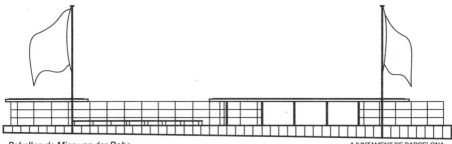

Pabellon de Mies van der Rohe

The **Cementiri Nou**, or **Cementiri del Sudest**, on the seaward slope of Montjuïc also dates from the city's Modernist days, when leading middle- and upper-class families commissioned architects to build elaborate tombs that provided sculptors and iron-workers an additional opportunity to show off their skills. Some outstanding examples are the **Panteó Batlló** (1885, **Josep Vilaseca**); the **Panteó La Riva** (1891, **Antoni M. Gallissà**); the **Panteó Terrades** (1917), **Panteó dels Barons de Quadres** (1917), **Panteó Macià** (1917) and **Panteó Damm** (1897) by Puig i Cadafalch; and the tombstones of **Gibert-Romeu** (1910), **Planells** (1916) and **Sansalvador** (1919) by **J.M. Jujol**.

Architectural Odds 'n' Ends

Sensitive to the impact of architecture on urban life, Barcelona has historically taken great care with its large-scale development projects, the first of which created the Eixample and was further fueled by the 1888 Universal Exhibition, which left the city with its **Arc del Triomf** and several installations in the **Parc de la Ciutadella**, including the **Casada** and Domènech i Montaner's cafe-cum-**Museu de Zoología**.

In preparation for the 1929 World's Fair, the city again geared up architecturally. Many of the structures of Montjuïc (the **Venetian Towers**, the **Palau Nacional**, the **Poble Espanyol**, the recently rebuilt **Pabellon de Mies van der Rohe**, the charming **Fuentes de Mont-juïc**, and the newly refurbished **Olympic Stadium**) date from this time.

In getting ready for its greatest international event ever—the 1992 Summer Olympic Games—Barcelona undertook the most extensive urban overhaul of our century. Among its structural contri-butions are the **Palau Sant Jordi** and the other sports and recreational installations of Montjuïc's **Olympic Ring**; the ambitious **Olympic Village** project with its contingent of marinas, new beaches and coastal parks; and a general upgrading of the municipal infra-structure, including new ring roads, a new airport, the new **Plaça de les Glòries Catalanes**, the **Moll de la Fusta**, and a compendium of new and revived parks, plazas and museums.

Olympic Village Project

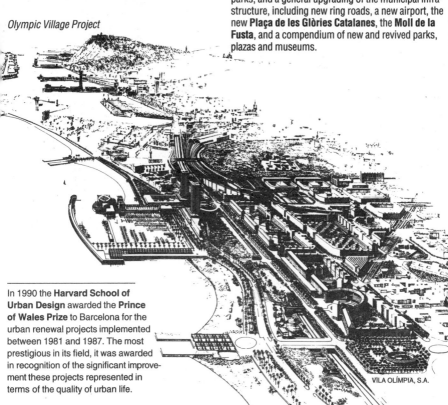

In 1990 the **Harvard School of Urban Design** awarded the **Prince of Wales Prize** to Barcelona for the urban renewal projects implemented between 1981 and 1987. The most prestigious in its field, it was awarded in recognition of the significant improve-ment these projects represented in terms of the quality of urban life.

VILA OLÍMPIA, S.A.

147

History

400 BC—Evidence suggests that the Iberian tribe Laie was established on Montjuïc.

230 BC—**Amílcar Barca**, a Carthaginian, takes over a former Phoenician settlement to establish the town of Barcino.

218 BC—The first evidence of Roman occupation.

133 BC—Barcino becomes the Roman Colonia Favencia Julia Augusta Pía Barcino.

AD 300—The Romans build a wall around Barcino.

415—**King Ataulfo** makes Barcelona the capital of his Visigothic kingdom.

717-18—The Muslim conquest of Barcelona.

801—**Luís el Piadoso**, king of the Franks, liberates Barcelona from Muslim domination and imposes Carolingian rule.

874—The **Condes de Barcelona** (Counts of Barcelona) win local independence.

878—The heredity of earldoms is established, allowing properties to be united through carefully planned marriages; Barcino becomes the capital.

985—The Muslim vizier **al-Mansur** destroys Barcelona.

986—The Franks withdraw their aid against Arab hostilities, and the seeds of Catalunya's autonomy are planted.

1137—The Kingdom of Catalunya and the Kingdom of Aragó merge through the marriage of Barcelona's **Ramón Berenguer IV** and Aragó's **Petronila**.

13th c—**King Jaume I** builds a second set of city walls.

13th-15th c—Catalunya dominates the Mediterranean and builds a colonial empire. Barcelona, at the hub of the empire, flourishes in what is today the Barri Gòtic.

1213—**Saint Francis of Assissi** creates Christianity's first manger scene in Barcelona on Christmas Eve.

1234—The Inquisition comes to Barcelona.

1245—King Jaume I conquers Mallorca, Ibiza and Valencia.

1249—King Jaume I allows the city to elect its own administrators and councilors.

1258—The Treaty of Corbeil between King Jaume I and **Louis IX** of France liberates Catalunya from its theoretical vassalage to the French throne.

1259—Barcelona produces history's first code of maritime law and custom known as the *Book of the Consulate of the Sea*.

1265—King Jaume I establishes Barcelona's **Consell del Cent** (Council of the 100) as the city's highest governing body.

1282—**Pedro el Grande** conquers Sicily.

1283—Catalunya's parliamentary courts are established.

1289—The **Generalitat de Catalunya** (regional government) is created.

14th c—Catalunya conquers part of Greece and reaches its colonial peak.

1319—Barcelona stages Spain's first Corpus Christi procession.

1348—**The Plague** destroys 1/3 of the population of Catalunya.

15th c—The Catalan empire declines: banks go belly up, Jews are killed, the French invade, and colonial wars break out.

1401—Europe's first bank is established in Barcelona, and the city's first university institution, the **Estudi d'Arts i Medicina** (School of Arts and Medicine) is founded.

1450—**King Alfons the Magnanimous** founds the University of Barcelona.

1468—Barcelona begins printing books.

1474—Catalunya, long part of the Kingdom of Aragó, loses its independence after the marriage of **Queen Isabel** of Castilla and **King Fernando** of Aragó results in the political union of these realms. Construction of Barcelona's port begins.

1492—Spain is unified after the Muslims finally succumb in the south. All non-Christians begin to be expelled from the country. **Columbus** discovers America.

1493—Columbus returns triumphant from his first New World voyage and is received by the Catholic Kings either in Barcelona or in the Monasterio de Sant Jeroni de la Murtra near Badalona.

1493—Columbus is named *Admiral of the Indies* by the Catholic Kings on 28 May.

1513—Spain's **Núñez de Balboa** discovers the Pacific Ocean, and Spain embarks on 100 years of imperial splendor that embraces not only the New World but much of Europe as well.

1519—**Emperor Charles V** comes to Barcelona and makes it the first capital of his Empire. He holds the Assembly of the Order of the Golden Fleece in Barcelona's Cathedral.

1520—Spain's first book is published in Catalan.

1558—Defeat of the Spanish Armada; the empire begins to crumble.

1640—A bloody uprising against **King Felipe IV** erupts in the War of the Reapers, and establishes the Republic of Catalonia.

1653—The war ends with the triumph of Felipe IV.

1702-14—The War of the Spanish Succession between those supporting **Felipe de Anjou** (Madrid and France) and those supporting the **Archduke Charles of Austria** (Aragó, Catalunya and England) puts **Felipe V**, Spain's first Bourbon king, on the Spanish throne.

1714—King Felipe V takes Barcelona after a heroic 11-month struggle on the part of the city.

1716—Construction of Felipe V's **Ciutadella** begins in what is now the **Parc de la Ciutadella**, and Catalunya's autonomy is suppressed.

1768—**Carlos III** permits Catalan merchants to resume overseas trade.

19th-20th c—Increasing industrialization leads to urban expansion. At the turn of the century Barcelona is a hotbed of anti-monastic, anticlerical and anarchist activity. At the same time Modernism flourishes.

1808-13—The French occupy Barcelona.

1814—The **War of Independence** ends. Catalunya is left in ruins, but begins a period of growth and change.

1835—Widespread suppression of religious orders and confiscation of church properties.

1847—The **Gran Teatre del Liceu** is founded.

1848—The Iberian Peninsula's first train begins operation between Barcelona and Mataró.

1852—**Antoni Gaudí** is born in Reus. As the leading figure in the *Modernismo* movement, he changed the face of Barcelona.

1854—*Les selfactines*, a series of violent protests by laborers opposed to increasing mechanization, takes place in Barcelona in July.

1859—Barcelona adopts **Ildefons Cerdà**'s plan for municipal expansion into the Eixample henceforth known as the Cerdà Plan. The world's first submarine, invented by the Catalan **Narcís Monturiol**, is immersed in Barcelona's port.

1868—Revolution dethrones Spain's **Queen Isabel II** and a revolutionary *junta* takes control of Barcelona and decides to demolish Felipe V's Ciutadella.

1873—The first Spanish Republic is declared, as well as the regional state of Catalunya.

1874—**King Alfonso XII** is restored to the throne of Spain, and a new phase of Catalan patriotism is begun.

1881—**Pablo Picasso** is born 25 October in Málaga, and later spends many of his formative years in Barcelona.

1882—Construction of the Sagrada Familia is begun under the supervision of architect Antoni Gaudí.

1888—Barcelona hosts the **Universal Exhibition**.

1892—The *Principles of Manresa* is written by the **Unio Catalanista**, proposing a home-rule constitution. The Catalan Movement is spreading rapidly through artistic circles, with proponents such as poet Joan Maragall and architect Lluis Domènech i Montaner.

1893—**Joan Miró** is born on Passatge de Crèdit. He later becomes one of the most important members of the 20th-century avant-garde art movement.

1897—The **Barcelona Football** (Soccer) **Club** is founded.

1901—The city erupts in large-scale Nationalist demonstrations on 11 September.

1904—**Salvador Dali**, one of the foremost Catalan painters, is born in Figueres.

1909—Workers' protests, anarchist activity and general repression explode in what becomes known as *Semana Trágica* (Tragic Week).

1914—The **Mancomunitat of Catalonia** is established, uniting the 4 Provincial Assemblies of Catalunya. It assumes the role of Catalunya's governing body and begins the modernization and improvement of the region.

1914-18—Spain remains neutral during WWI.

1923—The installation of **Primo de Rivera**'s dictatorship means strong repression of Barcelona's working classes and, to a lesser extent, of its staunchly Catalan middle class.

1924—**Radio Barcelona**, Spain's first nationwide station, begins broadcasting.

1929—Barcelona hosts the **World's Fair**.

1930—Rivera's dictatorship collapses.

1931—The Generalitat is reconvened under the Second Spanish Republic, and Catalunya regains autonomy.

1936-39—The Spanish Civil War.

1937—Picasso paints his large mural *Guernica* for the Spanish Pavilion of the Paris International Exposition to protest the bombing of the town of Guernica during the Civil War.

1938—**General Francisco Franco** abolishes Catalan autonomy in April.

1939—Barcelona falls to Franco's Nationalist forces on 26 January.

1936-75—The Franco dictatorship. Strong repression of the Catalan language and culture. Spain remains neutral during WWII.

1950—Spain joins the United Nations.

1955—Barcelona hosts the second **Mediterranean Games**.

1959—The beginning of Spain's tourist boom.

1969—Franco names **Prince Juan Carlos de Bourbon** as his successor.

1975—Franco dies. **Juan Carlos I** is proclaimed king. The wheels of democracy begin turning.

1977—First general election in 40 years. Catalunya gains regional autonomy under Spain's new democratic government led by **Aldolfo Suárez**.

1978—Spain adopts a new Constitution, restoring civil liberties.

1979—The Generalitat de Catalunya is reconvened once again.

1981—An attempted coup d'etat in February is aborted through the personal intervention of King Juan Carlos I.

1982—Spain becomes a member of NATO.

1986—Spain joins the European Economic Community. It remains a member of NATO after a nationwide referendum.

1986—Barcelona is chosen to host the **1992 Summer Olympic Games**.

1990—Barcelona wins the Harvard School of Urban Design's Prince of Wales Prize for its urban renewal efforts.

1992—25 July: let the Games begin!

History

The cuisine of Barcelona was greatly influenced by Italian food in the 18th and 19th centuries and French food in the 19th and 20th centuries.

Restaurants

Only restaurants with star ratings are listed below. All restaurants are listed alphabetically in the main index. Always telephone as far in advance as possible to confirm your table and ensure that a restaurant has not closed, changed its hours, or booked its tables for a private party.

Research & Writing
F. Lisa Beebe

Associate Editor
Karin Mullen

Editorial Assistants
Margie Lee
Daniela Sylvers

Word Processing
Jerry Stanton

Art Direction
Lynne Stiles

Design
Cheryl Fitzgerald

Map Design
Michael Kohnke

Production Assistance
Tom Beatty
Julie Bilski
Michael Blum
Gerard Garbutt
Patricia Keelin
Chris Middour
Laurie Miller

Scanning
Nisha Inalsingh

Film Production
Digital Pre-Press International

Printing and Otabind
Webcom Limited

Special Thanks
Ron Davis
David Wallington
Joe Lachoff
Sanjay Sakhuja
Stuart Silberma

ACCESS®PRESS

President
Mark Johnson

Director
Maura Carey Damacion

Project Director
Mark Goldman

Editorial Director
Jean Linsteadt

Acknowledgments:
Antonio Alonso
American Chamber of Commerce in Barcelona
Arxiu Administratiu
Barcelona Patronat de Turisme
Barcelona Promoció, S.A.
Carlos Diniz Associates
Ediciones Campaña
Editorial Gustave Gili, S.A.
Editorial Teide, S.A.
F.C. Metropolità de Barcelona, S.A. (S.P.M.)
Fundació Caixa de Pensions
Fundació Joan Miró
Jose Luis Izuel Compaire
Maria Fernanda C. Nogueira
Promoció de Ciutat Vella, S.A.
Miguel Romero Rey
Ricardo Bofill, Taller de Arquitecture
Richard Meier & Partners
Tourist Office of Spain, New York
Vila Olimpica, S.A.

CIUTAT VELLA, LA ISLA DE LOS TESOROS

View of Iglesia de Santa María del Mar from Calle Argenteria

Printed in Canada